THE NARCISSISTIC BRIDE OF CHRIST

9 CHARACTERISTICS OF NARCISSISM, HOW THE BRIDE OF CHRIST IS LIVING THEM OUT, AND STEPS TO HEALING

Stephanie Jordan

CROSS OVER JORDAN
PUBLISHING

DEDICATION

TO THE BRIDE OF CHRIST

This book is first and foremost dedicated to each one of you who are pursuing a passionate relationship with our Groom! Keep running toward the lover of your soul! Jesus is absolutely worth falling in love with. God loves you so much that He sent Jesus to rescue you in every way imaginable. May you learn about the greatest love story on each of these pages.

TO GOD, HOLY SPIRIT, AND JESUS

All of me is all Yours. I have nothing to bring to you other than a contrite heart that is passionately in love with You. I honor You by sharing this message that You have placed on my heart. May it be light in the darkness for everyone who reads it. Thank you for choosing me! I love you!

To my mom, Kaye

Boy! I truly couldn't do anything without my mom's support. If you all just knew how many hours she has spent listening to me edit, you would buy her a cupcake. She has always had to listen to my stories and big ideas. She has endlessly prayed for me my whole life. One time when I got mouthy to God complaining about her gentle spirit, He told me that my relationship with Him is a direct reflection of her relationship with Him. So this book, and all its contents, are also a direct reflection of a prayer warrior mom that has set the foundation for me to love the Lord so passionately. Mom, I will carry on the legacy! Thank you! I love you.

To my children Nautas, Nyah, Hammuel, Rebekah, and Shiloh

You guys have been so patient as I work on sharing this prophetic word to the world. Thank you for the grace to write when I probably should have been cooking dinner. You all are my greatest gifts and I am a better person because of each of you. You have taught me to laugh when crying seemed all there ever might be. You have taught me to get over myself more times than you will ever possibly know. May God bless each of you endlessly as you journey to know Him better. I love you all so much!

To my heartbreak

So many words gone unsaid, but I know they don't matter. I have filled these pages with thousands of those words. Whether "lesson" will be the best description I have for our time, know that you are worthy to be loved. I have loved you with my whole heart, but I choose to love me too. I choose me.

TABLE OF CONTENTS

PREFACE

¹⁷ 'AND IT SHALL BE IN THE LAST DAYS,'
God says,
'THAT I WILL POUR FORTH OF MY SPIRIT ON ALL
MANKIND;
AND YOUR SONS AND YOUR DAUGHTERS SHALL
PROPHESY,
AND YOUR YOUNG MEN SHALL SEE VISIONS,
AND YOUR OLD MEN SHALL DREAM DREAMS;
¹⁸ EVEN ON MY BONDSLAVES, BOTH MEN AND
WOMEN,
I WILL IN THOSE DAYS POUR FORTH OF MY
SPIRIT AND THEY SHALL PROPHESY.

—Acts 2:17-18

Hold on to your britches because we are going on a ride through the Bible, and deep diving into the Bride and why we must rescue her—I mean, us! The Church, *Ekklesia* (ek-klay-see-ah) as the Bible refers to it in Greek, is the body of believers that make up the Bride of Christ. If you claim Jesus as Lord and Savior, believe He was born from a virgin, lived a sinless life, went to the cross to be propitiation for our sin, died to conquer Death and Hades, and rose again as a victor with the keys to Death and Hades, and is our advocate sitting at the right hand of Father God, then this book is for you, Saint. Our belief, as Christians, is that one day Jesus will return to gather His bride and take her to heaven with

Him (1 **Corinthians** 15:51-52). There are various beliefs about when this event will occur: whether sometime before, during, or after the tribulation. Whenever it happens, we need to be prepared for our Groom. Failure to do so will not change that He will come, but it will change who is going with Him when He leaves. The Bible describes what the Bride looks and behaves like. Jesus is returning for that Bride, not the one that is prevalently operating today.

My heart breaks for the modern day *Ekklesia* because she looks way more like a narcissist than a beautiful, unblemished bride that Jesus expects. We have gotten so far away from the heart of our Father that it is hard to know how to love the Son. When our sin is louder than Jesus, we are very sick. My oldest son, Nautas said something so profound and I have to share it. He said, "Christianity has become a mask in the modern Church. You get all the showmanship without the true intentions." I saw a meme the other day on Facebook that made me laugh; it says, "If Paul were here, America would be getting a letter."

So, to you, America[1], from the Great I Am through me, this is your letter. This book is the divine revelation that God has given me to help make the Bride aware, to break the demonic spirit trying to lure her away from

---

[1] I am writing to the American church primarily, but this book (letter) is applicable for any nation, church body, or individual that is struggling with narcissistic tendencies. Other countries that have similar cultures most likely will experience very similar unhealthy relational traits.

her Groom, and to bring about healing. I am calling Christians to the table to discuss the evil in our midst. The pain we cause and the deception and lies that we hide behind have done enough damage. It is time for us to shape up. We cannot live in truth and be saturated in falsehood. We must choose to shed or choose to be delivered from the evil spirits that will try to destroy our testimony to the world, but to do so, we must recognize that they exist. We must be OK with saying, "We are not OK." We are active participants of this process when we claim Christ as savior. We have a Redeemer, a Savior, and a lover of our soul that wants to heal and fix all the mess, if we will allow Him to. He is Who we are preparing ourselves for, and one day He will come back in that cloud of glory and every ounce of effort you made to live out a spotless life will be worth it! We are made spotless by His work, but we put action to our faith by our works.

I most likely won't be using names for specific incidents that I talk about. This book isn't about calling out shame or trying to further scar the Bride's reputation. I am not talking about any individual; I am talking about a Body. When one part is hurt, we are all hurt. When one part of the Bride is blemished, we are all blemished. When there is a cancer of sin in the Bride, we all suffer.

²⁰ As it is, there are many parts, but one body.

²¹The eye cannot say to the hand, "I don't need you!" And the head cannot say to the feet, "I don't need you!" ²² On the contrary, those parts of the body that seem to be weaker are indispensable,²³ and the parts that we think are less honorable we treat with special honor. And the parts that are unpresentable are treated with special modesty, ²⁴ while our presentable parts need no special treatment. But God has put the body together, giving greater honor to the parts that lacked it, ²⁵ so that there should be no division in the body, but that its parts should have equal concern for each other.²⁶ If one part suffers, every part suffers with it; if one part is honored, every part rejoices with it.²⁷ Now you are the body of Christ, and each one of you is a part of it.

—1 Corinthians 12:20-27

I had a conversation with someone the other day and she argued that the persecuted Church does not act like a narcissist. I told her that the Bride is a collective whole and if any part of us is sick, it affects all of us. She disagreed. If her logic is right that the narcissism within the Church doesn't affect the persecuted Church, then we could argue that the persecuted Church is irrelevant to those of us who are not being persecuted. I believe removing any part of the Body of Christ from the Bride is dangerous and creates a "them vs us" mentality. The great divide of who is doing it right and who is wrong. I believe this is unhealthy thinking and allows the Bride to be attacked from many directions. All humans are subject to unhealthy relational patterns and should be willing to measure themselves by scripture. Pride has corroded people since the beginning of time. Everything that happens to the Bride should be important to the collective whole of the Church.

I was in a motorcycle accident a few years ago. I landed on my knee cap when I went down. Thankfully I didn't break my knee cap, but I had to get stitches and I had to lay in bed until the immense swelling and tissue damage had had a chance to heal. Now, the entire rest of my body wasn't hurting or having issues, but my bruised, swollen knee rendered the rest of my body ineffective. My neck didn't say to my knee, "You are unimportant, I am going to ignore your issues." Nope, my neck laid in bed right along with my knee. Because when one part of the body is hurt, the entire body is hurt. When the persecuted Church is experiencing numerous horrible things, it ripples out to all of us. When the Church has the cancer of spiritual corruption of narcissism, it affects the entire rest of the global Church. Maybe this divided thinking is an usher to the narcissistic spirit being able to triangulate[2] the Bride and making us believe that one

---

[2] Triangulation is a deceptive behavior used by narcissists to separate and divide people against each other. Narcissists will manipulate each person against each other until they have negative feelings toward one another or do not communicate to understand each other. This creates division.

part is separate therefore not affected by the troubles or conflicts we face.

Narcissism is one of the sneakiest, deadliest, spiritual cancers in the body of Christ. It is a spirit that has made its way into our lives with such stealth that it is destroying marriages, church environments, and our legacy as Christians. I want you to self-reflect as you journey through each section. If you see yourself in each of the areas we are talking about, consider how you can make changes in your life to heal and move forward readying yourself for Jesus. Pointing fingers at others because you haven't done the same thing is part of Ruach Narcissus[3] that will deceive you into thinking that you aren't them, and they aren't you...therefore, you aren't as bad. I fully discuss everything about this spiritual narcissism in chapter 2. Stay with me. I am not saying you are responsible for someone else's sin, that would be codependence because we cannot control others. However, we are responsible for how we handle the sins that are committed around us. If we turn a blind eye or help cover it to keep the sin hidden instead of being exposed into the light of Christ, we are complicit to the damage that sin creates.

By law if a group of people go to the gas station and someone in the group decides to rob the gas station and a murder happens in the process of the robbery, but no one else in the car knew that it was going to happen, everyone in the car can be charged with the murder. It

---

[3] (Ruach=Spirit/Hebrew) (Narcissus=proper name/Greek)

doesn't matter if they didn't know about the heinous intentions and it doesn't matter if they weren't even in the building. They are considered complicit to the crime of murder merely by being associated with the person who committed the crime. I believe this type of dissociated behavior is what we need to be aware of in the Bride. We may not have committed the sin, but if we don't hold it accountable or call it out to be dealt with by the entire Body of Christ, then we are being involuntarily complicit to the sin. We have a responsibility to hold each other responsible for the call we have when we claim the name of Jesus.

¹¹ But now I am writing to you that you must not associate with anyone who claims to be a brother or sister but is sexually immoral or greedy, an idolater or slanderer, a drunkard or swindler. Do not even eat with such people. ¹² What business is it of mine to judge those outside the church? Are you not to judge those inside? ¹³ God will judge those outside. "Expel the wicked person from among you."

—1 Corinthians 5:11-12

The Bible tells us we are a collective whole, so it is not true that we can separate ourselves. Jesus is coming back for His Bride, the *Ekklesia*, the collective whole of His followers. I hope that by the end of this book, you will have a heart of repentance and a refreshing and renewal of encouragement to pursue your first love, Jesus.

Is there grace? Is there redemption for this bride? What is the hope for her future? Will Jesus come back for this bride, or will he expect her to have cleaned herself up? The goal of this book is that you will be desperate to make the Bride ready for her Groom, starting with you and your realm of influence. We always have hope through Jesus Christ because of His redemptive work on the cross to change our trajectory back toward Him. Jesus longs to be with us; He is passionately in love with us. When we realize how much He loves us, if we truly belong to Him, we cannot continue in an unhealthy relationship pattern. Will you take this journey with me?

I would like to approach honest expectations for this book. This book is *not* a book to learn about Narcissistic Personality Disorder (NPD) and/or how to manage a narcissistic relationship with a human. I am not a counselor, psychiatrist, or psychologist. I share and explain narcissism on a surface level in chapter 2 to help give you a basic understanding of the experience of being in a relationship with a narcissist. I use an article that lists the personality traits of narcissism to correlate to the behaviors of the Bride of Christ in modern society.

You will not find denominational theology anywhere in this book. I use reference terms occasionally, and some even in jest, but this book is not about a particular denomination or what the denomination believes. As a matter of fact, denominations aren't even biblical, so I am not interested in focusing on any particular one. The Bride is made up of everyone who calls on the name of Jesus as Lord and Savior. You can maintain differences respectfully, and still apply everything this book shares about healing unhealthy behavior patterns.

This book is a book for the saints of Jesus Christ who are tired of being a sick Bride. I share behavioral issues that the Church has become commonly known for and the antidote to help each of us with self-reflection and changing our ways. This book is for you if you have a passionate hope to be in a genuine relationship with Jesus. The content will challenge, convict, and change you if you will let the light of truth shine into your life. None of us are always able to see our own flaws, so becoming curious about how any of these personality traits may fit into your life is ideal.

All scriptures are New International Version (NIV) unless stated otherwise. I believe this is a commonly used version in many church services. I use scripture to encourage you to understand how to seek a closer relationship with Jesus. Some sections have more scripture than others, but I implore you to dig into the Bible and study it for yourself. Please invite Holy Spirit to take the journey through this book with you. This is the divine revelation that God gave me to write this book and help me understand and teach the spiritual side of narcissism that affects humanity and the Bride of Jesus Christ.

Note from author: *This book is written to Christians who make up the body of the Bride of Jesus. If you are not a Christian, yet find yourself reading this book, my hope is that you find the redemptive power of God throughout it. I hope that you find that God is so compassionate to those who do not understand His love. He absolutely has a standard for those who call Him Father, and if you have been mistreated by any of His children, He did not take it lightly. He will absolutely hold the behavior accountable. I apologize for any way we hurt you!*

CHAPTER 1

THE BRIDE

THE PARENTS

Parents always have expectations for their children's marriage to be happy, good, and beneficial. They dream and pray for a spouse that is going to honor, respect, and cherish their children. Sometimes our parents may have even higher expectations than we do for ourselves. Parents have the innate ability to know their own children's flaws and can be objective enough to see the flaws in their child's potential mate. Loving parents will share concerns about a potential dark side to the upcoming marriage if they were to see one.

I don't know a parent that doesn't feel compelled to warn against impending disaster that could happen in an upcoming marriage. Parents tend to have the ability to know how difficult marriage can be and also how rewarding. Healthy parents desire marriage for their children because God designed and created us to be in partnerships with each other. To prevent narcissism from corrupting us as the Bride, we can look to the Bible.

In Genesis, God realized that it wasn't good for man to be alone (*The LORD God said, "It is not good for man to be alone. I will make a helper suitable for him."* **Genesis 2:18 NIV**), so He created for him a helpmate, woman. When man and woman come together, it is supposed to be extremely beneficial for both people. Our American culture has made this desire messy and these days we rarely see it live out its full potential. Marriage itself isn't flawed; it is the people in the marriage that are flawed.

How can flawed people create a healthy bride of Christ when they can't create a healthy marriage on Earth? Well, we can go back to the parents of the Bride-and Groom-to-be. The parents can be beacons for us.

The relationship that we can follow in the Bible is the relationship between God and Holy Spirit. Their relationship is so precious. There is a constant dance between God and Holy Spirit as parents. God is the Father and at the helm of all decisions. God is the one that spoke the Word (Jesus, **John 1:14**), and then creation happened. We see Holy Spirit make anything happen that God wills—the constant support and follow-through of God's design. Holy Spirit is the reminder of all of God's ways. God speaks and Holy Spirit activates. When God sent Jesus, Holy Spirit delivered Him to earth. God and Holy Spirit are able to be modeled by Jesus and the Bride.

14 The Word became flesh and made his dwelling among us. We have seen his glory, the glory of the one and only Son, who came from the Father, full of grace and truth.

—John 1:14 *NIV*

When Jesus is in ministry, He regularly comments that He is not here for His will but because His Father sent Him. The Bride is called to be the flesh example of Jesus for others. When the Bride is in line with her Groom, we see a healthy earthly example of God and Holy Spirit's relationship. The Bride is meant to follow Jesus' commands and ways of living that He modeled for us while on earth.

26 But the Advocate, the Holy Spirit, whom the Father will send in my name, will teach you all things and will remind you of everything I have said to you.

—John 14:26

We can see the support that Holy Spirit gives to God and then reaching down to God's children. Holy Spirit is sent out to teach us all things and bring to remembrance everything that Jesus said to us. Jesus, the Son, is going to have the expectation of having a good marriage because He has been able to see how the functionality of the dynamic, in which we are made in the image of, was meant to operate.

WHO IS SHE?

How do we get to know this mysterious bride? Can we see her? Touch her? Yes! All Believers make up the church who is the Bride of Christ. We are also known as the Body of Christ.

1 Therefore, I urge you, brothers and sisters, in view of God's mercy, to offer your bodies as a living sacrifice, holy and pleasing to God—this is your true and proper worship. 2 Do not conform to the pattern of this world, but be transformed by the renewing of your mind. Then you will be able to test and approve what God's will is—his good, pleasing and perfect will.

3 For by the grace given me I say to every one of you: Do not think of yourself more highly than you ought, but rather think of yourself with sober judgment, in accordance with the faith God has distributed to each of you. 4 For just as each of us has one body with many members, and these members do not all have the same function, 5 so in Christ we, though many, form one body, and each member belongs to all the others.

—Romans 12:1-5

I liken this to the rib exchange in Genesis.

20 But for Adam no suitable helper was found. 21 So the LORD God caused the man to fall into a deep sleep; and while he was sleeping, he took one of the man's ribs and then closed up the place with flesh. 22 Then the LORD God made a woman from the rib he had taken out of the man, and he brought her to the man.

23 The man said,
"This is now bone of my bones
and flesh of my flesh;
she shall be called 'woman,'
for she was taken out of man."

24 That is why a man leaves his father and mother and is united to his wife, and they become one flesh.

—Genesis 2:20-24 *NIV*

The Church was not taken out of Christ per se, but we are a part of Him.

Just like a woman is part of man. You don't see her full set of ribs and the lack of a man's rib. There is no exchange of the rib when you meet your wife. No one actually gives their woman their rib, she just came with it because God set it into the creation. This is the same for the Bride and the Body. We are a part of Jesus because God set it into our creation design, and we are the bride because we are made to be joined with Him.

Jesus came to Earth, leaving heaven and all its glory, to rescue His bride. It is the greatest love story of all time. While we were sinners, Christ died for us.

*8 But God demonstrates his own love for us in this:
While we were still sinners, Christ died for us.*

—Romans 5:8

We didn't love Him, just like a man pursuing a woman in the beginning of a relationship. She doesn't love him, but he is pretty sure that he wants her to. So he comes for her, romances her, and shows that he is worthy of her love. Jesus did that for us; while we were at our worst, he showed us that He will always love us so much. He put aside His own desire to be rescued from the devastation of the cross and crawled up Golgotha for His beautiful Bride.

We became the body of Christ by being made for Him by the miracle of redemption. He will leave heaven and all its glory again and come to retrieve us for the final time.

7 Let us rejoice and be glad
and give him glory!
For the wedding of the Lamb has come,
and his bride has made herself ready.

—Revelation 19:7

We cannot remove the spiritual element out of this conversation. Actually, this entire book is going to be filled with spiritual concepts. We cannot deny the fact that the spirit realm is the realm where we will spend most of our existence. We struggle with the spirit realm because we cannot see it, but faith is required to even believe in Jesus as Messiah. Faith is required for us to understand who we are as the Bride and the Body and how important it is for us to live out our lives accordingly to honor that call. I have used a lot of parallels between earthly marriage and the spiritual concept of the Bride. This scripture also compares earthly marriages to the marriage of Christ and the Church. We meet some of the expectations of the Bride here.

25 Husbands, love your wives, just as Christ loved the church and gave himself up for her 26 to make her holy, cleansing her by the washing with water through the word, 27 and to present her to himself as a radiant church, without stain or wrinkle or any other blemish, but holy and blameless. 28 In this same way, husbands ought to love their wives as their own bodies. He who loves his wife loves himself. 29 After all, no one ever hated their own body, but they feed and care for their body, just as Christ does the church—30 for we are members of his body. 31 "For this reason a man will leave his father and mother and be united to his wife, and the two will become one flesh." 32 This is a profound mystery—but I am talking about Christ and the church.

—Ephesians 5:25-32 *NIV*

We have some powerful words listed for the Church: cleansing her, presenting herself as radiant, without stain, wrinkle, or any other blemish, holy, and blameless.

Jesus has done his part by making us holy, blameless, and stainless from sin. He has washed us with His Living Water and is our Light. Are we doing our part to be presented as radiant, without stain, wrinkle, or blemish? Are we holy and blameless?

Paul realizes his mission with the Bride. As he plants new *ekklesia* groups and implores them through his letters to stay true to the path he shared with them, he states:

> ² *I am jealous for you with a godly jealousy. I promised you to one husband, to Christ, so that I might present you as a pure virgin to him.*

> **—2 Corinthians 11:2**

We are part of the Bride the moment we accept Jesus. It is critical for us to do our part to encourage our fellow brothers and sisters to stick to the path of life. We are a combined unit. You could think about it like a military unit: many people, one whole. If we try to separate ourselves, if we try to not be a unit, we have lost the vision of God for His children. The Bride is in her most beautiful state as a unit.

Have you ever seen photo mosaic pictures that from a distance are a single picture of a face, but when you look closer you realize that the large picture is actually made up of a bunch of tiny pictures? Look up that art form. It is so cool and may inspire you to understand how you fit in the unit of the Bride of Christ. You are one of the pictures. Your life makes up the picture. Not every picture will be bright; we need depth to make a captivating picture. Do not be afraid of diving in deep with your Groom. I hope by the time you finish this book, you will be able to go deeper. You will crave deeper. Your Groom is worth it. He is the ultimate experience of all our senses and, when we fall passionately in love with Him, we want Him to consume all of our senses much like we felt when we fell in love the first time.

THE FALL OF THE BRIDE

On publication of this book, it is 2024 and the Church is a mess. We do not look anything like this description of the Bride. We are full of sinful behaviors, cover-ups, slanders, fights and quarrels, and so many terrible things. But I think the most heinous of them all is that we are a black hole–consumers of the Light of Christ but incapable of reflecting that light back. We consume so much of the grace and mercy of Jesus. We continue to sin, knowingly, willingly, foolishly and to our own demise. We make excuses for gossiping, cheating in business, cheating on taxes, not sharing with those in need, racism, divorces, abortions, drug and alcohol addiction, pornography, homosexuality, affairs, mole-station and so many sexual perversions. This isn't even an exhaustive list. We justify and excuse away so that we do not have to sacrifice our wants or desires, or change ourselves.

We allow Satan to twist terms like "perfect" and "hypocrite" that puts us on the defensive when they are used against us. We then scream from the mountaintops, "We are not perfect, look at our sins!" We should be screaming from the mountaintops, "Jesus has died for us, cleansed us from those sins, and we all need Him." There are memes on social media that say, "I am not perfect. I sin too," and then the meme may have various lists of people's sins. The idea behind this is to show solidarity with others who also are sinning, but the point of salvation is not *that* we sin, it is that we are *delivered* from the power of sin. Many Christians feel the need to share their sins first, as though that is the only validation to their story of salvation, instead of redemption with God. There is no such thing as perfect on this side of heaven outside of Christ. It is not by our sin that we are meant to be known. When we feel the need to defend ourselves by amplifying our sin, we give into Satan's deception against us. For example: A family that is active in church and looks put together, we will label as a "perfect" family. We create pressure for that family to maintain an unrealistic reputation. The idea of a "perfect" family prevents people from getting help and support they need to heal during a hard season of life. Though there is no such thing as a perfect family, the *idea* that a family that looks put together is struggling seems to throw people off kilter. We mustn't allow labels like "perfect" to create fear and deception to win over truth and authenticity.

Satan has twisted "hypocrite," and so we are scared to call out others' sins. The fear Christians experience is that they will be labeled a hypocrite so they stay silent about their faith, hoping no one is looking as they stumble through their sanctification journey. As though the very idea that we know we need a Savior of our wretched hearts could ever offer perfection or lack of hypocrisy. Church leadership is allowing the flying of flags filled with sinful representation to compel people who want approval of their sin instead of being challenged to align under His ways. But if the church challenges the sin, aren't they all hypocrites? *"Cause they sin too."* You aren't justified in your sin because others sin too. You are cleansed from sin because Jesus defeated the power of it. Sinning is never the focus, or meant to be justified, but it is exactly what we are delivered from when we accept the redemptive work of Jesus Christ. Again, getting distracted by the words "perfect" and "hypocrite" are just deceptions by our enemy to keep us quiet, timid, and ineffective. We begin to magnify our sins instead of magnifying our Groom.

6 All of us have become like one who is unclean, and all our righteous acts are like filthy rags; we all shrivel up like a leaf, and like the wind our sins sweep us away.

—Isaiah 64:6

Our best is filthy rags.

We have forgotten that we bring nothing to the table to begin with. We want to defend ourselves because we can't handle the onslaught of lies from our greatest enemy. We are weak in knowing who God is and we are fearful of what others will say when we are called to the table of our own sin. We have sat in seats at tables we were never designed to be at and have forsaken our place at the feet of Jesus.

I heard a message one time from Pastor Adrian Cleetus at Deliverance Bible Church in Hurst, Texas, with such incredible imagery of this concept of the table. He said, "You set the table with your finest of everything. You have used your best table, tablecloths, finest china, and it is beautiful. Then you invite the Holy Spirit in and the next thing you know, your table is kicked over because it is not clean or usable."

If you ever see Pastor Cleetus, you will see that he is extremely tall and slender. As he spoke, he demonstrated the kicking over of this table and that vision sticks with me to this day. The moment we think we bring something usable to the table, we have fallen into the narcissistic black hole that is consuming the modern church, the Bride. We are usable because God wants to use us for His glory, not because we bring anything worth using to the table. A contrite heart is the most usable part of us and the ultimate antidote to narcissism. When we put any of our works, behaviors, and intentions above remaining humble, we believe that we bring something usable that others need. As though we have any power to save someone, instead of salvation being the beautiful miraculous work of Jesus.

As the Bride, we are meant to be dependent on our Groom. We are to prepare ourselves for Him, not to think that we are already ready. We must continuously be in a state of searching for His direction. He is preparing our eternal place.

2 My Father's house has many rooms; if that were not so, would I have told you that I am going there to prepare a place for you?3 And if I go and prepare a place for you, I will come back and take you to be with me so that you also may be where I am.

—John 14:2-3

Our primary goal is to be ready for Jesus to come and take us to be with Him forever. But He is not coming back for a narcissistic, sick, black hole Bride. He will return in God's timing, but just because we have His name on our lips, doesn't mean we have submitted to the relationship with Him. We cannot manipulate the Most-High God. The Ekklesia will not fool Him into thinking we belong to Him because we are dressed in white with crosses dripping from our necks. Oh no! He will push past the whitewashed tombs and sweep up the lovers of Him.

²⁷ "Woe to you, teachers of the law and Pharisees, you hypocrites! You are like whitewashed tombs, which look beautiful on the outside but on the inside are full of the bones of the dead and everything unclean. ²⁸ In the same way, on the outside you appear to people as righteous but on the inside you are full of hypocrisy and wickedness."

—Matthew 23:27-28

CHAPTER 2

There are four sections to this chapter. Each one is designed to give you a greater understanding of the spirit of narcissism primarily, but I only scratch the surface of Narcissistic Personality Disorder (NPD).

- In section one I explain that there is a natural and spiritual realm to narcissism. This section is to help you understand that the physical symptoms of narcissism are merely an outward expression of what is happening to a person who has the spirit of narcissism attached to them.

- In section two you will learn the dictionary definition of a narcissist and who Narcissus is in Greek mythology. Understanding these concepts will help you understand the pain that comes with dealing with the spirit of narcissism. This is important because the painfulness of the relational experience is what Jesus will reject. Jesus, unlike humans, will not be deceived or confused by the spirit of narcissism.

- In section three I explain everything about Ruach Narcissus, which means *spirit narcissus*. This is the divine revelation that God gave me to write this book and help me understand and teach the spiritual side of what is actually happening to a human with this spirit attached. The rubber meets the road as to the purpose of this book. The spirit realm is the eternal part of us, therefore the most important part, but natural behaviors can cause a lot of damage for us. We need to know our enemy so that we can fight it. Sometimes we need to study our enemy so we have a strategic plan in place to overcome the battle and not succumb to the attacks. It is important to understand that Ruach Narcissus is why there is so much pain when dealing with a narcissistic relationship.

- In section four, I explain the primary and secondary narcissistic personality traits that I will use for the explanation of how the Bride is acting like a narcissist. These traits are referenced for NPD, but I am using them as a correlation to the behaviors of the Bride in our modern world.

SECTION 1: THE NATURAL AND SPIRITUAL REALM OF NARCISSISM

UNDERSTANDING THE NATURAL REALM AND SPIRIT REALM OF NARCISSISM

You may or may not have heard the term narcissist. It is a hot term in American culture right now. If you haven't heard of or personally known a narcissist, you should be thankful. An experience with a narcissist will leave you feeling so empty, devoid of love, unsure of your own feelings, and desperate for something real and less . . . full of lies. It is possible that you have experienced a relationship that left you perplexed and feeling like you can't think straight. This is often how narcissism makes others feel. I was challenged to write this book after God took me through a long-term relationship with a man that I am sure qualifies as a covert narcissist. I am not a psychiatrist, he doesn't have a formal diagnosis, but all the behaviors and pain points match, and the effects of the damaging relationship left deep wounds that needed

Holy Spirit healing. It has been one of my greatest heartbreaking experiences because I believe the love was genuine, but tainted by the spirit of narcissism. Just like when we feel we genuinely love Jesus, but we operate out of a narcissistic spirit instead of Holy Spirit. We think we are in a good relationship, but it is tainted by our selfishness.

I have learned that sometimes, like with Hosea, God brings people into our lives to teach us spiritual principles. In the book of Hosea, he was married to a prostitute, and she represented Israel. Hosea's natural relationship with his prostituting wife was a representation of a spiritual relationship between God and Israel. I feel that this is what my experience with a narcissistic relationship served in my life. I use examples from my relationship to help clarify what dealing with this type of relationship might make someone feel like or what they might experience. I couldn't have known, or understood, the pain of the abuse had I not experienced it firsthand. As with all spiritual issues, we try to understand them in the natural realm by labeling them in some way. Alcohol/drug use/overeating/and similar problems can become addictions and psychosis is often labeled as mental illness, but we know that biblically these are often demonic possessions. Narcissism is called a personality disorder. I know spiritual vs natural is a complex concept, but the purpose of this book is to point out how the Bride is operating out of Ruach Narcissus, so I am merely scraping the surface of narcissism as a natural issue defined as a personality disorder. There are plenty of fantastic books that go into depth about narcissistic personality disorder (NPD) and how to understand it better. As God revealed more and more to me about the narcissistic spirit in the spirit realm, He shared His heart with me that this is how the Bride is operating.

Like a good Father, God is giving warning signs of the danger ahead if something doesn't change in the heart of the Bride. She has allowed herself to become tainted with the spirit of narcissism. It is damaging to her. The heart of this book is to call the Bride to wake up, break the spiritual mess off of her, and fall back in love with her Groom again. So hang in there with me through this chapter. It will challenge you, require you to have spirit-led eyes, and educate you if you are unaware of narcissism, and especially how the Bride is operating out of this corrupted spirit. Please pray that God will reveal to you what you need to learn or know from this book. Revelation always comes from Holy Spirit. You will need Holy Spirit to guide you through this book because it is all about spiritual concepts. We cannot remove the mysticism of Christianity and understand how much the spirit realm is consistently active in our lives.

An untrained person diagnosing someone as a narcissist, or with NPD, may or may not be legitimate, but you will know when you have experienced an interpersonal relationship with one. I studied narcissism extensively during and after my relationship, attempting to understand and make sense of all the insanity and confusion that I was experiencing within the relationship. The primary and most obvious trait is the lack of empathy a narcissist has for the people they claim to love the most. I watched a YouTube video about experiencing a narcissistic relationship and the host stated, "You may not be able to diagnose a narcissist, but you can judge whether you were in a relationship with someone who is very mean." Narcissism is an experiential, and devastating, situation.

Have you ever watched the TV show *House*? I think this show reflects the complication of a diagnosis of narcissism. In *House*, the doctor's name is House and he consistently solves mysterious illnesses that no one else can seem to figure out. The patients will come in with random symptoms and unknown causes, and House will use his out-of-the-box thinking to solve the issue and create a diagnosis and solution to save the patient. Because narcissism is experienced interpersonally, the person experiencing the relationship will be the only one who can give the symptoms, because a narcissist is incapable of seeing any issues within themselves. Not being able to see the symptoms of our sickness is the danger for the Bride because Jesus sees all of these unhealthy behaviors clearly. We need to make sure that we are willing to listen to our Groom's warnings before He has to walk away and claim that He never knew us. We don't need a proper "diagnosis" of the Bride to see that she is indeed operating out of this spirit. However, we do need the ability to put on our spiritual eyes so we can have the Light shining in them properly to prevent ourselves from being lured by this demonic spirit.

Most people are not narcissists by the standards of the counseling/psychology world. Many people are not setting proper boundaries and may not be operating in a healthy relational style, but that does not make them a narcissist. Thinking someone is a jerk does not make them a narcissist. We need to be careful to not casually label people as narcissists because it removes the impact of the level of abuse that comes along with someone who has survived this particular kind of abuse. Unhealthy relationships, even abusive relationships, do not always qualify the person as a narcissist. You will only be able to recognize narcissism in someone else if you are the one in the close interpersonal relationship with them. However, this book is not about diagnosing an individual person with narcissistic personality disorder (NPD), but about the collective whole of the Bride of Christ and how she is operating like a narcissist. I am only using the clinical correlation to give concrete concepts to quite an abstract concept, like God using a prostitute and Hosea to represent Israel and Himself.

Because narcissism is a spiritual corruption that is trying to be helped through the mental health society, it is a very complicated situation to "diagnose." Mental health advocates and practitioners do not necessarily recognize spiritual elements to their work with the mind. Often there is not a correlation to the mind, body, and spirit, though they may acknowledge mind and body together. Narcissism is a spiritual issue first, then one of the mind, and lastly of the body. If it is not dealt with in the spirit first, the mind and body will have no response to any treatment, if there is even any possibility to get a narcissist to listen to anyone in the first place.

I realized I was in a relationship with a narcissist for the first time by accident. I had an employee that surely is a narcissist and I began to study how to handle a narcissistic employee. This was my first exposure to any information about narcissism. While I was reading through an article and it was listing the traits and characteristics, I looked over to my right where he was laying, and Googled "nice narcissist." To my utter and complete surprise, the term "covert narcissist" popped up on my screen. I began to research and was completely shocked at the accuracy of what I was experiencing in my relationship. All the withholding, all the lies piling up, all the confusion of what just happened to our relationship...right there on the screen in black and white. I felt like Alice in Wonderland that had just fallen down the narcissistic rabbit hole. I had to keep researching to try and understand all that I am sharing with you. This was the beginning of my journey to share all of this information with you and how we mustn't let the Bride become the nightmare in the spirit realm. God began to reveal more and more to me about narcissism as a spirit and how it operates in the spirit realm after my relationship ended. I had no idea what I was up against in my relationship or how to fight for or against what was happening to us. Another casualty of the dark forces of this world—we didn't make it through the storm unscathed. Between my studies, and God given revelation through the Holy Spirit, I am able to write this book, and challenge the Bride to turn and run back to her Groom.

SECTION 2

WHO/WHAT IS A NARCISSIST?

I believe that it is very important to understand who and what a narcissist is to be able to fully understand the danger of the Bride of Christ falling into this spiritual hellhole. I am going to give you all the information that I know about this spiritual issue and what a human suffers once they are oppressed by this spirit.

The Dictionary.com definition of a narcissist[1] is:
noun

1. *a person who is overly self-involved, and often vain and selfish.*

2. *Psychiatry. a person who has narcissistic personality disorder.*

Narcissistic personality disorder (NPD) is primarily what we will focus on for the purpose of this book. There are nine primary personality traits of NPD. We will look at those nine, plus another four secondary issues associated with narcissism. These traits are what I will use as a roadmap to help clarify how the behaviors in the modern-day church are operating the same way as a narcissist. I am going to be referencing an article written by Suzanne Degges-White for psychologytoday.com called *The Thirteen Traits of a Narcissist: What do the clinical signs look like in everyday life?* [2] to gather the traits we will discuss and how the church fits into these characteristics. I like the way Ms. Degges-White simplifies a very complex subject like narcissism. She breaks it down into bite size pieces for more easy clarification. She is using these traits to explain human behavior and how they operate in daily life.

I have taken the nine primary traits and created full chapters for each of them, and then a single chapter to complete the final four secondary traits. All of my use of these traits is in contrast to spiritual attributes the Bride *should* have versus the behaviors that she is practicing. I begin each chapter with the practiced trait of narcissism, and then offer an antidote to the trait that would reflect Jesus, our Groom. Seeing how the traits are being practiced in the church helps us to understand how we operate out of the spirit of narcissism and looking into our own behaviors will challenge us to break the pattern.

From my studies I have learned the natural world says the only way to handle narcissism is to leave and save yourself. The main advice in secular culture is that narcissists can't be helped. There are many social media pages to help victims of narcissistic abuse and the primary advice is to leave the narcissist. Articles, YouTube channels, and nearly all the content you can find about narcissism is going to suggest that your only recourse is to leave. As a matter of fact, you will not find support groups and rarely find counselors for narcissists because they are virtually impossible to treat. I know, because I looked! However, you will find plenty of support groups and counselors for victims of narcissism. The narcissist is considered hopeless.

The reason for the hopelessness is because narcissism is a spirit. There is no other way to control a spirit, except through the Holy Spirit. The person that has the spirit attached to them will need to be willing to have the narcissistic spirit broken off of them by the Holy Spirit for complete healing to happen. There is no answer in the natural/material world that can help. The spirit of narcissism attaches itself and corrupts. This is how the Bride of Christ, which is a spiritual principal, can be attacked by this spirit. It attaches itself to humans, which make up the Bride. This doesn't mean that everyone who makes up the Bride of Christ has NPD, but much of the collective whole of the Bride in America, especially, is operating like a narcissist. The majority of us may not qualify under the traits of NPD, but yet our spiritual walk looks more like these traits than the ones that reflect God. An article by Crosswalk. com[3] states, "It's sad to say, but not everyone who claims to be Christian is really a follower of Christ. Many are simply pursuing their own agendas, be it money, fame, or political influence. These false disciples come in many shapes and forms, but perhaps none is more dangerous as the Spiritual Narcissist. A Spiritual Narcissist is someone who uses the Gospel to build themselves up while they tear others down. If left unchecked, their actions can inflict devastating harm on both Christians and non-Christians alike."[3] I like the term "spiritual narcissism" used in this article. It is a spirit, operating in the spirit realm, which affects humans in the natural realm. The issue may remain a spiritual issue alone, which is what this book is revealing and offering solutions, or it may become an issue so ingrained in the human, that the spiritual corruption is inseparable from the human's experience. This spirit cannot prevail, please do not misunderstand. Those who claim to be Christians but have allowed this spirit to activate in their lives, will not be taken as the Bride (**Matthew 7:21-23**). Jesus is not coming back for a black hole. A narcissist operates like a black hole. There is a never-ending consumption of the "supply" that a narcissist needs. A black hole does not reflect light, but consumes it. We are called to be Light. Jesus will not be fooled or manipulated, but He will be aware of His Father's warnings against the Bride. This is how the seven letters in Revelation correlate to this book.

The seven letters are written to different churches: Ephesus, Smyrna, Pergamum, Thyatira, Sardis, Philadelphia, and Laodicea. Jesus challenges and encourages each of these churches by calling out their acceptable and unacceptable behaviors. He also explains the consequences for both types of behavior. The unacceptable behaviors have harsh consequences and this is why the Bride needs to keep a look out so that she does not practice them. Ruach Narcissus will easily deceive us into practicing each one of these unacceptable behaviors because each is disguised by looking "churchy," meaning the behavior looks deceptively acceptable because it is done in the church. The good behaviors that Jesus acknowledges in the letters are rewarded quite powerfully and they are what the Bride needs to strive toward. Our salvation is not contingent on behaviors, meaning we cannot earn our salvation, but Jesus will know *who* has actually attained salvation by *how* we respond to Him. The Bible is very clear that if we love God, we will obey Him and keep His commandments (**1 John 5:3**). I do a deep dive into each letter in chapter twelve, and I had some great revelations myself that I am excited to share with you.

First Corinthians 11:29-32 helps us navigate the importance of judging our own hearts. This scripture tells us that we bring judgment on ourselves if we do not judge ourselves righteously and that it causes sickness and falling asleep (physical death). This scripture also informs us that God will discipline accordingly, so that we will be corrected and live according to His will—and not be condemned with the world. We must be honest with ourselves about who we are, which is how we will know whether we are operating like a narcissist. It will require each of us individually to repent, so that as a collective whole, we break off the spirit that is hurting the Bride.

After being in a narcissistic relationship, you will feel like you have just come through a storm. I equate this storm with a tornado and call it a spiritual tornado. It leaves your head spinning when you exit. Your heart will be depleted and your mind will be reeling looking for any form of stability. You will question yourself, your reality, and whether you are ever going to be sane again. Your trust will be shattered into a million pieces and you will be skeptical of anyone and everyone. Narcissists often talk in riddles or use backhanded compliments and statements leaving you wondering if you heard that correctly or are you crazy.

Cognitive dissonance keeps you from being able to clarify your thoughts. Cognitive dissonance is defined as anxiety or discomfort that results from simultaneously holding contradictory or otherwise incompatible attitudes, beliefs, or the like, such as when someone likes a person but disapproves strongly of one of their habits. [1] Cognitive dissonance will have you thinking two conflicting thoughts at exactly the same time. It is very hard to think clearly when this is your experience. You'll think to yourself:

"Was I supposed to or not supposed to feel insulted by that statement?"

"Is he/she honest, or is he/she a liar?"

"Did he/she abuse me emotionally, or am I being overly dramatic?"

These questions will be on repeat, every day, for the majority of the day as the narcissist gaslights you, confusing your reality. It is the constant questioning of your reality that makes you not quite able to realize whether it is real, or whether you are just making up the experience. Your body and spirit know it is real, but your mind is very confused. You will not understand how evil got so far under your skin that you can't shake it. You will long for the person, knowing that certainly there was a spark, love, something real! Or was it all just made up? (Head spinning, questioning what was real?) You will begin to study everything you can find trying to make it all make sense, and to understand what is happening, only to be left with the best advice the world has to offer, "You'll never understand it, so move on."

You will begin to see that you were merely supply. Supply is what narcissists need to function, because it feeds their ego and elevated sense of self-worth. Supply is the term used for the people that narcissists prey upon, it is the light that the black hole seeks to consume. Narcissists find endless supplies of all needs: financial, emotional, and physical. As long as you are providing that supply to them, they find you useful. If you cannot fulfill all the supply needs, they may find more relationships to engage in to help fill the void of your supply. They may find extra sexual partners, codependents that will give them money, or anyone they can use in addition to their main supply if they feel a void in their endless consumption of people. The moment that your supply runs out, or becomes more costly than useful, they will discard you like you are trash. This causes the victim to question their worth and value as a human being. They may question:

"What did I do wrong?"

"Why didn't they love me?"

"How can this relationship not matter at all?"

But the truth is, when the narcissistic spirit is operating, you only have value to the narcissistic spirit as long as you offer supply. Once you are no longer a supply from which it can feed, well . . . what do you do with an empty paper plate? Throw it away. That is exactly what Ruach Narcissus, the spirit of narcissism, will do. The supply person is treated like an object, merely discardable, instead of a person with complex emotions, feelings, and ultimate value. Being able to "throw away" someone you claim to love is a cold, heartless, and devastating action that only someone like a narcissist is able to do without remorse. The coldness by which the discarding happens is why the action is so devastating for the person it happens to. Now your dimmer light (soul) will leave feeling completely violated and stolen from. Trust issues are mounting for the survivor of the discard as the relationship lies are revealed along with the fact that the person never actually cared about the victim, and that everything in the relationship was a farce. This is how the Bride is treating Jesus when we claim the name of Christian, but our lies are mounting up; we never actually cared about Him or keeping His commands, and the entire relationship was a farce, only a show for the world to see.

The lies that the narcissist tells are often petty when they are revealed, but sometimes can be catastrophic. Typically, the lies are about how much money their paycheck is, or what they spent their money on, but they are not above stooping as low as stealing someone's identity or destroying another's credit. These lies begin to flood out of hiding like a leaky bathtub that has been ripped out of a bathroom. I was stunned at some of the lies that were hidden in my relationship, but really hurt by some of the bigger ones. It is hard to be in an intimate relationship with someone when you begin to realize that everything they say is most likely untrue in some way, if not untrue completely. As these victims get farther and farther away from the crazy making cognitive dissonance, there is clarification dawning on how messed up things really were in the relationship. The utter lack of care from the narcissist is a marker of being in a narcissistic relationship.

When I realized that my ex did not care about me at all, but only cared about what he could get from me, it broke my heart into a million pieces. I had overlooked all the times he could care less about me. I justified it, poured more of my energy into it, hoping that somehow he would begin to care, that certainly he must care. But nope. He didn't.

I posted an entire series, with only the victim being the focus, on Instagram about how to heal from narcissistic abuse. The narcissist makes every single thing about them, and they expect everyone else to make everything about them as well. They consume every aspect of life while they are in it, so when healing begins, don't let them be a part of the process at all. Healing from the abuse can be all about the victim. Instead of focusing on the narcissist and trying to rectify the abuse and confusion, focus on yourself and heal what can be controlled. There is no understanding why the narcissist does what they do, unless you can look at it through spiritual eyes. It still won't make sense, because it is a demonic spirit, but at least as healing comes, the victim will be able to reconcile the little bit of sanity still left after the relationship has ended.

I call narcissism a black hole because I have never met a human that actually has a spiritual entity attached to them, who sucks light and tries to snuff it out like narcissism. This revelation of dealing with a block hole human is what sparked this journey into leaning into God and trying to understand what was happening to me and my relationship. I have dealt with addiction in a relationship and its dragon-like, ugly head. Addiction is awful, but it is not like narcissism. Addiction and narcissism are both spiritual attacks from the enemy of our souls. I needed to understand what was happening and why my relationship was so crazy-making. God began to reveal the spiritual side to narcissism through dreams and spiritual visions. The spirit of narcissism is a black hole that sucks in all the light it can possibly find because it has no light of its own and is desperately trying to consume all it can. I didn't realize that what I was dealing with was a spirit until God revealed it to me after the relationship ended. You go into that relationship a bright light, but you come out much dimmer. The good news, the encouraging news, YOU ARE STILL A LIGHT! It may take time to regain your glow, but never give up. Your worth is set by God, your Maker, Father, and lover of your soul. It is worth taking the time to heal from this kind of relationship, because you have been dealing with an evil spirit attached to your human. Let the Holy Spirit do some deep inner healing work to get your heart back into shape to love again. At the end of the book, I share five steps towards healing from this abuse.

Jesus is the Light of the World. ¹² *When Jesus spoke again to the people, he said, "I am the light of the world. Whoever follows me will never walk in darkness, but will have the light of life."*

—John 8:12

He will not be attaching Himself to a black hole. Jesus is not interested in darkness. We are.

¹⁹ *This is the verdict: Light has come into the world, but people loved darkness instead of light because their deeds were evil.*

—John 3:19

Because of this attraction to darkness, we open ourselves to be subjected to this awful spirit. Jesus expects His Bride to be full of light, blameless and without blemish. Jesus will only accept the Bride that carries those traits.

WHO IS NARCISSUS?

Narcissus is a Greek demi-god who is described as very beautiful like a marble statue. He is a hunter. He receives a prophecy from a seer about himself as a young child that he will live a long life if he never comes to know himself. Once he is grown, a young man falls in love with Narcissus and is angry that he doesn't return his attention. Nemesis, the goddess of revenge, curses Narcissus, on behalf of the man, so that his love will never be returned by the one he loves. Narcissus is heartbroken that he would never have that love. When he is separated from the other hunters, Narcissus becomes thirsty and finds a pool of pure water that no animal has ever approached before. He sees a reflection and falls deeply in love with it, not realizing it is his own reflection. Both the prophecy and the curse came true at that moment. Narcissus fades away, or commits suicide when he knows that his love can never be returned and fails to realize that it is him that he was in love with. [4]

SECTION 3

WHO IS RUACH NARCISSUS?

I have spoken a lot about the spiritual aspect of narcissism and this next part is when you get to read all the meaty, interesting information about it. Now, put your spiritual eyes on. You may even need to pray before you start this section and ask God for help to understand. Often when new concepts are brought across our path, we struggle to understand them. Comprehending the human experience of narcissism may be already causing your brain to stretch, but let's go a bit farther together. This section explains how the spirit of narcissism operates in the spirit realm where we cannot see without divine revelation. **Ephesians 6:10-19** explains that we are fighting a spiritual battle of evil principles and dark forces. If we do not have any information on who/what we are fighting, it would be careless of God to put us in a battle we are ignorant to. God is revealing this evil entity so the Bride can be battle ready, and defeat this spirit trying to lure her away from her Groom.

God has called me to share this revelation about Ruach Narcissus, which means Spirit Narcissus. I asked him why He told me the name in Hebrew (Ruach = spirit) and Greek. He told me that the spirit wasn't around before Greek culture. Mind blown!

Our culture looks very similar to ancient Greek culture. The ancient Greeks have had an incredible influence on our foundations as a modern society. We value their establishment of philosophy, democracy, art, architecture, and military. Our government is established from the Greek concept of democracy, and their architecture is seen throughout our buildings and structures, especially the use of columns. Their passion for philosophy is still quoted and inspires deep discussions today as we question existence, knowledge, values, reason, mind, and language to establish who we are individually and as a collective whole. As Christians, we establish all of these from God. He sets the design of all of these into place and we align with it, knowing He is our creator. The Greeks had their mythology for their religion with many deities. As stated above, Narcissus was a demi-god in Greek mythology. His father was a god, but his mother was not. I am not well educated in Greek mythology, nor is ancient Greek religion the point of this section, so I am not going to digress. What I do know as a Christian is that there is only One true God, and He is in authority.

I don't believe that Ruach Narcissus is some kind of spirit reincarnation of the demi-god Narcissus. I believe the mythical story was the ancient Greeks' way of explaining the existence of this demonic spirit in their culture, like I am doing here for our modern culture but with Holy Spirit guidance. I don't know if ancient Greeks used the term "narcissism" to explain their experience with this spirit, but clearly they were having enough of an issue with it to recognize it in their own philosophical understanding. God revealed in the revelation to me that it wasn't active (notice I did not say it didn't exist, just that it was not active) prior to the ancient Greeks, so they must have had a significant problem with it, like us. They were the reigning culture at that time with large territory and strong opinions. Sound familiar? Remember, they were a pagan culture and Christianity had not become of any importance to Greece yet, or was still practiced in small subculture, so they only had their own religion as a way of understanding the spirit world.

When you meet a human that has Ruach Narcissus attached to them, you may not even realize it unless you are capable of seeing in the spirit realm with Holy Spirit vision. I am asking God to give me vision to see this spirit so that I can take authority over it and rebuke it off of the human and give them freedom by the grace of God. When the Bride is operating in her strength, we will be able to deliver people from this spirit, but not if we are operating from it ourselves. Mary Magdalene was delivered from demonic spirits that humans only saw as crazy behaviors because they were not capable of seeing what was actually happening in the spirit realm. At that time, humans didn't have Holy Spirit living inside of them, but now we do, so we need to begin to see deeper, past the natural and into the spirit so we can make a difference for humans who are suffering with Ruach Narcissus. You think you are dealing with the human, and just merely their very poor and sour behaviors, and to some degree you are, but the spirit is the primary influence for the human and the operating force behind the human's relationships.

Ruach Narcissus is a podded spirit, which means it completely encapsulates the person. This is why it is basically impenetrable, and mental health counselors don't really know how to address it and can't "heal" it. The spirit seals itself around the person. The person was podded as a child, possibly through severe emotional neglect (most likely covert narcissists) or through idolatry worship (most likely overt narcissists). The spirit is familiar to the child, and the spirit has preyed on the child for so long that the human inside the pod feels completely void and depleted of himself or herself. Typically, the human will feel that they are completely unworthy of love, even if they want it or desire it. They are not capable of accepting love because the spirit has corrupted that part of them for so long. They do not believe that they can be loved.

The spirit manifests itself when the person experiences, as a teen or early twenties and in an intimate relationship, the same or similar emotions they did as a child when the spirit attached. For example, if the child was emotionally neglected, that is a familiar feeling. So when the child grows into a teen/young adult and gets into a relationship with someone who emotionally neglects them, the spirit manifests itself, almost like a trigger. This relationship would have either been emotionally neglectful or overly worshiping, just like their childhood experiences, and the spirit would activate itself without the human ever knowing it happened. The spirit is so familiar—because the child has had it his or her entire life—that the beginning manifestation feels common also, especially if triggered by the same feelings. This becomes the pattern of all intimate relationships from that point forward. The human will leave many in the wake of their damaging relationship patterns but completely unaware of *why* this pattern exists. Frankly, it doesn't seem like they ever even care *why* they have this pattern.

Have your brains melted yet? Hang in there with me! This is lifesaving information.

The outside of the pod is covered in mirrors. This is how the Ruach Narcissus mirrors your behaviors and you basically fall in love with yourself, your hopes, your dreams, and your future goals. The pod spins. Slowly at first when you first meet your person podded in the spirit. It is almost like the mirrors magnetize you and you can't, don't want to, get away. As issues arise, especially if you can recognize something is wrong and call it out, the pod spins faster and faster. This creates a lot of confusion. This is also the storm that comes along with Ruach Narcissus. It looks much like a tornado. The path of destruction is very direct and everyone and everything around the narcissists may be left completely untouched by the tornadic storm, except for the person that is closest to the narcissist. The victim will not only be attached to the storm, but in the eye of it. Spiritually spinning out of control with their human, wondering what is going on. The discard often happens after this experience, and it will leave the victim dizzy in the head wondering what just happened.

If you saw someone spinning around in circles trying to function, you would tell them that they have to stop if they want to do anything. But because the spinning is happening in the spirit realm you can't see it happening, therefore, you will hop right on the crazy tornadic pod until it rejects you and validates all the sickness in your own heart: rejection, abandonment, and any other pain you've ever had. This is part of the devastation that one experiences after a relationship with a narcissist. It is almost like the tornado stirs up all the victim's own hurts and insecurities from every corner of their heart and now they are left with trying to filter through all the unexpected pain.

The primary question that resounds from victims is: "Do narcissists know how badly they hurt people?" Based on my God-given wisdom and personal experience, I believe the answer is fairly, no. They hurt people because they are not operating out of their fully conscious mind, but like drug and alcohol addiction, there is a greater pull outside of themselves that propels the behavior. Because this spirit is podded, they are not able to see what all is going on around them, but I believe if you look deep into the eyes of a narcissist, you will see the genuine human begging to get out. There is a saying: "The eyes are the gateway to the soul," and I believe that is true for narcissists. There is a genuine human inside of them that wants to be delivered, loved, and in a good, functional relationship. They just maybe don't realize that they will have to fight hell to get there. Fighting hell is what Jesus already did after the cross, so He intends to come and retrieve a fully healthy Bride who has readied herself for her groom.

If you are in a relationship with someone you think is struggling with Ruach Narcissus, begin to pray for that pod to burst open and the mirrors to be shattered in Jesus' name. You can fight for your loved one. You may need to get to a safe place to do so, because the confusion and craziness that come along with a narcissistic relationship can leave you in deep despair. Cognitive dissonance is a huge issue when dealing with a narcissist. You will have two conflicting thoughts at the same time:

Are they nice? Are they mean?

Is that a compliment or an insult?

Did we just have a fight, or did I just get upset?

Do I love them? Do I hate them?

Cognitive dissonance is one of the ways that the spirit confuses you so that you can't think straight about the relationship. The narcissist will make the victim believe that they are too sensitive, too emotional, and just too much as a person. Everything the narcissist says within the interpersonal relationship (communication about the relationship, relationship issues, or situations you are facing in the relationship) will be said in a way to make you confused or question yourself and your perspective of them. This includes "future faking," which is a tactic used by narcissists to make you believe they are planning for the future, but they will not actually make any steps to work toward making the future a reality. The victim will hang onto the idea, like a fishing lure thrown out by the narcissist, to keep him/her hooked, but the narcissist will not ever make good on any future growth. The victim will waste years of their lives without moving forward, hoping that it will change, because the person they loved made promises they never intended to keep. The entire time, like the fishing lure tricks fish into thinking there is a meal to enjoy, you will be hooked on a hoodwinking idea. It is critical that you get clarity from the cognitive dissonance. Jesus will not suffer from cognitive dissonance and will be very clear about the thought process of the Bride. We will not confuse Him with deceptive internal thinking that we are clean, when we are really filthy rags. We will not be able to future fake with the One who holds the future in His hands.

We don't need a proper "diagnosis" of the Bride to see that she is indeed operating out of this spirit. However, we do need the ability to put on our spiritual eyes so we can have the Light shining in them properly to prevent ourselves from being lured by this demonic spirit.

All narcissistic behaviors are out of rebellion. Our pridefulness leads to rebellion, which then leads to the open door for a spirit like narcissism to attach itself to us. Rebellion, led by pride, was the very act of the first sin in the Garden of Eden. We are still fighting the same sin today, but when we allow our pride to lead us into rebellion, all sorts of evil will manifest. That is what this book is explaining about the Bride. The evil that we have allowed to become prevalent in ourselves. This book, the evil actions of the Church, and the Bride aren't about the outside world, or pagans. We cannot hold pagans to our standards; they do not believe in our standards, and we cannot excuse or justify our behaviors because we see pagans doing them too. *We*, Jesus followers, make up the Bride; therefore, we choose how she operates and behaves, and when we drop our defenses, opening our eyes to the possibility that we are living in pride and rebellion, we can begin to heal and repair the Bride. We want to be spotless, blameless, and without wrinkles for our Groom. He speaks to our behaviors in the letters to the churches in Revelation. I share these letters in Chapter 12.

SECTION 4

NARCISSISTIC PERSONALITY TRAITS

I don't believe that it is ironic that the Ruach Narcissus and the Greek mythology story have so many things in common. Ruach Narcissus prevents the human it has attached to from being able to be loved, similar to the curse given to the hunter. Also, the hunter was warned not to "get to know himself," which is the ultimate challenge of every human dealing with narcissism. They are incapable of self-reflection and self-accountability. The narcissist is incapable of getting to know himself/herself. They will refuse, deny, or blame-shift any issues that are brought before them. The victims of narcissism will often claim that their narcissistic partners are self-absorbed and grandiose, much like the very handsome Narcissus.

The "masks" of a narcissist make them incognito to others. The mask refers to the behaviors they display in the beginning of the relationship that help you fall in love with them. Typically these masks consist of the mirrors that cover the spiritual pod that encapsulates the human. These spiritual mirrors allow the podded human to mirror your behaviors, wants, desires, and needs so that you ultimately fall in love with yourself because they are mirroring everything you say and do. Because narcissists are black holes, they do not know themselves at all. They will only like things that other people, who they have around them as supply, like or love. However, the mask slips and eventually falls off, leaving the victim confused. The unsuspecting person will eventually wonder what happened and question how they used to have so many things in common, only to be left doing most things alone or miserable because the narcissist will punish them for having to participate in the very thing they claimed to "love" during the dating phase. For example, say a person likes to go tubing on the river every weekend. When he/she meets a narcissist looking for supply, the narcissist, too, will like to go tubing on the weekends. During the dating phase, the happy couple will go tubing every weekend. The unsuspecting victim will feel like they have met their soulmate. It will feel like the best relationship ever because the entire time, the narcissist is mirroring the victim. It is heavenly to have someone with so many things in common and so many of the same desires for the future. Hooray! A match made in heaven! They get married. At first, tubing starts only happening once a month. The victim will ask the narcissist why they aren't going tubing as often and will be met with some shallow excuse, like there isn't enough time. Except just a month ago, there was plenty of time. Come to think of it, for the last year, there was plenty of time. Now all of a sudden, there is no longer enough time, except the only change is that they have gotten married. As time moves on, the victim finds that not only does the narcissist *not* love tubing but will punish him/her in very awful ways for still wanting to go tubing. So tubing becomes less desirable to pursue, not because the love for tubing has waned, but because the punishment from their partner is so painful and consistent, that tubing becomes not worth the emotional torture. What once seemed like such a dream, turns into the greatest nightmare, seemingly with no escape. This situation encompasses every aspect of the victim, not just one hobby. The narcissist will treat the victim this same way about everything the victim loves, cares about, and desires. During the dating stage, there was so much support, only for the victim to find out that they fell into a black hole of void and are now struggling to free themselves from the vortex of relationship hell. The black hole wears a mask that looks like light, but it is only a mirror. This is what makes narcissism so cunning, and so very demonic. The hoodwinking is real.

There are two primary types of narcissists: overt and covert. The overt narcissist is usually going to exhibit very demonstrative, captivating, "in your face" behavior and potentially be flamboyant. The overt narcissist does not see themselves as a victim, but more like the "king/queen of the world." They are not vulnerable. The covert narcissist is underhandedly sinister because the behavioral traits are the same as an overt narcissist in nature, but they live in the "poor me, woe is me" victim mentality, and are vulnerable. Sometimes covert narcissists are referred to as "vulnerable narcissists." Both of them rage at their victims. An overt will most likely show their rage outwardly in all sorts of ways, while a covert seethes on their inside toward the person they are in relationship with.

Why do these two identities matter? They can help you identify which one you may be dealing with personally as the Bride or even in a relationship with someone else. The overt narcissist is often going to be one that grabs the spotlight and needs to hold everyone's attention. This behavior seems like they are obviously messed up, especially when it comes to the thought that Christians should be humble. We must be careful though; just because someone *can* command a room, doesn't mean that they *need* to command a room. The overt narcissist will desire to absorb all the light in every single room they occupy. They may be demanding of it if they are not naturally given what they think is their rightful place— the best place, wherever that may be. They will be incredibly jealous and controlling.

The covert narcissist will seem humble, even gentle, and seen as kind and possibly shy. However, underneath they seethe with rage and anger and are like a toxic gas. You inhale it long enough and you will be poisoned beyond belief. Many people stay in relationships with covert narcissists for long periods of time because the behaviors are so subtle and hidden, that though they know something is wrong and something doesn't feel right, they can't quite put their finger on *what* is going on. How can someone who is so nice be so awful? And why am I the only one who sees it? These are the questions that someone dealing with a covert narcissist may ask themselves. Typically a covert narcissist doesn't need the attention of the entire room, but will demand the attention of the one person they have their eyes set on. They can be incredibly jealous and controlling under the radar where no one else knows. Think about the term "covert operation" purposefully meaning to be hidden. Covert narcissistic behaviors are always very well hidden.

Narcissists cannot handle others' emotions, especially an outburst of emotion. This will cause a catastrophic blow to their ego and will potentially cause them to punish you in some horrific way. The options are limitless, but will be painful for the victim and may include physical abuse, ghosting (vanishing without communication), the silent treatment, complete character assassination without any consideration of the ramifications for the victim, utterly withholding everything their victim may want or need, gaslighting (changing the perception of a situation to make someone not trust their perception, creating doubt in the victim about their own sanity/reality), and a hard discard leaving the victim feeling like they've been thrown away like trash.

Listed below are primary and secondary traits of narcissism, totaling thirteen traits. This list describes the traits that would be used to determine if someone is suffering with NPD. I use these same traits in the following chapters as they correlate with the behaviors within the Bride (Ekklesia) to show how we are operating out of Ruach Narcissus. The spirit leads behaviors. We are spirit beings having a natural experience. So the proper alignment is always spirit, mind, and then our bodies. The spirit we follow will be what we choose to operate out of with our mind and then our bodies will follow. When we are operating out of Holy Spirit guidance, our behaviors align with Jesus properly. When we are operating out of Ruach Narcissus, our behaviors will align with this list of narcissistic traits instead of Jesus' ways. The nine primary personality traits that are associated with narcissism according to the article in psychologytoday.com by Suzanne Degges-White Ph.D.[2]:

1.Grandiose sense of self importance

The belief that your contribution and presence are essential to the happiness, success, or equilibrium of other people and enterprises or relationships.

2.Preoccupation with fantasies of unlimited success, power, brilliance, beauty, or ideal love.

This describes the belief that you are capable of exceptionally high levels of achievement even when your skills or abilities provide no evidence of this being possible.

3.Belief that he/she is special and unique and can only be understood by, or should associate with, other special or high-status people or institutions.

This resembles the "I want to talk to the manager" mindset in that narcissists firmly believe that they should only have to deal with the top-level person in any institution. They try to insert themselves in high-status cliques, meetings or social groups even if they are unwanted.

4.Need for excessive admiration

The narcissist isn't satisfied with a compliment or pat on the back when others offer them as part of the natural conversation. They demand that others admire their appearance, accomplishments, skills, or existence. The admiration of others is what feeds the narcissist.

5.Sense of entitlement

Narcissists may believe that success takes hard work—but only for others, not for them. They totally believe that they deserve the best tickets, top score, the nicest room, or the best seat in the house. They don't ever have to verbalize this belief as their behavior and actions clearly communicate their sense of entitlement.

6. Interpersonally exploitative behavior

Narcissists see other people as tools. Their lack of self-awareness is paralleled by a lack of awareness that others exist as individuals with feelings, needs, and desires.

7. Lack of empathy

This is the cold inability to accurately recognize how other people feel. This speaks to the narcissist's lack of emotional awareness or depth. It is not always that the narcissists don't "care" about another's feelings, it is just that they are unaware that others might even have those feelings.

8. Envy of others or belief that others are envious of him/her

This describes the narcissist's constant comparison of themselves to others, wishing for themselves the success others experience, and the false belief that everyone else is envious of them. That's how they keep their egos intact. Being perceived as "normal" or "subpar" would represent an ego wound they could not handle.

9. Demonstration of arrogant and haughty behaviors or attitudes

Arrogance and conceit are traits that are often noticed first in narcissists. This is evidenced by disrespect for the positions or rights of others and the narcissist's willingness to demand and expect that others will bend to their will. Like exploitative behavior, this behavior can be easily noticed without the narcissist having to say a word. They break in lines, use patronizing tones, and act as if they have every right to take away what is rightfully someone else's.

The secondary four areas that we will also touch on are: identity, self-direction, empathy, and intimacy. These are consistent relational trouble spots for narcissists. Degges-White describes these four areas in greater detail as well. She states in her article[2]:

- **Identity**—For narcissists, this is excessive focus on others to support their own self-definition and excessive reference on others as means to maintain their own self-esteem, as well as overly estimated self-appraisal and a tendency to be overly pleased or inordinately displeased with oneself. For narcissists, it's not what's inside that matters, it's what outsiders perceive when they faze on the narcissist that shapes their identity.

- **Self-direction**—Narcissists tend to keep their eyes on the prize that they feel others would prize. They are driven by a desire to prove they are superior to others. This drive is often coupled with a sense of entitlement that leaves them feeling that they should be above having to work for any goal.

- **Empathy**—This area of functioning is what allows humans to connect with and understand the plights of others. Unfortunately, narcissists only reference the reactions or actions of others as they relate to the narcissist's own behavior. Even these "readings" of others are out of focus, as narcissists aren't able to accurately assess their effects on others. They may attend to someone's expressed feelings in order to leverage the person to the narcissist's own benefit, but there's no awareness that goes beyond the practical.

- **Intimacy**—This is where the narcissist's true nature and shortcomings often hurt others the most. Narcissists are unable to forge or maintain more than superficial relationships. They don't have the emotional capacity to relate in authentic, intimate ways. Every relationship is seen as a tool to fuel the narcissist's ego.

CHAPTER 3

GRANDIOSE SENSE OF SELF-IMPORTANCE

The belief that your contribution and presence are essential to the happiness, success, or equilibrium of other people and enterprises or relationships.

The Church has had such a prominent place in society for a very long time. It should be that way, but not for the reasons that it has been that way. The Bride and the government were never meant to be in a premarital affair. The Bride was never meant to be the government's mistress. The Church in the New Testament was not involved in politics or in regulating society. The Bride is to ready HERSELF *for the Bridegroom.* The focus is to train other image bearers[4] how to know God, follow Jesus, and live out their lives with the power of the Holy Spirit.

---

[4] The term "image bearer" is always in reference to us, humans, because we are made in the image of God; therefore, we are image bearers of God

We got in over our heads when priests and pastors became woven into the societal fabric. The Protestant Reformation was birthed because of corruption. We still see the Pope and his elbow rubbing that has now created deep sin inside the Catholic arm of the body. We have pastors who use their power and influence to regulate cities, towns, and potentially even states. The Church was never designed to regulate everyone. The standards the Church was established to set up and uphold are the ones that God set in place for His Bride. Nothing more, nothing less.

Our involvement in regulating society has removed our ability to hold the Bride properly accountable. We've become so focused on the sin of a fallen world that we quit looking at the sin that has become a cancer within our own body. The Bible is clear that we must take the plank out of our own eye before we can take the speck out of another's eye (**Luke 6:42**, NIV). The plank is the overwhelming amount of sin we have in the church and the very reason the terms "hypocrite" and "Christian" have become so closely associated. We allow this grandiosity to go on without calling it down, calling it out, or ironing out the crevasse of a wrinkle we created in the fabric of our wedding gown.

For example, some churches use their power to control whether a city has a restaurant or bar because it serves alcohol. The good intention here is that they will prevent people from succumbing to alcoholism or make alcohol less accessible to them. However, the grandiose sense-of-self-importance issue is that preventing someone from drinking alcohol is not the Church's responsibility. It is conviction by the Holy Spirit that will make a person choose to refrain from behaviors that hurt them or others. Now is it wrong for the church to encourage itself not to drink? Absolutely not! The facilitators of teachings within the Church, most likely a pastor, should encourage their fellow image bearers to not consume alcohol excessively and the "why" behind it. **Ephesians 5:18** encourages not getting drunk on wine because it leads to debauchery, but to be filled with the Spirit instead. The "why" we shouldn't get drunk is because it leads to debauchery and also physical destruction to our liver and brains, but every man and woman must choose for themselves whether they will submit to God and honor His ways. The Church cannot do it for them and shouldn't be trying to do it for nonbelievers. But the Church's stance towards alcohol falls on a spectrum from the "Whiskeypalians" to the "Tee-totaling Baptists."

So let's discuss this spectrum, including church denominations that are against alcohol entirely. They will guilt and shame others for consuming alcohol and somehow pretend that Jesus didn't drink alcoholic wine. My first question is, "How in the world would that liquid at the wedding in Cana not have been alcoholic?" Fermentation was the primary process by which things were preserved; not only that, fermentation is the primary way that fruit around the world spoils, which can easily be demonstrated by drinking directly out of an orange or grapefruit juice bottle and leaving it to sit out at room temperature for a week. So, the assertion that Jesus drank nonalcoholic wine seems silly and makes little sense, yet it gives some of the more conservative denominations some sense of validation and control. Truly, it would be best if they would just say they abstain from alcohol because they recognize the potential for addiction for believers and also offer that potentially people can drink without being alcoholics and destroying their lives. They don't have to try to make absurd claims like the wine in the Bible isn't alcoholic. This place, the one of recognition of the potential problem alcohol can cause and recognition of freedom in Christ, is a healthy way of balance.

While we are on politics, I'd be remiss not to touch on the current political climate in the United States of America. Donald Trump IS NOT the savior and offers no one salvation. The idolatry that has developed over the last few years for one man is obtuse. I am not saying who you can and cannot, should or should not, would or would not vote for. I am saying that Donald Trump is merely a man and should not be put on a pedestal greater than any other man. As Christians, our salvation comes in the form of Jesus Christ and Him alone. When we have put a mere human in some place of deliverance from evil, we are setting the exact stage for the antichrist. That is the deception that humans will have. The world will be so bad off and desperate that people will beg to have relief and a savior, looking anywhere but to Jesus. The Bride must keep her focus on her Deliverer. There is no other answer.

Yes. I do believe that Christians should vote and be involved in the process that our country offers of having a voice. The Mosaic Law didn't regulate us very well, and that is why God sent Jesus. It is no different today. Laws still don't regulate people. People regulate themselves. Instead of making a bunch of laws to regulate people, I believe in freedom. There should be absolute consequences for crimes, so that when someone is found guilty they cannot buy their way out of facing the conviction. There should be an understanding that if you make a victim, you will be punished without rebuttal if found guilty. But whether you are Democrat or Republican is irrelevant if your heart is so skewed by the Ruach Narcissus. You will be completely ineffective in changing your sphere of influence with hypocrisy dripping off your lips that your approach to politics becomes toxic.

I believe this is what we have seen come to pass over the last few years. The toxicity of the political climate, and how politics have been able to successfully make image bearers enemies, is proof that what we have been doing isn't working and we need to do it a different way. We *must* do it a different way. Starting with falling back in love with Jesus and letting Him be our primary focus. Knowing that everything we see, all we are fighting about, will pass away.

The arguments over race, the battle of the sexes, and many other cultural disagreements are merely smoke and mirrors issues. When we focus on these temporary issues, we lose sight of our long-term position in the spirit realm. We are all equally important and have a role to play in this incredible love story of Jesus coming to rescue us from eternal damnation. **Ephesians 6** tells us that our battle is not with flesh and blood, but the evil spirits and principalities of this fallen world. So if our conflict is not with each other, then we must remain focused when all we can see is the fight with another human in our face. The issues of abortion, transgender, gay marriage, and so many others are all spiritual issues, not political ones. Putting policies in place either to accept or reject these things does not prevent anyone from doing exactly what they want. What we do is win hearts. Win hearts for God and let the Holy Spirit do the work of healing. Sin then cannot prevail against the person. But because the Bride has such a gigantic plank in her eye, every time we are trying to help our brother/sister remove theirs, we are hitting them with the plank sticking out of our eyes! We just keep ramming our plank into their face, bloodying their nose, hoping that they will see it our way.

Faux humility is when we think of ourselves as lesser than we should or lesser than others. When we practice self-deprecation as a form of humility, it is a lie. This type of thinking falls in line with covert narcissistic behavior. If someone brings something to your attention that has hurt them, faux humility might respond with,

"I'm sorry. I suck," or "I'm sorry. I'm just a piece of crap," reducing one's self to an artificially low status. This is a false apology with faux humility dressed up as an apology with humility. The person who was wronged might then think they need to build up the person who hurt them. This becomes very confusing emotionally.

Faux humility is self-grandiosity in the negative. A church practicing faux humility will always leave their people feeling "less than," so that the leaders can feel "greater than." The leadership may act like they are humble but expect the people they minister to to feel lesser and not as equipped to share the message of Jesus Christ. The very purpose of a pastor is to equip the people, Bride, to spread the message and to be disciples. A leader with faux humility will not be able to handle the blow to his/her ego and the fact that they may get questions they don't know the answers to. These types of church leaders will enjoy their influence and power over others. Instead of fostering authentic and genuine conversations, if they are confronted with new information, they will become defensive and most likely try to make the interlocutor feel like they have somehow violated God just by asking questions.

There are certain denominations that have put pastors on pedestals as though they are infallible and cannot be questioned. No one should ever be afraid of questioning God and allowing Him to reveal Himself. Jesus came and tore the veil so that we never have to go through a human to access Him. We get direct access to God through the blood of Jesus and the redemption of his sacrifice on the cross. When we are not able to be in the pursuit of truth due to ego, sin has moved in and Ruach Narcissus can thrive.

There is absolute truth. It is that sin leads to death, and Jesus died on the cross to pay that debt on our behalf. The Bride's goal is to fight against sin by loving each other well. We cannot go in with an attitude of grandiosity, as though that summons hearts, and expect to leave with Jesus.

28 "Come to me, all you who are weary and burdened, and I will give you rest. 29 Take my yoke upon you and learn from me, for I am gentle and humble in heart, and you will find rest for your souls.

—Matthew 11:28-29

THE ANTIDOTE TO GRANDIOSITY IS HUMILITY

We see that Jesus is humble in heart. But what does humble mean? What is humility? Dictionary.com defines humble as:

1. not proud or arrogant

2. having a feeling of insignificance, inferiority, subservience, etc.

3. low in rank, importance, status, quality, etc.

4. courteously respectful.

Jesus, the Son of God, sent to Earth did not consider himself of great importance. He did not rub elbows with the higher ups or the most important people. He was known for hanging out with people who weren't significant. He attended events that no one really cares about, but he cared for the people. He already knew that He had all of heaven at His disposal but chose to arrive in a stable, to be placed in a manger, to live as a carpenter and then itinerant minister, and to die on a cross. All for us. This looks nothing like a King, much less a King of Kings, but it was the most powerful, and earth-changing experience possible.

Jesus didn't need all the accolades because he knew that accolades don't summon hearts. Accolades don't impress people who are broken to their core. Jesus came for the broken, weary, and burdened. I don't know about you, but when I have been in some of my lowest places, seeing people who are doing amazingly well and are just so "perfect" didn't inspire me, it disgusted me. Not because I was jealous and wanted to be like them; no, it was that they couldn't even possibly relate to the trenches I was in. They seemed completely out of touch. I believe the feeling or belief of being out of touch with the weary and burdened is what Jesus made an effort to prevent.

We should make an effort to prevent being out of touch with the weary and burdened as well. Does this mean that we can't have money and influence? Not necessarily. You can have those things if you can also retain your grasp on humanity with some humility.

9 Believers in humble circumstances ought to take pride in their high position.10 But the rich should take pride in their humiliation—since they will pass away like a wildflower.

—James 1:9-10

I have a precious woman in my life, a huge gift from the Lord named Betsy Kopecky. She is the epitome of humility. She has money, she has had a place of influence, but she remains deeply planted in the world of the weary and burdened. She consistently works with rehabs, reentry from prison programs, and broken and downtrodden women. She is an encourager to do better, to know better, to live better, and to be uncompromisingly passionate for Jesus. She was never in those physical places herself; she was never an addict (mostly because the Holy Spirit protected her and told her to stay away from alcohol), but she didn't have to be there to know that she needed to go there. The love of Jesus summons her heart to dwell with the weary and burdened of humanity. Betsy has remained in humble circumstances, regardless of what her bank account looks like. It is beautiful to watch and I am honored to get an up-close and personal seat. Oh! How much she has taught me to see people, to guide, and to teach.

The moment we feel like we are bigger than, better than, and not like "them," we are on the slippery slope to self-aggrandizement. It is a repulsive look for the Bride of Christ. We must fight it with everything in us. If that requires extreme measures like giving everything away that you cherish, so that you are free to go and do what God has put in front of you, then that is what you need to do. If it requires you getting out of your comfort zone, squishing your pride, and getting uncomfortable then you need to take courage and go. You will have to get real and authentic before the Lord and go ahead and plan for Him to wreck your world. It isn't your kingdom you are trying to build anyway. Pride and ego are the driving forces of Ruach Narcissus. That deceptive spirit will always make you believe that your kingdom matters the most. Your kingdom will burn in the refining fire, but as saints, you are the Bride to a kingdom that will stand forever.

6 *Humble yourselves, therefore, under God's mighty hand, that he may lift you up in due time.* 7 *Cast all your anxiety on him because he cares for you.*

—1 Peter 5:6-7

God will see you. He is the only One that matters when it comes to assigning your worth and value. Building ourselves up to be more important than we are meant to be may prevent us from having our Heavenly Father lift us up in glory. Humility was once described to me as thinking less of yourself, but not of yourself as less. We must not fall into the trap of self-grandiosity or covert, faux humility.

⁶ But he gives us more grace.
That is why Scripture says:
"God opposes the proud
but shows favor to the humble.

—James 4:6

God will stand in opposition to those who think they are more than they are, especially when they are part of the body of Christ, because we are meant to be representatives. We need to be willing to embrace less of us, more of God. He will show favor to you in that space, and you will have ironed out one wrinkle in the Bride's pursuit of the lover of her soul, Jesus.

REFLECTION QUESTIONS

1. Do you see moments or situations where you have practiced grandiosity?

2. How have your actions hurt others?

3. List 3 practical ways to show humility.

4. Pray for revelation from God for wisdom to show humility when you want to be grandiose.

CHAPTER 4

PREOCCUPATION WITH FANTASIES OF UNLIMITED SUCCESS, POWER, BRILLIANCE, BEAUTY, OR IDEAL LOVE.

This describes the belief that you are capable of exceptionally high levels of achievement even when your skills or abilities provide no evidence of this being possible.

UNLIMITED SUCCESS

Let's talk about church buildings! The amount of money that is going toward buildings is insane. The Ekklesia isn't a building, the Bride isn't a building. People, image bearers, are what comprise the Ekklesia and the Bride. Yet, there are millions of dollars every year spent on buildings.

"Well, Stephanie, we have to put the people somewhere." That's a true statement, but can't that "somewhere" possibly already be built? Or not as fancy? Or less huge? Or in homes or businesses? For nearly two thousand years, the Church establishment never had huge fancy air-conditioned buildings with hot coffee and doughnuts. If that is what it takes to get us together, then we have been corrupted with Ruach Narcissus.

We are called to gather together.

24 And let us consider how we may spur one another on toward love and good deeds, 25 not giving up meeting together, as some are in the habit of doing, but encouraging one another—and all the more as you see the Day approaching.

—Hebrews 10:24-25

We are meant to be together to encourage each other. Where we gather shouldn't matter as much as the quality of what is happening when we gather. We want others to see the success of the Church too many times. If the Church looks like it is thriving, then maybe it is and more people will want to come. It is the trap of unlimited success that makes us build, and build, and build these buildings that we have to upkeep, insure, and take care of. Yet we neglect the very call that we have to go into all the world and make disciples (**Mark**

16:15). There is a lot of world out there that hasn't had the chance to hear the Gospel of Jesus Christ, but we spend money for buildings instead; we also require our missionaries to raise their own capital. Imagine what missionaries could do with just one year's worth of insurance payments.

Do we believe that people won't come if we don't make it attractive and comfortable? Do we think that if the Church doesn't look successful that people won't be a part of it? Do we think that our success is marked by how fancy a space we meet in appears?

I do not have anything against making beautiful places of worship for God. What I have a problem with is when the space becomes the focus and God becomes the secondary reason we have made the space. The success of the Church solely relies on the submitted heart of the Bride and her diligent pursuit of readying herself for her Groom.

POWER AND BRILLIANCE

We could mirror the self-grandiosity information here, but there is no reason to repeat when there are so many issues. The Church's power should only reside in the Holy Spirit; however, we see much less of the fruits of the spirit and so much more of human will and endless desire for power.

I attended a church, the closest thing I've ever personally seen to a cult, that was a complete and total nightmare. Thankfully our family left before the narcissistic storm went completely out of control. He tried to curse us and condemn my now late-husband for leaving. The term narcissist wasn't even around (or at least commonly used) when we were in this church, but the founder and lead pastor is encapsulated in Ruach Narcissus. He thinks so incredibly highly of himself. I know countless couples and people that he has harmed with his arrogance and hunger for power. He has stolen identities, taken advantage of his members for free labor for selfish gain, cursed families who spoke up against him, plagiarized sermons, and even got physically aggressive with one male member.

His endless need for power over the people in the church was so intense that the leadership was attempting to arrange marriages, tell people how many children they should have and how to birth their children, and all sorts of other behaviors that are terribly controlling. People wanted to believe in him and meet Jesus through him, but instead they met hell. He has fallen from high places he set up himself more times than anyone I know, yet he fails to see how corrupt his own heart is.

Unfortunately, I don't think that he is an exception to the rule anymore, but maybe falls right in line with many other pastors. They get a taste of power over hungry people who are looking for answers to the brokenness in their lives, and instead of showing them

Jesus and His love, they get hungry for more power. These pastors are weak in their own self-discipline and their egos need a lot of stroking to keep them from feeling weak. But the Lord is strong in our weakness.

> *9 But he said to me, "My grace is sufficient for you, for my power is made perfect in weakness." Therefore I will boast all the more gladly about my weaknesses, so that Christ's power may rest on me.*

—2 Corinthians 12:9

If pastors and leaders of the church can become authentic, and not only recognize their weaknesses but share them with those they are teaching, the Lord's strength shines through. Our own arrogance tells us that we have to be strong. Leadership positions require a certain level of strength, but not when it is deceptive or corrupted.

Too many pastors have taken great falls from pedestals they were never meant to be on in the first place. One may argue that the pastors are meant to be on the pedestal because of the position they took as a leader. A valid argument, however, humans are not meant to be worshiped. In Acts, Cornelius bows to Peter when he shows up after God told Cornelius to send for him. Peter immediately corrects him and says not to do that because he is merely a man, just like Cornelius (**Acts**

10). Pastors are merely human, just like the rest of us, and not meant to be set on pedestals to be worshiped. They are an influence, and should be worthy of being followed, but that is the importance of being authentic. Instead we place them on pedestals and worship them, then feel the impact of their fall. Sometimes that fall shatters the entirety of the ground we were standing on. We no longer trust the pastor, but worse, we no longer trust God. We conflated the two together as though they were one and the same.

There was a well known pastor many years ago who was busted having an affair with a male prostitute. When the news came out, everyone was so angry and disappointed in this pastor. They shunned him and canceled him. He had become a huge disgrace . . . to everyone but me. I felt relief for him. I believe it was the first time in so many years that this man had the opportunity to become raw, genuine, and broken before the Lord. What others saw as a great fall, I saw as an opportunity for him to hit his knees and recenter.

THE CONGREGATION POWER

We can't put pastors on pedestals. The ONLY One meant for worship is the Triune God. The congregation is at fault for putting pastors up in high places when they have no business being there. The followers need to always be aware that pastors are humans, experiencing the same issues and problems all of us face. If we do not allow them to be honest, we are also guilty of their lies. When we can't extend grace and mercy for them as they travel a complex road called life, then we do not deserve grace and mercy either. We can't expect more from others than we expect for ourselves.

No one can live under the weight of someone else's expectations that are unrealistic. A pastor's role is to equip, lead and guide, and encourage the saints. It is the responsibility of the congregation to be teachable in these areas. There should be a beautiful dance between the pastor and the congregation that builds up both parts.

The hurt and pain that people have caused for pastoral families by having unrealistic and high expectations is a devastating casualty of the mission field. Mission families have an incredibly high divorce rate and extreme trauma from dealing with church congregations. According to www.pastoralcareinc.com [1], 80% of pastors believe ministry has negatively affected their family. The congregation holds a lot of power to make or break the experience for the family. If the congregation is full of criticism and judgment, they will tear apart a pastoral mission family. I use the terms "mission family" and "pastoral family" synonymously here. All pastoral families are missionaries to our local communities.

I have a friend who told me a story just the other day about something that her church is experiencing now.

They have a woman who is stirring up strife and now they are facing a split . . . or a broken bone in the Bride. The pastor committed a heinous sin about twenty-five years ago, *prior* to becoming a Christian. The pastor and his wife no longer consider it an issue, and through Christ he has complete forgiveness. The information was new to this busybody lady, so she started trying to move other members against the pastor. Instead of Jesus' sacrifice being sufficient to pay for this sin, she wants this pastor to be held accountable to her. She wants him to pay for his sin today and will not release grace and mercy toward him. The whole church is now sick and toxic. Instead of this lady being held accountable for the sin of self-righteousness, she fails to see how her own self-righteousness is the very same, or worse since she is a believer, as the sin he committed. She wants to use his sin against him to hold him accountable as though she is the one who can stand in judgment of another. She is using her power to be destructive instead of life-giving.

And another pastoral mission family will leave a church broken, hurt, and feeling like they should just give up. They will be one of many feeling the sting of the congregational power operating by Ruach Narcissus being used to hurt and corrupt, instead of looking to their Groom and knowing how to extend grace and mercy. Sometimes it is OK for us not to have to answer for other people and their sins. We can allow God to be God—and live in the space of grace.

How is this biblical when the Bible tells us to hold others accountable? IF the pastor was in active sin at the moment, like caught in the act, that is when the church holds the pastor accountable, not twenty-five years later. However, even when a church catches a pastor living sinfully and harming the Body, there is a way to go about it that isn't eating the person alive or with a witch hunt. The church should be a relatively soft place for hurting and broken people to land. Most of the time it is like landing on a diamond surface, and it shatters the heart into a million pieces. We will talk more about this with the situation of empathy, or lack thereof.

BEAUTY

The unfortunate situation is that we have the gift of THE greatest love story of all time, which we say we believe, yet we summon our hearts toward all sorts of other gods. The Church has become easy to be swayed by idols. We are no different than the ancient Hebrews who built the golden calf while Moses was still up on the mountain scribing the Ten Commandments.

We build golden calves out of our homes, cars, clothes, pets, and bodies. We have begun to worship those things as though they have significance. We buy things we can't afford, but then don't have the money to take care of other image bearers. We prioritize things like lip fillers and false eyelashes, or maybe large trucks, fast cars, and fancy shoes while we choose to overlook the needs of others. And I don't just mean the homeless; the homeless and overtly poor people always need care and have many ministries that focus on helping them regularly. I mean that young mom who may need someone to buy her lunch and speak encouragement and life into her and her family. I mean the man who sits alone and may need an invite to Christmas, even though he looks like he is well outside your social status. I mean the people struggling with paying for high school fees so their kid can graduate. There are so many people not looking for help that need it and would probably take it if it were offered from someone who has taken the time to build a relationship with them.

I see people spend an exorbitant amount of money on their pets. They will buy them clothes, fancy foods, medicines in large amounts, and many other things, while image bearers are desperate for attention. Yes, your pet is your responsibility, but it is not an image bearer. Having, loving, and caring for a pet is not the issue. By all means, have a pet. Just remember that it is a pet. People can often get very defensive about this topic of pet care, as it clearly hits a trigger point for people's good intentions. There is no eternal significance for your furry, scaly, or slimy pet. Basic needs and care are plenty for the pets. Instead of using the money that you indulge on a pet, use it to have an impact on someone who needs it is what Jesus would do. When we put animals in positions that only humans should have, we get on a slippery slope of missing the heart of God.

Pets are not people. We cannot move them into having the same significant role. Many Christians would be stupefied to be correlated to Hinduism or Native American animal worship. We certainly do not worship our animals, or do we?

25 *They exchanged the truth about God for a lie, and worshiped and served created things rather than the Creator—who is forever praised. Amen.*

—Romans 1:25

If we value our animals above our fellow image bearers, we have closely tread the line of worshiping what is not eternal over what is eternal, worshiping the created over the Creator. People are made in the image of God, animals are not. Where we invest our hard earned income is very much a reflection of what or who we worship.

17 *You say, 'I am rich; I have acquired wealth and do not need a thing.' But you do not realize that you are wretched, pitiful, poor, blind and naked.*

18 I counsel you to buy from me gold refined in the fire, so you can become rich; and white clothes to wear, so you can cover your shameful nakedness; and salve to put on your eyes, so you can see.

—Revelation 3:17-18

We are building golden calves while our insides are rotten, then we call it Christianity and taint our entire spheres with toxic lies. We confuse the notions that if a thing is beautiful to our eyes that it must be beautiful in an absolute sense. However, there is a difference between what the world accounts as beautiful and valuable and what God considers beautiful and valuable. God wants our hearts to be fully submitted, so that what He values, we value. God does not focus on what you look like on your outside. The focus is always what is on your inside.

7 But the LORD said to Samuel, "Do not consider his appearance or his height, for I have rejected him. The LORD does not look at the things people look at. People look at the outward appearance, but the LORD looks at the heart."

—1 Samuel 16:7

You won't impress God with the beauty of this world. He is the maker and creator of all the most glorious beauty in creation. Ruach Narcissus will fool you into thinking that the beauty it draws you to is real, but it is a lie and deception.

I used to do education for a hair product company. I would travel around the region to salons and hair conventions and teach color techniques. I had a dress code to uphold, and I love fashion! So I wanted to have really nice clothes to teach in and hopefully impress those I was teaching. I wanted to look fashionable and cutting edge. One day, I had a conversation with God about it. I was feeling a little conviction about how much money I was willing to spend on the clothes, and I found myself wanting to create an image to impress. I asked God what His thoughts were on it. He said, "I don't mind you having nice things. What I mind is when you put your identity in it." OK God. Point made. I chose then not to equate my value and identity with what I was putting on my body. I stayed in the place of a humble heart before the Lord and it didn't really matter how much I attempted to impress humans, it was God's heart that I consistently pursued. I could have easily fallen into the trap of being wrapped up in the world's love of beauty. Heck! I have been in the beauty industry for over twenty-five years! I lived to make people beautiful and consumed all things beauty. But man, did I meet some wretched hearts in that journey of being saturated in beauty.

Gossip is a common act of bonding in the salon culture. When I was younger, I would often indulge in the juiciest gossip. I knew all sorts of things about people and their lives. I think it made me feel powerful. I wasn't following God very closely in those days and it took many years before I realized that I was actually hearing a lot of hurt and pain in people's lives. Now when someone shares with me their pain, I don't relish in it and enjoy it, instead I pray with them. I will encourage them and walk through some hard moments with them and always point back toward Jesus. My heart was wretched for so long, until I realized that the beauty I was giving them didn't matter nearly as much if the inside didn't matter. I named my salon storefront Beauty for Ashes Salon and Colorbar because I wanted people to come in with their ashes (life's woes) and leave with beauty (a restoration on their inside and outside). The work we do in salons is such a powerful and impactful work on the people who sit in our chairs. I love to see beautiful things, but I no longer find it beautiful if it is just surface.

When we fail to see our insides because we think our outsides are what matter, we are not honest with ourselves. I have a neighbor whose house is all pulled together. It is cute on the outside and the yard is kept up nicely. From the outside, you would think that it is a cozy little home. If you could see the heart on the inside, the humans that live there, you would think differently. There is so much brokenness and terrible stuff. There have been so many days that I would pray for that home to find Jesus because I knew no matter how manufacturedly beautiful the outside was, the inside was rotten, and causing harm and pain. They have given in to the illusion that being pulled together and impressing others matters more than what is happening on the inside of them.

IDEAL LOVE

Unfortunately churches, for so many years, have been promoting grace and mercy like it is the only characteristic of God. We need grace and mercy. We like grace and mercy. We devour grace and mercy. We abuse grace and mercy. We think we can just do whatever we want and it doesn't matter because of grace and mercy. We lift the proverbial rug and shove all the sins under like it was just covered by grace and mercy and there is no place for holiness and justice.

[1] What shall we say, then? Shall we go on sinning so that grace may increase? [2] By no means! We are those who have died to sin; how can we live in it any longer? [3] Or don't you know that all of us who were baptized into Christ Jesus were baptized into his

death? *4* *We were therefore buried with him through baptism into death in order that, just as Christ was raised from the dead through the glory of the Father, we too may live a new life.*

—Romans 6:1-4

We love Jesus as Savior. He is safe as Savior. He is welcome as Savior. Savior works for us because it serves us. Saving us from ourselves sounds awesome! And it is given freely!! Sign me up! I am good with being saved.

But there is a second part. Jesus is also Lord. As Lord, He requires submission. Lordship requires that we are no longer in charge, but He is. This isn't as comfortable. This isn't really welcome because it takes control away from us. Ruach Narcissus can't let us feel safe without control—then it will lose control over us, the Bride.

9 *If you declare with your mouth, "Jesus is Lord," and believe in your heart that God raised him from the dead, you will be saved.* *10* *For it is with your heart that you believe and are justified, and it is with your mouth that you profess your faith and are saved.*

—Romans 10:9-10

Jesus as Lord comes first, then we are saved. Jesus without His lordship is not our salvation at all and we cannot fool ourselves into thinking that all we need is grace and mercy. We cannot fall in love with ideal love that tells us we are OK just as we are. We cannot romanticize a Savior that doesn't call us to repentance. We cannot trust a Savior that is not also Lord. How could Jesus save us if he requires nothing from us?

We are masters at making messes out of ourselves and our lives. To save us from ourselves but to continue to let us make messes would make Him a very irresponsible and foolish Savior. God, Jesus, and Holy Spirit are neither irresponsible nor foolish, and will not be persuaded to compromise to make us feel like we have ideal love that fits us. The Ruach Narcissus demands that we continue to live however we want, yet we should still be saved. This spirit spits in the face of Jesus' lordship and claims that if He is grace and mercy that he cannot possibly require holiness.

We cannot have mercy without sacrifice. We cannot have grace without justice. We cannot have love without holiness. We cannot have salvation without lordship. Mercy, grace, love, salvation, sacrifice, justice, holiness, and lordship are all characteristics of God. We cannot pick one or two and say we know our Trinity. We must break the sickness of idealizing love that kills and accept true Love that changes, challenges, and saves us.

THE ANTIDOTE TO PREOCCUPATION WITH SUCCESS, POWER, BEAUTY, AND IDEAL LOVE

First, we must recognize our propensity to fall into a preoccupation with success, power, beauty, and ideal love. We need to get an honest and genuine assessment of our lives and see where we can get real with ourselves and before the Lord. Once we recognize and confess, Jesus is diligent to forgive and redirect us to a better way.

We must trust that God is in control of the success of the Church. He founded the Church, the Bride, and He has a vision for us. Let God reveal to you what His vision is for your part and begin to take the bold, brave steps to walk in it. You may be surprised where it takes you. It may be into a greater position than you ever could have dreamed, or it may take you into the lowest position that you never could have imagined. Either way, if God is orchestrating it; you are in safe hands and the beauty that will come out of it will be the greatest blessing of your life.

We may need to ask how we use our power in a tainted way and then have enough humility to allow our behaviors to align with what God shows us. We may need to make some apologies to people whom we have hurt, even if we didn't mean to or know we did it at the time. God can bring to light anything that we have done. Sometimes we don't even realize that we have used our power at all. We may think that because we are passive and quiet that we didn't hurt anyone, but maybe we needed to stand up for what is right, and we didn't because we didn't want to cause trouble. Each of us still used our power—we just used it in a passive form. If you allowed an injustice, and didn't stand up, repenting from that behavior is a great way to begin to change your ways. When you see an injustice, speak up!

We have power because we are made in the image of God. We do not get to choose whether we possess power, it is innate, but we do get to choose how we use our power. We will use it to build or destroy. We will use it to show others that we love God, or we will use it to show that we love ourselves. There is no neutral ground when eternity is at stake.

21 The tongue has the power of life and death,
and those who love it will eat its fruit.

—Proverbs 18:21

Breaking out of the beauty deception is freeing, though at first it may seem scary. There is no right or wrong physical appearance as a Christian. There is no perfect mold. We need to look at people's hearts. We need to think through how much energy and identity we put into the things that fade away and how much we overlook the things that are eternal. It will make a difference for our heart toward others when we recognize that beauty is truly so much more than outer appearance.

We will be compelled to be in buildings that feed our spirits for the battle that is before us, instead of seeking places that make us feel comfortable and satisfy our flesh. The Church is designed as a gathering place so that the Church (Ekklesia) can come together and equip each other. We mustn't need it to be overly beautiful to the eyes and forget that the soul is what should be moved. I wonder if in some of the great cathedrals of the world people who go in are in awe of God, or are just in awe of the artwork from man? I wonder how many times someone has fallen to their knees because of the dense presence of the Holy Spirit and a new understanding of how much God loves them.

I believe in preserving these works of art for the sake of the art, but not because these cathedrals are necessarily bringing people closer to God. It saddens me that we have allowed so much money to go to buildings that have no eternal significance while image bearers are overlooked. We must keep our focus, Bride. None of the money that we spend on things that will burn up or fade away matters. Let's not continue to build buildings and call it holy work, when truly it seems to be more about satisfying our endless need for beauty and comfortable surroundings.

The most important antidote for this section definitely defeats our notion of ideal love that was listed above, and that is to recognize Jesus as Lord and Savior. He must come first in our lives. We have to allow him to be the decision maker for us, even if that looks like sacrificing everything we have ever known to make it happen. We can trust in His Lordship so well that, even in the fear of letting Him have control, we are the safest there. Once He becomes Lord of your life, you realize that you have nothing to lose, but only gain.

20 I eagerly expect and hope that I will in no way be ashamed, but will have sufficient courage so that now as always Christ will be exalted in my body, whether by life or by death. 21 For to me, to live is Christ and to die is gain.

—Philippians 1: 20-21

Jesus becomes our savior only when He is lord first. We cannot expect to be saved by someone we will not listen to. Have you ever had a toddler or even been around a toddler? They are chaos in little bodies. Their endless desire for adventure and to learn everything is inspiring and terrifying for adults. If you have had one toddler, you may not have as few cares as someone who has had three or more. The first toddler you can coddle fairly well and there is still a ton of energy to go around. The second one might have a chance at receiving extreme life-saving measures. But by the time you get to toddler number three, or any consecutive ones, you are fully outnumbered and at the mercy of God to make it through. Why? Because toddlers . . . Do. Not. Listen. They don't. You tell them not to put something in their mouths and they do it anyway, while they are staring at you straight in the face. You tell them to sit on the potty, and they pee on your floor. You tell them to eat food that is healthy for them, and they are eating the plastic wrapper out of the trash. Toddlers do not care that we have their best interests in mind. They do not care that we absolutely without a doubt know more than they do. They do not care that we are guiding them for their own safety. What they care about is doing it their way. We are like those toddlers when we do not allow Jesus to be our Lord.

We were given guidelines, but not because God feels the need to control us. If that were the case, He could have just removed our free will. Easy peasy. God gives us guidelines because we are so prone to doing everything we shouldn't do and struggle to do what we are told to do. Choosing to allow Him to be Lord of our lives is us submitting our will to Him so that when He tells us something is bad for us, we are willing to listen. We are willing to do what we don't want to do, what we aren't prone to do, when we allow Jesus to be Lord.

Paul shares with us such a perfect explanation of this struggle in Romans:

15 I do not understand what I do. For what I want to do I do not do, but what I hate I do. 16 And if I do what I do not want to do, I agree that the law is good. 17 As it is, it is no longer I myself who does it, but it is sin living in me. 18 For I know that good itself does not dwell in me, that is, in my sinful nature. For I have the desire to do what is good, but I cannot carry it out. 19 For I do not do the good I want to do, but the evil I do not want to do—this I keep on doing. 20 Now if I do what I do not want to do, it is no longer I who does it, but it is sin living in me that does it.

21 So I find this law at work: Although I want to do good, evil is right there with me. 22 For in my inner being I delight in God's law; 23 but I see another law at work in me, waging war against the law of my mind and making me a prisoner of the law of sin at work within me. 24 What a wretched man I am! Who will rescue me from this body that is subject to death?

25 Thanks be to God, who delivers me through Jesus Christ our Lord!

So then, I myself in my mind am a slave to God's law, but in my sinful nature a slave to the law of sin.

—Romans 7:15-25

Paul asks, "Who will rescue me from this body that is subject to death?" and then emphatically answers, "Jesus Christ our Lord!" Lord. That is the key. He has to be Lord to deliver us from ourselves and our propensity to sin, which leads to death. This is the greatest love story of all time.

16 For God so loved the world that he gave his one and only Son, that whoever believes in him shall not perish but have eternal life. 17 For God did not send his Son into the world to condemn the world, but to save the world through him.

—John 3:16-17

8 But God demonstrates his own love for us in this: While we were still sinners, Christ died for us.

—Romans 5:8

We move from ideal love of Jesus Christ to authentic love when we desire Him to be Lord and Savior of our lives; when we truly submit to Him all of us. When we grow out of our toddler-like behaviors and choose to follow Him as Lord, He can help us grow into mature Christians who make an impact. He cares for us and He does not take the gift of us choosing Him lightly. It is so important to Him that He came and died for it. When we live in the concept of ideal love, God can just accept anything we think/act/or behave as acceptable, but that isn't real genuine love of a Father. Jesus consistently shows us that the way to the Father is through Him, and very narrow. Listening, learning, and accepting God's instructions will illuminate the narrow way. Jesus is looking for authentic love from His Bride.

REFLECTION QUESTIONS

1. Have you idolized success in an unhealthy way?

2. Are you allowing God to show what His idea of success looks like for you personally?

3. Is Jesus your *Lord* and Savior?

4. How do you practically live out Jesus as Lord in your life?

CHAPTER 5

SPECIAL AND UNIQUE

Belief that he/she is special and unique and can only be understood by, or should associate with, other special or high-status people or institutions.

This resembles the "I want to talk to the manager" mindset in that narcissists firmly believe that they should only have to deal with the top-level person in any institution. They try to insert themselves in high-status cliques, meetings or social groups even if they are unwanted.

Facebook, Instagram, TikTok, YouTube, and all the social media outlets have really given oxygen to the flame of feeling special and unique. This wildfire is somewhat out of control! If you see how Christians operate on social media, especially in relation to each other, it will make you detest the Bride quite quickly. So many slanderous and vicious comments. Arguments over nonessential items. The concept of "I am absolutely right and right absolutely" becomes the mantra of every keyboard warrior. The inability to realize that maybe you don't need to have an opinion is prevalent.

Gaining followers becomes the pursuit because we must get our message out there. We need more likes to be seen and heard. The Bride needs to show off every element of herself in hopes of luring people in, much more like a harlot than an anticipating bride without spot or blemish. We strip the message into palatable thirty-second clips that are easily twisted and corrupted to make the Bride look like a tease. We are showing off the most intimate parts of our lover's heart toward Jesus without any thoughts about how it gets taken out of context by those who do not love us or our Savior. We have turned the message of our first love into click bait and human worship. If we can only get seen, then we can be on top. If we can capture their attention, then maybe they will see us . . . I mean Jesus. Or do I?

I don't think Jesus is often the pursuit of the topic, though His name is used in the subject. So many teachings today make God a genie—if we just do something the right way, we will be able to get Him to do just the right thing for us. Ultimately, the message is human centered the whole time but wrapped in Jesus-embossed paper with a big fat bow of self-worship. Just like Ruach Narcissus hopes . . . keep her distracted by false words and faux illusions.

The power in Jesus' name stands in spite of us. Jesus alone harnesses the power of His name. We do not create the power in Jesus' name, and we do not own the power in Jesus' name. We are able to use the power in His name because He gives us permission, and that is one of the redemption gifts the cross offers us. When we say the name of Jesus, the power that moves in the spirit realm rests solely on the divine person of Who Jesus is, the Son of God. That is the reason people can perform miracles in His name and He will not even know them.

> 21 *"Not everyone who says to me, 'Lord, Lord,' will enter the kingdom of heaven, but only the one who does the will of my Father who is in heaven.* 22 *Many will say to me on that day, 'Lord, Lord, did we not prophesy in your name and in your name drive out demons and in your name perform many miracles?'* 23 *Then I will tell them plainly, 'I never knew you. Away from me, you evildoers!'*
>
> **—Matthew 7:21-23**

When we use the name of Jesus to make us feel special and unique and climb social ladders, we are corrupting the purpose of His name. We are using His name for our glory and not His. The relationship with Jesus summons us to a place of humility and the laying down of ourselves. Our pursuit should never be to honor man over God. We will often not feel very special or unique when we carry the cross laid out before us to share the Good News to everyone, even if they hate us for it.

Let me be clear that I do not think that being on social platforms and sharing the message of Jesus is wrong in any way. I believe that these platforms are an avenue that people who may not have other exposure can take to acquire some knowledge and understanding, but the heart's intention behind why you are there must remain humble and submitted to the Lord. What you say is also the message that you are sharing to the world. Does it glorify the human and make humans the idol of God's worship, or does this message glorify the Father? Is the post a gospel message that can be shared around the world, or is it just American rhetoric?

I am one that prefers calling a spade a spade. If you are going to share American rhetoric from the pulpit, call it as such, but don't you dare act as though it is biblical gospel teaching. American dream rhetoric teachings—from prosperity teaching to political rants to treating God like He is a genie do not align with the gospel. If it cannot be taught in the remotest unknown places in the world and stand true, it is not gospel preaching. If it doesn't stand true for every image bearer on the face of the planet, it is not gospel teaching. We must quit dressing up our feel-good messages of human worship in cloaks of deception and calling it the Gospel of Jesus. We cannot retain any dignity when we want to be special and unique through a guise of lies and deceptions that sound good, but do not have any call to repentance for sin and a promise of eternal life. Some Bible translations like the New American Standard (NASB) refer to this as "tickling the ears" and I think that is such a great word picture. This one, the New International Version (NIV), says, "itching ears."

¹ In the presence of God and of Christ Jesus, who will judge the living and the dead, and in view of his appearing and his kingdom, I give you this charge: ² Preach the word; be prepared in season and out of season; correct, rebuke and encourage—with great patience and careful instruction. ³ For the time will come when people will not put up with sound doctrine. Instead, to suit their own desires, they will gather around them a great number of teachers to say what their itching ears want to hear. ⁴ They will turn their ears away from the truth and turn aside to myths.

—2 Timothy 4:1-4

The Bride will not want her itching ears tickled; she knows that that leads to death because it suits our own desires. The Bride will preach the word to correct, rebuke, and encourage all those who are willing to hear. You cannot save someone else, that is the Holy Spirit's job, but you can share your testimony with all who will listen. If we are trying to impress others, we may withhold the very thing they need to hear: our story.

I have fallen into this trap before. I have been around people who made me nervous, and I wanted them to like me, so I stayed quiet. But what I found to happen in those circumstances is that they still didn't accept me. Why? Because I cannot separate Jesus in me. I still didn't talk like they talk, do what they do, act like they act . . . I was still different. I was still set apart. I will always remain set apart because when I accepted Jesus as Lord and Savior, He set me apart from the world and I am no longer able to blend in. My camouflage is heavenly, but it shines like a candle here on Earth.

14 You are the light of the world. A town built on a hill cannot be hidden. 15 Neither do people light a lamp and put it under a bowl. Instead they put it on its stand, and it gives light to everyone in the house. 16 In the same way, let your light shine before others, that they may see your good deeds and glorify your Father in heaven.

—Matthew 5:14-16

Jesus came as lowly as possible. He didn't come with all his glory shining for man to see a flashy king who thought highly of himself. He knew that our human tendency is to desire to be special and unique. God created us special and unique.

13 For you created my inmost being;
you knit me together in my mother's womb.
14 I praise you because I am fearfully and
wonderfully made;
your works are wonderful,

I know that full well.
15 My frame was not hidden from you
when I was made in the secret place,
when I was woven together in the depths
of the earth.
16 Your eyes saw my unformed body;
all the days ordained for me were written
in your book
before one of them came to be.

—Psalm 139:13-16

So what is wrong with thinking we are special and unique if we are made that way? Again, it is the heart behind our behaviors. God made us special and unique to shine His glory throughout the world—not so that we rub elbows with who we think are the most important people or those who "deserve" our presence.

THE ANTIDOTE FOR SPECIAL AND UNIQUE

Our antidote is to know that we are special and unique by God's design and we shine because of Jesus in us. Without Jesus, our hearts are so rotten. Because we are image bearers of God, we have some pretty cool components that are only brought to their fullness when we are in relationship with our Groom. Our initial human inclination is "me first." We always want to look out for ourselves first. There is nothing special or unique about that behavior pattern or thinking. We must fight the thinking that we are only special and unique when we feel like we are better than or above someone else. But when we submit ourselves to God and allow Him to develop us into maturity, we quit thinking like a child and become special and unique.

[11] When I was a child, I talked like a child, I thought like a child, I reasoned like a child. When I became a man, I put the ways of childhood behind me.

—1 Corinthians 13:11

This is called being holy. Holy means to be set apart. We are special and unique because we have the ability to become holy. Jesus' work of redemption on the cross is what gives us the ability to be holy. His cleansing blood wipes away all of our trespasses of sin, so that we are made clean in the spirit. We are able to be set apart from what is going on around us. We handle things differently. We see the world through God's eyes and not our own. We are brought out of the darkness of the world. Once our vision for humanity is illuminated, we are inclined to love harder, love better, and love more fully.

9 But you are a chosen people, a royal priesthood, a holy nation, God's special possession, that you may declare the praises of him who called you out of darkness into his wonderful light.

—1 Peter 2:9

REFLECTION QUESTIONS

1. Do you attack or mistreat fellow believers on social media?

2. List 3 ways that you are special because of God's work in you, not your own works.

3. What makes you feel the most special? Does it align with scripture?

4. Do you need to be noticed by the "most important" person to feel accepted in church, business, and events?

5. Pray that the Lord will reveal your unique characteristics that He wants to use for His glory, not yours.

CHAPTER 6

NEED FOR EXCESSIVE ADMIRATION

The narcissist isn't satisfied with a compliment or pat on the back when others offer them as part of the natural conversation. They demand that others admire their appearance, accomplishments, skills, or existence. The admiration of others is what feeds the narcissist.

This chapter piggybacks on the last chapter well. The overwhelming need to be seen as special and unique by the world will always lead you to grapple for its admiration. Much like the great cathedrals I was talking about, people come to look, but not actually approach God. But how do we get a world to admire us when we have the name of Jesus all over us? We can't. It is a futile pursuit.

18 "If the world hates you, keep in mind that it hated me first. 19 If you belonged to the world, it would love you as its own. As it is, you do not belong to the world, but I have chosen you out of the world. That is why the world hates you. 20 Remember what I told you: 'A servant is not greater than his master.' If they persecuted me, they will persecute you also. If they obeyed my teaching, they will obey yours also.

—John 15:18-20

What does worldly admiration look like in the Church? I asked this question on Facebook to see what my friends would say. The resounding two answers were: the Church justifying sin and the lack of power in worship. Justifying sin is the Bride's compromise and the lack of power has made our worship wayward.

So let's dig into these two primary issues. But first, I think one of the core issues the Bride has struggled with that has opened the door to these other issues is relevance. The Bride is trying to be relevant to an enemy, not the lover of her soul (Jesus). This is when the Bride has been courted by a narcissistic enemy and allowed the tainting to tarnish her.

33 Do not be misled: "Bad company corrupts good character." 34 Come back to your senses as you ought, and stop sinning; for there are some who are ignorant of God—I say this to your shame.

—1 Corinthians 15:33-34

The Bride will not be able to hide herself from this truth. When we have allowed ourselves to be courted by our enemy, we will think, act, and behave like he does. The temptation is great because there is something enticing about darkness. We are drawn to darkness because of sin in us. Just like Paul said earlier in the passage in Romans (**Romans 7:15-20**) when he talked about doing what he doesn't want to do because of sin in him. The sin in us naturally draws us to self-destruction. Then we choose to dance with the devil and see where he will take us. The Bride was never designed to be relevant to the culture; as a matter of fact, it has always been counterculture. We are deceived in softening the message of Jesus so that we are relevant to an enemy. Trying to trick people into coming to know Jesus with treats and comfort will only lead them to resentments. Satan is the enticer of humanity; Jesus wants to be Lord and Savior.

There are many songs written about the bad boy and the good girl. It is almost like a self-fulfilling prophecy.

WAYWARD WORSHIP

Satan, Lucifer (Lucifero, Latin), Helel (Hebrew), was anointed guardian cherub in heaven. He is known as the "son of the morning" or the Hebrew term meaning "shining one." The Latin term means "light bringer."[1] **Ezekiel 28:13** (NKJV & NIV hybrid) says that his timbrels and pipes were made of gold on the day he was created. Cherubs are guardians of the throne of God. Helel was one who worshiped God as a guardian of His throne. When God created him, his instruments of worship were created with him. Helel's entire existence was worshiping God until he rebelled against God and was thrown out of heaven. God tossed him to Earth and has allowed him to roam freely, but now Satan hates God—and us as His image bearers. Satan will do anything to lure us away from God and deceive us. Corrupting us, our worship, and our minds is Satan's way of continuing to give God a giant birdie finger.

It is not a surprise that he tries to corrupt through music. There is nothing in the Bible that says he lost his talent with music when he was thrown out of heaven. He was given the gift of music and worship in the most powerful space in existence, the throne of God. Yet, Satan is stuck here on earth with people he hates. What better way to get back at God than to corrupt with the very gift he was given? Kind of mimics exactly what is happening to Christians who are given the gift of worship only to twist it to worship themselves, or humanity, first. Certainly Satan has the ability to encourage us to make music that feeds the sinful part of our soul and call it worship.

> 10b *You also have become weak, as we are;*
> *you have become like us."*
> 11 *All your pomp has been brought down to the grave,*
> *along with the noise of your harps;*

—Isaiah 14: 10b-11a

This scripture says that all his respect and status was thrown down to death, the grave, along with the noise of his harps. Why wouldn't he use what he has talent in to corrupt against God? See, angels, cherubs, they don't have redemption through Jesus. We are made higher than the angels through redemption in Jesus (**Hebrews 1:4-5**). We are called sons and daughters of God once we become saints. Angels do not ever have that title. So once they have sinned or defiled themselves, they are forever bound to Death. They may have a time to torment on this Earth, but ultimately, they are limited in authority. Helel, Lucifer, Satan's only power is to deceive. He is a master deceiver and master genealogist, so he will use everything in your genetic lineage to try to destroy you. Satan is not equal to God in any way. He is a defeated foe, a conquered adversary. Think of him as a pest that has a vendetta against you. His entire goal is to steal your vision, kill your God-given talents and dreams, and destroy your testimony.

It seems like he is having his way with worship leaders as many of them are seeking self-glorification over utter humility. They want to be rock stars and have clout instead of remaining in places of contrite heart, knee bending, leading. Many lyrics have low impact to summon one to their knees before the Lord. We went from incredible songs like *Amazing Grace* and *It Is Well with My Soul* to songs that repeat the same lyrics over and over with no umph of power. The songs don't have impact because they are written by people who are too comfortable and forget that they are to usher in the presence of God. I don't think that the people who are writing the songs mean to make them somewhat shallow; I think as a general whole the Christian population is just too comfortable on enemy territory. There are some incredible songs that have been birthed in modern worship. I don't want to overlook them, but I think so many of the modern songs still make humans the object and God the genie. Modern worship songs are often about how God is going to build us up more because we still need more of Him because we don't understand our fullness in Him from the moment we accept Him as Lord and Savior.

Where is the fear of the Lord? It isn't in the performance of man. We have made productions as though the presence of God isn't enough. We need smoke machines, dancing lights, and pretty people with the best voices. I can't sing, so I have great respect for those who can sing on key. God has given people incredible talent that He wants to use for His glory. He delights in our worship . . . when we make it about Him. When these beautiful voices and the music come together, I believe heaven moves. But if it is about the show, the people, the secondary components that are just required to make music happen, then we have become wayward in worship. Ruach Narcissus will confuse a genuine heart once the admiration of people begins to happen. I believe many people start worshiping for the right reason but end up getting corrupted along the way. Pure intentions are always tarnished when a spirit like narcissism touches it. Worship is a spiritual experience, so it is easily open to being corrupted if we aren't diligent in protecting it.

If God wanted performance, trust that He would've sent Jesus in that form. But He didn't because performance is all about human glory, not God's. Worship is about submitting ourselves, lowering ourselves, and praising God. Making a noise that honors Him because He is worthy to be praised. He should be the focus of our hearts, words, and music.

We must do better as the Bride to teach the 'what' and 'why' behind worship. Each of us should feel the weight of the Lord on our shoulders as we come into His presence so that we cannot help but fall to our knees in His glory. If all of the angels of heaven are in constant worship, there is something to be learned from their example. We are made to worship. It is in our God-design. We cannot choose whether we want to worship, but we choose what we worship.

*21 the people I formed for myself
that they may proclaim my praise.*

—Isaiah 43:21 (2)

*6 Come, let us bow down in worship,
let us kneel before the LORD our Maker.*

—Psalms 95:6 (2)

23 Yet a time is coming and has now come when the true worshipers will worship the Father in the Spirit and in truth, for they are the kind of worshipers the Father seeks.

—John 4:23 (2)

Praise the LORD.

1 Praise God in his sanctuary;
praise him in his mighty heavens.
2 Praise him for his acts of power;
praise him for his surpassing greatness.
3 Praise him with the sounding of the trumpet,
praise him with the harp and lyre,
4 praise him with timbrel and dancing,
praise him with the strings and pipe,
5 praise him with the clash of cymbals,
praise him with resounding cymbals.

6 Let everything that has breath praise the LORD.

Praise the LORD.

—Psalms 150:1-6 [2]

We are created to worship God, not ourselves and not each other. We need to keep our praise pointed solely at the One who deserves it, and that brings us closer to the heart of our Groom. This is worship that moves the heart of the Father.

THE BRIDE'S COMPROMISE

I don't think we can overemphasize the detriment of accepting sin within the Church and calling it good, OK, acceptable, and 'not that bad' because "Jesus is love."

Y'all.

This may be one of the greatest, most damaging, most dangerous things that is happening in the modern-day church, the Bride. I cannot think of anything more devastating to the heart of our Groom, and God the Father, than telling people, other image bearers, that their sin is acceptable to the Lord. So let's dig into a hefty amount of scripture to get our hearts aligned with what words truly matter: God's Word.

18 The wrath of God is being revealed from heaven against all the godlessness and wickedness of people, who suppress the truth by their wickedness, 19 since what may be known about God is plain to them, because God has made it plain to them. 20 For since the creation of the world God's invisible qualities—his eternal power and divine nature—have been clearly seen, being understood from what has been made, so that people are without excuse.

21 For although they knew God, they neither glorified him as God nor gave thanks to him, but their thinking became futile and their foolish hearts were darkened. 22 Although they claimed to be wise, they became fools 23 and exchanged the glory of the immortal God for images made to look like a mortal human being and birds and animals and reptiles.

24 Therefore God gave them over in the sinful desires of their hearts to sexual impurity for the degrading of their bodies with one another. 25 They exchanged the truth about God for a lie, and worshiped and served created things rather than the Creator—who is forever praised. Amen.

26 Because of this, God gave them over to shameful lusts. Even their women exchanged natural sexual relations for unnatural ones. 27 In the same way the men also abandoned natural relations with women and were inflamed with lust for one another. Men committed shameful acts with other men, and received in themselves the due penalty for their error.

28 Furthermore, just as they did not think it worthwhile to retain the knowledge of God, so God gave them over to a depraved mind, so that they do what ought not to be done. 29 They have become filled with every kind of wickedness, evil, greed and depravity. They are full of envy, murder, strife, deceit and malice. They are gossips, 30 slanderers, God-haters, insolent, arrogant and boastful; they invent ways of doing evil; they disobey their parents;

31 they have no understanding, no fidelity, no love, no mercy. 32 Although they know God's righteous decree that those who do such things deserve death, they not only continue to do these very things but also approve of those who practice them.

—Romans 1:18-32

16 There are six things the LORD hates,
seven that are detestable to him:
17 haughty eyes,
a lying tongue,
hands that shed innocent blood,
18 a heart that devises wicked schemes,
feet that are quick to rush into evil,
19 a false witness who pours out lies
and a person who stirs up conflict in the community.

—Proverbs 6:16-19

1 See what great love the Father has lavished on us, that we should be called children of God! And that is what we are! The reason the world does not know us is that it did not know him. 2 Dear friends, now we are children of God, and what we will be has not yet been made known. But we know that when Christ appears, we shall be like him, for we shall see him as he is. 3 All who have this hope in him purify themselves, just as he is pure. 4 Everyone who sins

*breaks the law; in fact, sin is lawlessness. ⁵ But you
know that he appeared so that he might take away
our sins. And in him is no sin. ⁶ No one who lives in
him keeps on sinning. No one who continues to sin
has either seen him or known him.*

*⁷ Dear children, do not let anyone lead you astray.
The one who does what is right is righteous, just as
he is righteous. ⁸ The one who does what is sinful is of
the devil, because the devil has been sinning from the
beginning. The reason the Son of God appeared was
to destroy the devil's work. ⁹ No one who is born of
God will continue to sin, because God's seed remains
in them; they cannot go on sinning, because they
have been born of God. ¹⁰ This is how we know who
the children of God are and who the children of the
devil are: Anyone who does not do what is right is
not God's child, nor is anyone who does not love their
brother and sister.*

—1 John 3:1-10

We cannot justify sin and honor our Groom. He took
our sins upon Himself, to deliver us from them, not so
we can make excuses for our sins. We are fooling
ourselves, lying to ourselves, if we say that our sinful
behaviors do not matter. We must live in truth to honor
the Lord, and recognizing and then repenting is the call
that all Christians will have to submit to.

I cannot possibly say anything better than **Romans 6** does on this matter:

¹ What shall we say, then? Shall we go on sinning so that grace may increase? ² By no means! We are those who have died to sin; how can we live in it any longer? ³ Or don't you know that all of us who were baptized into Christ Jesus were baptized into his death? ⁴ We were therefore buried with him through baptism into death in order that, just as Christ was raised from the dead through the glory of the Father, we too may live a new life. ⁵ For if we have been united with him in a death like his, we will certainly also be united with him in a resurrection like his. ⁶ For we know that our old self was crucified with him so that the body ruled by sin might be done away with, that we should no longer be slaves to sin— ⁷ because anyone who has died has been set free from sin.

—Romans 6:1-7

¹¹ In the same way, count yourselves dead to sin but alive to God in Christ Jesus. ¹² Therefore do not let sin reign in your mortal body so that you obey its evil desires. ¹³ Do not offer any part of yourself to sin as an instrument of wickedness, but rather offer yourselves to God as those who have been brought from death to life; and offer every part of yourself to him as an instrument of righteousness. 14 For sin shall no longer be your master, because you are not under the law, but under grace.

—Romans 6:11-14

The very beginning of this scripture is imploring us to recognize that when we continue to sin it will not increase grace for us because we have died to sin and can no longer practice it. We cannot attain any more grace than what we received the moment we submitted to follow the Lord. When we became Jesus followers we chose to accept His death inside of us, that we would no longer sin, so that we will live a new life in His resurrection power. We must not continue to walk the pathway of sinful ways. Water baptism is a representation of this spiritual concept. We are laid back in the water as a semblance of death, then brought up out of the water as a semblance of resurrection. One of the coolest revelations I have had about baptism is that the moment we are laid back into that water is the *only* taste of death a believer will ever experience. It is the very moment we die to sin, and we are reborn in the name of the Father, Son, and Holy Spirit.

But I sin every day, Stephanie, what does that mean for me?

Once we are believers, the Bible never refers to us as sinners again. The only term used for Christians other than Christian is saints. The term "sinner" is only for nonbelievers. Do saints sin? Absolutely we do. But not with the same heart or with the same thought process about it. While we are in these meat puppets, our flesh, we will always struggle with our propensity to sin. The difference is that we will repent. We will live in truth and acknowledge the sin as sin, then allow the forgiveness that comes with the cross to propel us in a better direction. So if you are still actively participating in the same sin twenty years later, after you have given your life to the Lord, you probably have not fully submitted that area to God. We cannot justify, excuse, or wallow in sin and truly be followers of Jesus. We must practice judging our hearts righteously and honestly through the lens of the Bible.

15 *What then? Shall we sin because we are not under the law but under grace? By no means!* 16 *Don't you know that when you offer yourselves to someone as obedient slaves, you are slaves of the one you obey—whether you are slaves to sin, which leads to death, or to obedience, which leads to righteousness?* 17 *But thanks be to God that, though you used to be slaves to sin, you have come to obey from your heart the pattern of teaching that has now claimed your allegiance.* 18 *You have been set free from sin and have become slaves to righteousness.*

19 I am using an example from everyday life because of your human limitations. Just as you used to offer yourselves as slaves to impurity and to ever-increasing wickedness, so now offer yourselves as slaves to righteousness leading to holiness. 20 When you were slaves to sin, you were free from the control of righteousness. 21 What benefit did you reap at that time from the things you are now ashamed of? Those things result in death! 22 But now that you have been set free from sin and have become slaves of God, the benefit you reap leads to holiness, and the result is eternal life. 23 For the wages of sin is death, but the gift of God is eternal life in Christ Jesus our Lord.

—Romans 6:15-23

We are slaves to the one we obey. If we continue to make excuses for sin, tell others they can sin, and think we can cover it up all under grace, we are liars. The truth is not in us. We will stumble and have some really crappy days, but we must be honest in our trespasses. This honesty opens the door for grace and mercy to do their beautiful work.

¹ My dear children, I write this to you so that you will not sin. But if anybody does sin, we have an advocate with the Father—Jesus Christ, the Righteous One. ² He is the atoning sacrifice for our sins, and not only for ours but also for the sins of the whole world.

³ We know that we have come to know him if we keep his commands. ⁴ Whoever says, "I know him," but does not do what he commands is a liar, and the truth is not in that person. ⁵ But if anyone obeys his word, love for God is truly made complete in them. This is how we know we are in him: ⁶ Whoever claims to live in him must live as Jesus did.

—1 John 2:1-6

Grace and mercy are part of what we cling to with the gift of salvation, but we do not have grace and mercy without Jesus as Lord and Savior. Grace is not getting what we deserve and mercy is getting what we don't deserve. Grace prevents us from having to pay for our sins by going to hell. Mercy is that we get to experience eternal life though we don't deserve it. We squander these beautiful characteristics, just like a narcissist will consume the light of their victim, when we think we can live however we want, and teach others the same thing. Jesus defeated sin and death once and for all so that His Bride would never have to experience what they bring to the table. To continue sinning, openly, unapologetically and excusing it away is the biggest slap in the face to the work of Jesus on the cross. The Bride might as well spiritually slap Him in the face and confess, "We do not want You or anything you have to offer." Because that is *exactly* what we say every single time this foolishness is allowed to continue.

THE ANTIDOTE TO THE NEED FOR EXCESSIVE ADMIRATION

Confession. Why have we lost the art of confession? We should be confessing our trespasses against ourselves and others openly and regularly. Satan works in secrets, and when we keep our sins in secret, we give him ample room to pursue our heart to veil it with more lies and shame. Ruach Narcissus will never allow confession. Confession is accountability and the ability to self-reflect. The act of confession is humility.

The Catholic church has been faithful to the art of confession, but unfortunately, they have made it a religious practice and twisted it into a ritual as though we have anything to do with the forgiveness of the sins. A priest cannot offer forgiveness. Saying a rosary that holds no power or honesty in the heart of the one saying it can't forgive sins either. Only through the blood of Jesus and our honesty can sin be forgiven. The Bride should always be searching for the Light of the World, her Groom. Sin cannot reside in the light. So when we bring it into the light, it must be dealt with. What does the Bible say about confession?

16 Therefore confess your sins to each other and pray for each other so that you may be healed. The prayer of a righteous person is powerful and effective.

—James 5:16 (3)

9 If we confess our sins, he is faithful and just and will forgive us our sins and purify us from all unrighteousness.

—1 John 1:9 (3)

6 Confessing their sins, they were baptized by him in the Jordan River.

—Matthew 3:6 (3)

18 Many of those who believed now came and openly confessed what they had done.

—Acts 19:18 (3)

13 Whoever conceals their sins does not prosper, but the one who confesses and renounces them finds mercy.

—Proverbs 28:13 (3)

¹¹ But you, man of God, flee from all this, and pursue righteousness, godliness, faith, love, endurance and gentleness. ¹² Fight the good fight of the faith. Take hold of the eternal life to which you were called when you made your good confession in the presence of many witnesses. ¹³ In the sight of God, who gives life to everything, and of Christ Jesus, who while testifying before Pontius Pilate made the good confession, I charge you ¹⁴ to keep this command without spot or blame until the appearing of our Lord Jesus Christ.

—1 Timothy 6:11-14 (3)

The Bible has a ton to say about confession. It is a requirement for repentance and for living in truth. We could spend all day listing all the sins that we are facing; we would run out of hours if we tried to list them all. The Holy Spirit is faithful to convict us of our un-righteousness. We will allow that work, for the light to be shone into the dark recesses of our heart, so we can heal and live in truth. God is not looking for anyone to think they have it all together and never stumble; that is a lie, and not God's way. Instead, God is looking for faithful hearts that are submitted to Him so, when they do stumble, they are quick to notice, confess, and repent.

When I first met a man that I started dating, we were having a discussion about certain anti-God possessions like albums and books. He asked me why it mattered why he listened to or read these items. I told him, "I don't talk to other men because I am in a relationship with you and it would hurt our relationship if I did. In the same way, I don't do things that hurt my relationship with God because I don't want to hurt Him. I love Him. I value my relationship with Him. If something doesn't support that relationship, then I will remove it." He had never heard it put that way. He didn't understand that our relationship with God is more important than any relationship with a person can ever be but especially over holding onto sinful behaviors or items that are against Him.

The Bride will want to prepare herself solely for her Groom. That means there is no room to court another. There is no space for the Bride to entertain evil and sin. Sin courts Death. Sin is writing love letters to the masterful destroyer of our hearts, minds, body, and, ultimately, our souls.

Our worship will always reveal the depths of our heart towards God. Matt Redman has a wonderful song called "Heart of Worship." In the song he explains that he is bringing worship back to God, and God alone. He realizes that he has nothing to offer in and of himself, that all of worship belongs to God. He passionately expresses that he will bring God more than a song because the song in itself is not what God is looking for, but instead, it is the heart of the man behind the song.

We need to remember this every time we come to worship, collectively and individually.

If you don't know where to start, guess what? There is a whole entire book of songs in the Bible called Psalms. A perfect beginning place to sing the songs out to God. I am always thankful that God says make a joyful noise because noise is about the best I have. I carry a tune about as well as I can carry a horse. I often ask the Lord if my heavenly body will have an amazing voice because I will sing with all diligence. Maybe with the fellow choir of people in heaven, my voice will fit into the exact note it was meant to, but I am fairly certain no one on Earth wants to hear that note.

But I sing. I sing to the heart of my Father. I sing to Him because He is worthy and I am made and designed to do it. I will find my place in worship that creates humility in my heart and reminds me of His glory shining. Coming before the Lord with thanksgiving for who He is, not what He does, but just *Who He is. The Great I Am.* We do not need admiration because we are wicked in our hearts, but oh how worthy the Lord of Hosts is because He is Truth, Light, Life, Salvation, and a Good Father.

¹ Shout for joy to the LORD, all the earth.
² Worship the LORD with gladness;
come before him with joyful songs.
³ Know that the LORD is God.

It is he who made us, and we are his;
we are his people, the sheep of his pasture.
4 Enter his gates with thanksgiving
and his courts with praise;
give thanks to him and praise his name.
5 For the LORD is good and his love endures forever;
His faithfulness continues through all generations.

—Psalms 100:1-5

You may not know today how to get to that place of worship, but I hope by the time you have finished this book, you are so passionately in love with our Groom that you feel compelled to worship. It doesn't have to be perfect, remember how we talked about that word being a lie when it comes to humans. Only the Trinity is perfect, and we can rest in the fact that we aren't expected to be. We only need to be really good students, willing to learn new things and new ways, and mostly have faith to walk the road of life that leads to eternal life with our Groom. You may be out of tune, and that may be in a few areas of your life, but you can get in tune with the help of the Holy Spirit. One step. One moment. One new adventure as a Bride anticipating her Groom. No shame. No one else matters. Just the passion for our forever. This is where the need for excess admiration goes to die and our candle shines so incredibly bright for all the world to see.

REFLECTION QUESTIONS

1. Do you need excessive admiration?

2. If so, what is the root of this behavior?

3. If you don't know what the root is, ask God to reveal it to you.

4. Find someone or a small group of fellow believers you can trust and begin to practice confession and ask them to pray with you.

CHAPTER 7

SENSE OF ENTITLEMENT

Narcissists may believe that success takes hard work—but only for others, not for them. They totally believe that they deserve the best tickets, top score, the nicest room, or the best seat in the house. They don't ever have to verbalize this belief as their behavior and actions clearly communicate their sense of entitlement.

12 *They have harps and lyres at their banquets,*
pipes and timbrels and wine,
but they have no regard for the deeds of the LORD,
no respect for the work of his hands.

—Isaiah 5:12

Talk about having to fight a cultural tidal wave! Entitlement is almost in our blood here in America. We have everything we could possibly want and need and then an overflow of a ton of things that we don't need; even the poor in America are more rich than anywhere in the world. We think we deserve whatever we want, even if it is not good or productive for us, and we will be forceful to attain it if necessary. It is nearly impossible not to be sucked in by this undertow of corruption of heart. It will truly take so much effort to prevent the corruption of our heart from taking over.

OUT IN THE WORLD

If you think that entitlement isn't an issue, next Sunday when you leave church, go eat at a restaurant and ask the wait staff how they are treated by the "church" crowd. It is known among the service industry that the "church crowd" are the biggest nightmares to deal with. We leave a church service that didn't summon us into the presence of God and go to a meal where we have no inclination to exhibit the presence of God for those who couldn't join us because they are working. The staff is left with a sour taste of our entitlement as they see the Bride in all her narcissistic glory of self. *Serve me. It's all about me. Look at me. I am better than you. Do better, your service is not enough.* Oh man! What a horrendous nightmare we have created.

If you want to think that it's just others, it's just "them" because you don't act that way, you have forgotten that we are a collective. No, we cannot control everything that everyone else does, but we can stand against looking away if we see a fellow believer mistreating someone else. We should confront that behavior. I said earlier that how we use the power we are given matters, and when we openly see someone mistreat someone else, we have a duty to step in and do things differently. Do not let fear stop you from making a difference for someone else. Now please do not take this as becoming the restaurant vigilante that has to fix everything. We aren't looking for hyperbole, but balance.

I admit this next part is one of my greatest personal struggles. The road. Driving and having to share the road with other humans can just about send me through the roof of my car. I have often said that if shooting out tires was legal, I would be taking out quite a few cars. God is really having to work on my heart in this area. I do not ride in the left lane unless I am passing someone or exiting left, but many take up residency in that lane and feel like they own it. This will then send electricity to just about every driver that is having to maneuver to pass them in some other lane.

Entitlement for both drivers causes clashing and at times becomes deadly. The driver that has taken residence in the left lane is living out entitlement, and the one who gets angry is also in entitlement; otherwise, what is there to be angry about? We are both cruising down the road at approximately the same speed, getting to our destinations at around the same relative time. The truth is that none of us even deserve to have these incredible roads and these expensive cars in the first place, but we quit being grateful because we just have them . . . and expect them. We can afford them, we bought them, we deserve it. Yet our hearts mistreat those around us with this privilege.

I have had to ask for forgiveness so many times when my entitlement swells my pride into foolish territory. It is like entitlement is the hot air to the pride balloon and the next thing you know, you are in an altercation with someone you don't know, have never met, to fight for space that neither of you own. There have been people who killed others over this type of situation. I have heard people say they are scared to honk the horn because they may get shot. The idea that someone thinks they could take a life over being honked at is the epitome of entitlement.

The other day I went to Trader Joe's—and ours is in an affluent part of town. After almost getting run over, I thought to myself, this is the cesspool of entitlement. This Trader Joe's is off of US 280. I do not have the emotional maturity for that road because of my lack of ability not to get angry behind the wheel. Nearly everyone in Birmingham, Alabama, will tell you how awful it is to drive on US 280. It isn't just the level of traffic, though there is plenty of that, it is the attitude of the people driving. It is "me first, only me first, and I do not care about you at all" mentality. I used to work down that road and decided it was good for me to leave because of the stress it caused me to get to work. I take ownership that my entitlement, a part of me that I am still filtering and working through with the Lord's help, played a role in that situation.

Let's talk about King Saul in **1 Samuel 15**. He is a good example of entitlement. He was chosen to be the first king over Israel after they entered the Promised Land. God told him to go and completely destroy the evil Amalekites. Every single person and animal was to be destroyed, but Saul thought he knew better. He took the choicest of the animals and spared them and he took the king captive. Samuel goes to meet Saul, who is basically proud of himself. He took the animals to sacrifice to God after all, so why wouldn't God be happy with that?

22 But Samuel replied:

"Does the LORD delight in burnt offerings and
sacrifices as much as in obeying the LORD?
To obey is better than sacrifice,
and to heed is better than the fat of rams.
23 For rebellion is like the sin of divination,
and arrogance like the evil of idolatry.
Because you have rejected the word of the LORD,
he has rejected you as king."

—1 Samuel 15:22-23

Our arrogance of entitlement is the evil of idolatry. *WE* are the idol of worship in entitlement. We think that we are better than others and we deserve to serve ourselves, regardless of others. The restaurant and the driving examples are just two of many, many examples that we could list here. Some others are: standing in line at a store, not putting the grocery cart back in the proper place, not being kind to customer service people on the phone, dealing with doctors' offices and utilities, waiting for the green man to illuminate before crossing the intersection, waiting in line to enter the elementary school parking lot, and the list goes on and on. We have many potential frustrations we face every day, but the frustration mostly comes from not getting our way or not getting it fast enough. Smartphones and the information age have made some things faster than ever, meaning that we are quicker to feel entitled than ever before.

[1] *What causes fights and quarrels among you? Don't they come from your desires that battle within you?* [2] *You desire but do not have, so you kill. You covet but you cannot get what you want, so you quarrel and fight. You do not have because you do not ask God.* [3] *When you ask, you do not receive, because you ask with wrong motives, that you may spend what you get on your pleasures.*

4 You adulterous people, don't you know that friendship with the world means enmity against God? Therefore, anyone who chooses to be a friend of the world becomes an enemy of God. 5 Or do you think Scripture says without reason that he jealously longs for the spirit he has caused to dwell in us?

—James 4:1-5

We do not trust God to meet our needs. When we are not trusting Him to meet our needs, we are a groomless Bride. We feel desperate to fill that space with anyone, including ourselves, when we practice this kind of entitlement behavior. We become a "thirsty" Bride. The term "thirsty" is a new slang term that means "desperate, easy, whore-like." We have lost sight of our greatest Love and are now looking to the left and the right hoping that we will somehow find someone, anyone, to love us and choose us. Our entitlement gives us a sense of control about our lives. That makes us feel better than leaving our lives in the hands of a God we can't see, can't touch, and don't trust. We fear being uncared for by the Lover of our souls. Until we harness that fear led lie and bring it under submission of the cross, and speak truth to it, we will remain in the entitlement mindset. It will bring so much damage to the Bride, and Jesus is not coming back for a thirsty Bride.

Narcissists are often seeking supply the same way that a groomless bride acts. They will take anyone they can take more from. Their entitlement attitude is "what is mine is mine, and what is yours is mine." They are absolutely unapologetic about it too. Ruach Narcissus will entice the Bride to merely consume more out of desperation, because the Bride has forgotten that Jesus is her portion. She is lacking in nothing, therefore does not need to feel entitled.

Entitlement in the Church

It seems like the title of this section is an oxymoron, and truly it should be. But I would not be writing this book if entitlement in the church were not present. Entitlement is not reserved for any one specific aspect of the church environment. It can be from the leadership all the way to the mostly invisible attendee.

Leaders often see themselves as celebrities these days. Though I am not sure that this is a new concept because power tends to corrupt people. I am certain we can look back through the beginning of the Church and find plenty of entitlement issues from leaders. Celebrity status always comes with perks. Past to present, it must be a challenge for any of the celebrity pastors to keep their humility.

Pastoral Leadership

I have attended churches before where I didn't even know who the pastor was because I only saw him on the stage, but never mixed in with his people. He only shook hands with those who had status and basically overlooked those he didn't deem as important to notice.

If you haven't noticed by my author's picture, I have vividly colored hair. I am not easy to miss in person, somewhat like a walking art piece. So when I see a pastor just a few feet away from me and he deliberately will not make eye contact, I know exactly what kind of entitled pastor I am dealing with. He will always be looking over everyone to see who looks expensive or who is "popular" among the staff.

I understand that Sundays and service times can be busy for staff members. I do not expect to be coddled, but certainly a smile is in order. Certainly a nod isn't too much to ask when you are supposed to be the leader that I am supposed to be following. Personally, I find it hard to follow someone who doesn't seem the least bit interested in getting to know me in some sort of fashion. When the shepherd of a church doesn't know one iota about his sheep, he is in the wrong position and potentially needs to step aside . . . but could his ego allow him to do so? Not with the example of entitlement that plagues the churches today.

I recognize pastors with extremely large church audiences may not be able to learn who everyone is in their church; that is just unrealistic. However, I don't see that huge church model anywhere in the Bible, so I am not sure that megachurches were ever even meant to exist for the Bride. Nonetheless, the megachurch is now part of American church culture, and I think it needs to be handled wisely. It is really easy to overlook the "have nots" among a huge crowd of "haves" and scripturally that is very dangerous ground. Judges with evil thoughts is how this kind of discrimination is described in James.

¹ My brothers and sisters, believers in our glorious Lord Jesus Christ must not show favoritism. ² Suppose a man comes into your meeting wearing a gold ring and fine clothes, and a poor man in filthy old clothes also comes in. ³ If you show special attention to the man wearing fine clothes and say, "Here's a good seat for you," but say to the poor man, "You stand there" or "Sit on the floor by my feet," ⁴ have you not discriminated among yourselves and become judges with evil thoughts?

—James 2:1-4

But if you go to many large churches today and ask people who attend, you will see a very distinctive difference between the groups. Pastors are afraid to lose the money that high earners bring but do not feel like the impact would be as great for someone who doesn't tithe as much. We will touch on this topic about money-hungry pastoral hearts more in the next chapter.

Why do people who are overlooked continue to go to large churches? Well, I believe you will find a high turnover rate for those people because they are looking for connection with their body of believers. They probably leave the church within one to two years, as opposed to members connected to leadership who probably stay much longer. They may continue to attend the church for the massive amount of resources many large churches have. Their children may also go to school with many of the other kids, so the parents continue to attend, though they have no additional connection beyond their kids' peers, so their children can hopefully be connected to fellow believers.

MEMBERS AND LEADERSHIP BOARDS

As if pastors haven't made an entitlement mess of the Bride, we certainly can't leave out the rest of the body that is just as guilty . . . maybe even more so at times. My friend Ellen gave me this term and I think it is perfect: "churchtainment." I mean, isn't that what we go for?? To be entertained? We want our coffee, doughnuts, comfy seats, a good singer, songs we prefer, and all the other first-world benefits we can pack into the place. We want to go and feel good about ourselves, comfortable with ourselves. We are able to completely forget that the whole purpose of church is to be equipped for war in the spirit. Last time I saw soldiers preparing for war, they didn't look comfortable at all. They certainly weren't being coddled.

The Church has become a playground for Christians, not a prepping ground for the reality of the darkness that is all around us. We are too drawn to allowing the darkness to dance with us. Our church gathering places look so much like everything else in this world. The only difference is the name says that we should be meeting God there, and instead we meet entitled spoiled children there.

We don't allow the Holy Spirit to move freely and take control of what we teach, say, or sing. We have our patterns set in stone so that God fits into our comfortable time box, including getting out in time to beat the other congregation from down the street to the lunch line.

Check.

We did our part on Sunday.

Now we can go to lunch and torture the workers with our poor attitudes, but they should just be glad that we are there giving them our hard-earned money.

Would you continue to go to a church where the pastor or teacher shows up and says, "I have nothing prepared today, but we are gonna just read scripture?" Would you feel like the pastor wasn't doing his job? Or would you sit in awe as the Holy Spirit showed up in amazing ways? What if it wasn't even for you? Could you handle sitting with someone else who just got wrecked by the Holy Spirit and dig into their journey with them? Or will you feel so shorted because you "didn't get anything out of that scripture"? Are you entitled to think that every single gathering should be all about you and what you get out of it? As though every single image bearer sitting around you isn't part of your journey too. What if that day was all about you learning how to walk along with someone else, so that God can use you to do that same thing at work?

When did the church quit being moved solely by the work of the Holy Spirit? There is no church without that movement. We don't need wise words of man nearly as badly as we need the Holy Spirit to shine light into all of our dark places and change us from the inside.

The church I grew up attending had some people in leadership that were extremely rigid. They made sure that their opinions were heard and, by God, heeded. There was no other way, or they would leave. There was no room for anything outside of their conformity. So I watched interesting people leave, committed people leave, families leave. Over time, there began to be a noticeable shortage of people.

Rigidity has no place within the Church. When muscles atrophy, they become useless. Same with churches who have rigid members that are inflexible to change, movement, and other's ideas that they may not love. Rigid thinking is firmly rooted in entitlement. It is the "I am right. You are wrong" mentality.

- The way I worship is right, your worship is wrong.

- How I want a church building used is right, the way you want to use it is wrong.

- I park there; it is my space. You park somewhere else.

- This is my pew. You sit somewhere else.

- This is acceptable because I say so, but what you want isn't considered.

If a church body allows this member to continue to atrophy their movement, the body will have no choice but to begin to pay the price and shed healthy people.

These are hard conversations to have, and they make people uncomfortable. Conflict isn't always a bad thing. Sometimes it is necessary when we are bringing sin out into the light. The Bible is clear on how to handle this sort of issue. You will find the biblical suggestions at the end of this book. Setting the culture of the church environment to one of Holy Spirit flexibility starts with leadership. A pastor may have a challenge changing a deeply rooted sinful culture, but if he will consistently call it out, consistently speak against it, and teach his followers why it is sinful, he will have a better chance of bringing life back into the church.

If he doesn't choose to do so, or cannot get the congregation to follow, it might be in his best interest to leave that particular body and not go down with the ship. Jesus won't be arriving for them. He is looking for His Bride who is preparing for Him. This means that He is Lord, not some member(s) that can't get over themselves.

Change is scary sometimes, but it is the way of growth. Change allows us not to get lost in our old ways but to allow the Lord to do His will in our lives and through our church body.

Zechariah 7 is such a great story about how rigidity doesn't bode well with the Lord. When we fall into the trap of religion and its disconnect from the Lord God, we have lost sight and God will give us the chance to turn back to Him. Unfortunately, humans are usually quite stubborn, as we are about to see. The good news is that you can choose to do things differently, knowing that your immediate tendency will be to resist change.

4 Then the word of the LORD Almighty came to me: 5 "Ask all the people of the land and the priests, 'When you fasted and mourned in the fifth and seventh months for the past seventy years, was it really for me that you fasted? 6 And when you were eating and drinking, were you not just feasting for yourselves? 7 Are these not the words the LORD proclaimed through the earlier prophets when Jerusalem and its surrounding towns were at rest and prosperous, and the Negev and the western foothills were settled?'"

—Zechariah 7:4-7

The people of Bethel are asking God if they should have a day of mourning for the anniversary of Jerusalem's fall as they had been doing for the last seventy years. But God answered, "Have you been doing these things for me? Or for yourself?" Then God tells them:

8 And the word of the LORD came again to Zechariah: 9 "This is what the LORD Almighty said: 'Administer true justice; show mercy and compassion to one another. 10 Do not oppress the widow or the fatherless, the foreigner or the poor. Do not plot evil against each other.

—Zechariah 7:8-10

Because the people refused to listen to God, he let atrophy happen.

11 *"But they refused to pay attention; stubbornly they turned their backs and covered their ears.* 12 *They made their hearts as hard as flint and would not listen to the law or to the words that the LORD Almighty had sent by his Spirit through the earlier prophets. So the LORD Almighty was very angry.*

—Zechariah 7:11-12

It doesn't bode well for them after that. Basically God scattered them far and wide and made the land desolate. This is what happens to a church that lands in the entitlement behavior of rigidity. You may wonder how being rigid falls under entitlement. Entitlement and rigidity refuse to accept the yield that God requires to follow Him. Being rigid is just a completely inflexible form of entitlement.

THE ANTIDOTE TO ENTITLEMENT

The parable of the "good Samaritan" is an example of getting involved when you see an injustice. He didn't just turn away like the religious. He stepped in and made a difference. If we are to love our neighbor as ourselves, that means we stand up for one who needs to be defended and we call out hurtful behaviors that we see happen.

25 On one occasion an expert in the law stood up to test Jesus. "Teacher," he asked, "what must I do to inherit eternal life?"

26 "What is written in the Law?" he replied. "How do you read it?"

27 He answered, "'Love the Lord your God with all your heart and with all your soul and with all your strength and with all your mind'; and, 'Love your neighbor as yourself.'"

28 "You have answered correctly," Jesus replied. "Do this and you will live."

29 But he wanted to justify himself, so he asked Jesus, "And who is my neighbor?"

30 In reply Jesus said: "A man was going down from Jerusalem to Jericho, when he was attacked by robbers. They stripped him of his clothes, beat him and went away, leaving him half dead. 31 A priest happened to be going down the same road, and when he saw the man, he passed by on the other side. 32 So too, a Levite, when he came to the place and saw him, passed by on the other side. 33 But a Samaritan, as he traveled, came where the man was; and when he saw him, he took pity on him. 34 He went to him and bandaged his wounds, pouring on oil and wine. Then he put the man on his own donkey, brought him to an inn and took care of him. 35 The next day he took out two denari and gave them to the innkeeper. 'Look after him,' he said, 'and when I return, I will reimburse you for any extra expense you may have.'

36 "Which of these three do you think was a neighbor to the man who fell into the hands of robbers?"

37 The expert in the law replied, "The one who had mercy on him."

Jesus told him, "Go and do likewise."

—Luke 10:25-37

Fear is a real issue in today's culture when relationships around us are crumbling at breakneck speed. How do we trust a God we can't see to care for us? We must get real before the Lord and express our fear. He is not afraid of our fear. He will comfort us and show us how to rest in His incredible care.

> *1 I will extol the LORD at all times;*
> *his praise will always be on my lips.*
> *2 I will glory in the LORD;*
> *let the afflicted hear and rejoice.*
> *3 Glorify the LORD with me;*
> *let us exalt his name together.*
>
> *4 I sought the LORD, and he answered me;*
> *he delivered me from all my fears.*
> *5 Those who look to him are radiant;*
> *their faces are never covered with shame.*
> *6 This poor man called, and the LORD heard him;*
> *he saved him out of all his troubles.*
> *7 The angel of the LORD encamps around those who*
> *fear him, and he delivers them.*

8 Taste and see that the LORD is good;
blessed is the one who takes refuge in him.
9 Fear the LORD, you his holy people,
for those who fear him lack nothing.

10 The lions may grow weak and hungry,
but those who seek the LORD lack no good thing.

—Psalm 34:1-10

The Lord is so trustworthy and so good! You can trust to lay yourself down, and He will be there. You can submit all of yourself to God without fear. Just because it is scary at first, doesn't mean that it isn't worth trying. It is tiring to have to be the watcher for ourselves. We are not omniscient, omnipresent, or loving toward ourselves. We are incapable of being god in our lives, but entitlement makes us think that it is possible. It makes us weary, tired, and soul tired. It is a tiredness that is unquenchable, and we feel it to our very core. Why? Because we are trying to fill shoes that are too big for us. It feels good for a period of time, but as the storms of life rage, we are depleted of the rest that they require to survive. Pride will tell us that we are OK, that nothing needs to change because we have it together. Inside, we are crumbling under the misery of anxiety, depression, unhealthy coping mechanisms, and various health issues. Resting in the Lord is what He asks of us, and to do that, we have to trust Him.

28 "Come to me, all you who are weary and burdened, and I will give you rest. 29 Take my yoke upon you and learn from me, for I am gentle and humble in heart, and you will find rest for your souls. 30 For my yoke is easy and my burden is light.

—Matthew 11:28-30

We go to church to be equipped to tackle the war that we face every day against darkness. The Bride of Christ isn't looking to be entertained by the things of this world. She has her eyes locked and loaded on the One who is the Lover of her soul and coming back to rescue her. She is not interested in the words of anyone other than her Groom and she will have the discernment to know the difference. The Bride also does not need consistent chocolate and roses from Jesus. We should not need to be reminded, as believers, over and over and over again about the sacrifice He made for us. That is foundational knowledge. When we need Jesus to pursue our hearts over and over again, almost like He is begging us to love Him, we are narcissists. That is what a narcissist makes you do, beg. They want you to grovel, and nothing is ever enough. Ruach Narcissus in full-blown spiritual corruption will fool you into thinking that Jesus will never be enough and that you need to consume Him and His Light. The black hole you created spiritually is of evil, not of God. You will have to recognize and acknowledge that you have a spiritual black hole and allow the Lord to reveal the way out.

Many Christians, because comfort is easier, refuse to acknowledge that the Bible consistently tells us that we are in a battle against hell. We are image bearers and have an enemy that wants to annihilate us, Death is the name. Then we have a very deceitful adversary that is trying to lull us to sleep on enemy territory by fattening us up on all the comforts he knows we desire.

42 Jesus said to them, "If God were your Father, you would love me, for I have come here from God. I have not come on my own; God sent me. 43 Why is my language not clear to you? Because you are unable to hear what I say. 44 You belong to your father, the devil, and you want to carry out your father's desires. He was a murderer from the beginning, not holding to the truth, for there is no truth in him. When he lies, he speaks his native language, for he is a liar and the father of lies. 45 Yet because I tell the truth, you do not believe me! 46 Can any of you prove me guilty of sin? If I am telling the truth, why don't you believe me? 47 Whoever belongs to God hears what God says. The reason you do not hear is that you do not belong to God."

—John 8:42-47

Lying is Satan's native language. It is all our enemy knows how to speak. When the Bride is captivated by these lies because we can't hear the truth, we do not belong to God. We cannot allow our entitlement sin to deceive us into falling for the enemy's schemes. We must be clear minded to see these schemes before they tarnish the Bride for her Groom.

¹¹ in order that Satan might not outwit us. For we are not unaware of his schemes.

—2 Corinthians 2:11

We are in a war against all of the devil's schemes and so much more. All of darkness and evil principalities want to harm us while we are here on Earth. Did you read that? Read it again. *ALL* of evil wants to come against us. Why? Because we are on enemy territory, and we are made in the image of God. Therefore we have some super powerful adversaries that hate us. While we sit around and think we are god, they (evil spirits and principalities of darkness) are having a field day with us, our hearts, and minds. We are at odds with each other and focusing on silly things, like attempting to pretend the whole world won't hate the message that Jesus brought, and we uphold.

The Bride has constant inner turmoil about non-primary, non-gospel issues: tattoos, women teachers/ pastors, perceived false teachers, and so many other topics that we could let rest on personal conviction. It's like a gluten and dairy intolerance in the body. An intolerance may bother the body, but it is not going to cause destruction for the body. Discussing an intolerance is noteworthy, but it is not going to be the most important element. These issues aren't primary issues that needs to be focused on and fought about. We can trust God to bring conviction to these areas if needed. If you feel that God is strongly putting it on your heart to share a message about it, share the message, but let God do the work of convicting hearts. The message you share may be for four out of a hundred people, or it may be for all one hundred. You do not know, nor is it your responsibility to make sure that everyone is aligned with what your convictions are. You are just responsible for sharing the message that God has entrusted to you.

If it is scripture, it is important. It should also be taken in the context of the entirety of the Bible and not piecemealed to fit a narrative that makes you the most comfortable personally. We have lost the ability to focus on the majors and instead get lost in the fight about the minors. Then the whole world watches us insult and tear each other down. We then look like fools because the primary issue of loving others well gets overlooked by minor issues like can we have tattoos.

Who is and who isn't going to hell is a primary example of this. We do not know. The *only* thing we have to go on is whether they call on the name of Jesus and what behaviors that we need to be made aware of, but it is not up to us to think we can know who is and who isn't going. We need to trust God to be the judge of the living and the dead. Our goal as the Bride is not to focus on who is and who isn't going, but to share our excitement over our Groom! If we are excited, and following His ways, we will inspire others to get to know Him too. Please do not confuse my statement with the mistaken concept that everyone is going to make it to heaven if they are good. That is *not* what I am saying because it is not a biblical concept. I believe there is a second death, where people will go to hell and spend an eternity away from God. I can't think of anything worse, which is partially why I am writing this book. The Bride can encourage everyone who meets her to get to know her Love. Have you ever talked to someone who is in the giddy stages of love? They just got engaged. They are gushy, sweet, excited, and can't wait to tell the world about it. That is how we should be as believers, the Ekklesia. Excited, anticipatory, and ready to share the beauty of the love of our Lord and Savior. Not sour, bitter, and indifferent to the passion of the gospel story because people aren't doing what we think they should do to go to heaven. We must fall in love with Jesus, and let the Holy Spirit do the work of convicting hearts, so that God is glorified, honored, and praised.

When we gather as a church, we should be as tight as the strongest military force on the planet. We should move as one element. Every need should be met and planned for. We should be so enthusiastic about each other that we are willing to self-sacrifice so each member is taken care of. Soldiers in any military aren't worth their weight if they are selfish and indifferent to their entire platoon. They have prepared their mind before they ever enter into war that at whatever cost, including their own life, they will fight alongside and for each of their fellow soldiers to accomplish a task. This is the attitude that we should have when we enter the church building each week. If we entered with this heart intact, we would change the entire concept of "churchtainment" into a powerhouse of spiritual revolution. Each church gathering should be equipping us for the war at hand: the one for the souls of all humankind.

10 Finally, be strong in the Lord and in his mighty power. 11 Put on the full armor of God, so that you can take your stand against the devil's schemes. 12 For our struggle is not against flesh and blood, but against the rulers, against the authorities, against the powers of this dark world and against the spiritual forces of evil in the heavenly realms. 13 Therefore put on the full armor of God, so that when the day of evil comes, you may be able to stand your ground, and after you have done everything, to stand. 14 Stand firm then, with the belt of truth buckled around your waist, with the breastplate of righteousness in place, 15 and with your feet fitted with the readiness that comes from the gospel of peace. 16 In addition to all this, take up the shield of

*faith, with which you can extinguish all the flaming
arrows of the evil one. ¹⁷ Take the helmet of salvation
and the sword of the Spirit, which is the word of God.*

*¹⁸ And pray in the Spirit on all occasions with all
kinds of prayers and requests. With this in mind, be
alert and always keep on praying for all the Lord's
people.*

—Ephesians 6:10-18

To break our tendency toward entitlement, we need to
keep our focus on who/what our enemy is and never
allow ourselves to be comfortable. Our church gatherings should always remind us of the awe of God. Not a
single second of it is about us. It is for us to be equipped
and ready for what we face. Until the current church
culture sheds this wicked skin, it will be a blemish on
the Bride.

When we go to the church building and gather as a
collective body, we should have power (**Acts 1:8**). People should enter with a sense of wonder and awe, even
fear is appropriate, because God is the Great I Am. If we
would embrace them, whoever enters, right where they
are, oh how we could change some lives! We expect
everyone to be in the same place in their journey with
God as we are. This is, unfortunately, an entitlement
mentality.

So let's fight this and recognize that everyone has a walk and a journey with the Lord. Some may saunter, some may sprint, some may quantum leap their way into miraculous knowledge, but if you're anything like me, my journey has been year after year of God peeling back the layers of my broken heart and healing me. God never went after my biggest issues first. I would have resisted. Our biggest sins are the ones that we hold dearest and closest. God knows how to penetrate our hearts in such a powerful way. He promises to be a lamp unto our feet and a light unto our path, so as we take one step at a time, we follow Him. A life-long journey begins.

105 Your word is a lamp for my feet,
a light on my path.
106 I have taken an oath and confirmed it,
that I will follow your righteous laws.
107 I have suffered much;
preserve my life, LORD, according to your word.
108 Accept, LORD, the willing praise of my mouth,
and teach me your laws.
109 Though I constantly take my life in my hands,
I will not forget your law.
110 The wicked have set a snare for me,
but I have not strayed from your precepts.

—Psalms 119:105-110

When we maintain humility of what God has brought us through, we are able to extend that grace to others. Now, do not confuse this with the modern distorted thinking that because everyone sins that it doesn't matter; this is a false humility that isn't from God. Sin absolutely matters and we must take an active measure to remove it from our lives as much as possible. But we need to be able to acknowledge that as people walk their journey, we cheerlead them and encourage them towards God. It is OK to trust the Holy Spirit to do the work in the heart of man. Let's declare the praises of our Lord. Let's be excited about our Groom!

9 But you are a chosen people, a royal priesthood, a holy nation, God's special possession, that you may declare the praises of him who called you out of darkness into his wonderful light. 10 Once you were not a people, but now you are the people of God; once you had not received mercy, but now you have received mercy.

—1 Peter 2: 9-10

We are to follow Christ's example. When a woman is engaged to a man, she will consistently be learning his ways, his desires, and what pleases him. Her heart will be a consistent student of him. Her anticipation to please him once they are married is exciting to her, and she intends to multiply everything he gives her. As the Bride of Christ, we should be inclined to be consistent students of His. We should be able to follow in His footsteps so that we begin to take on His image to the world. We are called to be servant leaders.

REFLECTION QUESTIONS

1. Do you recognize entitlement in your own life?

2. List 3 entitlement behaviors that you have practiced or are currently practicing.

3. Pray that God will shine His healing light into these areas so that you can be delivered from these deceptive behaviors.

4. Do you trust that God is good?

5. Start your day with telling God that you trust Him and you submit yourself to Him.

CHAPTER 8

INTERPERSONAL EXPLOITATIVE BEHAVIOR

Narcissists see other people as tools. Their lack of self-awareness is paralleled by a lack of awareness that others exist as individuals with feelings, needs, and desires.

Buckle up and hold on. This chapter is going to be a bumpy ride.

There is no condemnation in Christ, but this chapter should bring shame to all who call themselves believers, but have participated in any part of exploitative behavior, because you will not find Jesus in one single practice of exploiting people. The Ekklesia is riddled with shame currently because of the lack of self-control and because of the Ruach Narcissus having its way violating the Bride.

We cannot pretend to overlook this section because it is uncomfortable. We, as a collective whole, cannot turn a blind eye to the mass amounts of exploitative behavior the pastors, elders, leadership, and priests have committed in the church buildings and in the name of authority. And I can barely even type this out without wanting to vomit, but pasting the name of Jesus on their wretched and sinful behavior is the epitome of tragic and disgusting.

We have allowed religion to trump a relationship with Jesus and given too much trust and leeway to people who are supposed to be leading us. We turn a blind eye and cover up behaviors that "might put a blemish on the church" to maintain our lies. We fail to shine light on the sin and let all the world see that it must be dealt with. We become hypocrites and double the sons of hell because we allow this exploitive behavior to go on. We learn by these evil hearts to turn a blind eye. They will use their power and authority to shame and condemn anyone who speaks against them. They know they are sinning, yet do not care.

PASTORS, LEADERS, AND PRIESTS

13 *"Woe to you, teachers of the law and Pharisees, you hypocrites! You shut the door of the kingdom of heaven in people's faces. You yourselves do not enter, nor will you let those enter who are trying to.*

15 "Woe to you, teachers of the law and Pharisees, you hypocrites! You travel over land and sea to win a single convert, and when you have succeeded, you make them twice as much a child of hell as you are.

—Matthew 23:13&15

Priests have been given too much authority, and it has created chaos in the Catholic church. The wretched things that priests have done in hidden places and then tried to cover up is reprehensible. They used their place of power and a sense of entitlement to harm and hurt others in traumatic ways. The church gave them too much power and withheld their need for a wife, all in the name of entitlement and religion.

Southern Baptists have gained an equally bad reputation for sexual exploitations and the raping of women. These pastors, leaders, and priests become untouchables because they are "respected," and the victim goes unheard. Skid Row has a song called "In a Darkened Room" that absolutely describes the wretchedness of this behavior. I can't quote it here because of copyright issues, but I recommend you look up the lyrics. It is a devastatingly powerful song pleading for light in a darkened room. Indeed. Light. Let me assure you, Church, God sees every single second of it; every single perverted and sinful behavior. He sees the first inappropriate text, hears the first comment, and knows every thought that you would never take captive.

5 We demolish arguments and every pretension that sets itself up against the knowledge of God, and we take captive every thought to make it obedient to Christ. 6 And we will be ready to punish every act of disobedience, once your obedience is complete.

—2 Corinthians 10:5-6

God gave every single person who has exploited another the opportunity to back out. He gives us the chance and strength to refuse to sin. When we exploit others, and are complicit in these behaviors, we are guilty of that sin.

13 No temptation has overtaken you except what is common to mankind. And God is faithful; he will not let you be tempted beyond what you can bear. But when you are tempted, he will also provide a way out so that you can endure it.

—1 Corinthians 10:13

13 You, my brothers and sisters, were called to be free. But do not use your freedom to indulge the flesh; rather, serve one another humbly in love. 14 For the entire law is fulfilled in keeping this one command: "Love your neighbor as yourself." 15 If you bite and devour each other, watch out or you will be destroyed by each other.

16 So I say, walk by the Spirit, and you will not gratify the desires of the flesh. 17 For the flesh desires what is contrary to the Spirit, and the Spirit what is contrary to the flesh. They are in conflict with each other, so that you are not to do whatever you want. 18 But if you are led by the Spirit, you are not under the law.

19 The acts of the flesh are obvious: sexual immorality, impurity and debauchery; 20 idolatry and witchcraft; hatred, discord, jealousy, fits of rage, selfish ambition, dissensions, factions 21 and envy; drunkenness, orgies, and the like. I warn you, as I did before, that those who live like this will not inherit the kingdom of God.

—Galatians 5:13-21

18 Flee from sexual immorality. All other sins a person commits are outside the body, but whoever sins sexually, sins against their own body.

—1 Corinthians 6:18

I was originally going to focus on specific stories about awful things that people have done in the church. But God said to me, "Stephanie, this isn't about shaming anyone in particular. This is about the entirety of the Bride and how she is off the mark." Yessir.

So please do not get distracted by who did what, why they did it, what excuses they made in the process. All of that is irrelevant, really, when we have created, adopted, and supported a system that allowed all this to happen in the first place. The Church was never meant to be a religious system. Jesus says He is going to build His church on Peter, which doesn't sound much like a system, but on people. The design has always been freedom in Christ, sharing our testimony and the gospel. That is it. We have developed the rest of the trash, and now we need to take it out, and all the exploitative, toxic, and disgusting behaviors with it. Shame should rest on the shoulders of the pastors, leaders, and priests who have participated in these types of behaviors in the name of authority.

We cannot overlook the congregants who have also done these same behaviors, but maybe without having the title or status to go with it. Any exploitation of another is sin. All of the scriptures listed above are relevant for church attendees as well. You have the chance to back out of choosing sin and exploitation of others. You are called to back out and let the Holy Spirit convict you. You know you feel it, you know it is wrong, but does it become a challenge in your heart? Does your flesh tempt you to see how far you can go? So instead of using the tools you've been given in scripture, you indulge in sin.

May it never be that way again! Turn now! Repent now! You can absolutely change your sin trajectory today.

Love of Money: Ours and Others

Other's Money

Money. The downfall of so many good people with originally good intentions. Money isn't inherently wrong. God can do some beautiful things with money. But the love of money corrupts every single time.

> [10] *For the love of money is a root of all kinds of evil. Some people, eager for money, have wandered from the faith and pierced themselves with many griefs.*
>
> **—1 Timothy 6:10**

We exploit others when we see them as paychecks and endless bank accounts. There is a place to make a living in ministry, and I believe that staff should be paid livable wages. I believe there needs to be a balance between what we sell and what should be given freely when it comes to ministry. Three areas that are exploitative to charge monies for are: prophecy, prayer, and healing.

Prophecy: God's words are His and should never be sold. You should never pay to have someone tell you what God is saying. First of all, we can all hear God's voice. We are His children. He wants to talk to us, be in a relationship with us. Prophecy should be given freely. These are words that God has given and they do not belong to the human. For the human to charge money pretends to make God's word their own possession and is an abomination.

27 My sheep listen to my voice; I know them, and they follow me.

—John 10:27

Prayer: We should never pay for prayer. When people are charging for prayers, stay away. They do not have the heart of God and are exploiting people who are not strong in that area. We can all learn to be strong in prayer. It is a practice. If we practice it, we will become better and better at it. Prayer is communication with God.

Healing: Healing comes from Jesus' wounds (**Isaiah 53:5**) and the work of the Holy Spirit. If someone is charging for healing, they are corrupt and exploitative.

Reject anything that they attempt. Jesus says that many people will do miracles in His name, but He won't know them (**Matthew 7:21-23**). Why? Because Jesus' name carries power in spite of us. Anyone trying to monetize the work that Jesus did to give us healing is demonic and covered in Ruach Narcissus.

(Note: this is not referencing professional medical care. This is covering the miraculous work of healing through the divine Trinity.)

8b Freely you have received; freely give. 9 "Do not get any gold or silver or copper to take with you in your belts—10 no bag for the journey or extra shirt or sandals or a staff, for the worker is worth his keep.

—Matthew 10:8b-10

The expectation the world seems to have that no one in the church should make a living is kind of silly. Things that are OK to charge money for are music, books, creative endeavors, businesses, talents (possibly like playing in the worship band), and speaking engagements. Most people who are in ministry will have multiple jobs or streams of income to supplement what ministry cannot pay them. The majority of their ministry work is most likely pro bono or low pay. Certainly there are the "celebrity" pastors that make substantial incomes, but that is a very small percentage of people doing ministry. You may see them with the most facetime, but they are not the majority of ministers, nor do their incomes represent the majority of church staff incomes.

However, looking at fellow image bearers as endless bank accounts is not what God had in mind when he said to tithe. When we become retailers of God's message and gifts, we are on dangerous ground. Televangelists seem to be the catalyst for this behavior. The Bible never speaks specifically about television, so I guess it made them feel like they had leeway, but God does speak about greed and about the love of money. There is also a story illustrating how Jesus became very upset about God's house becoming a marketplace. Though the TV may not be a church building, the same principle applies everywhere that His name is the focus.

15 On reaching Jerusalem, Jesus entered the temple courts and began driving out those who were buying and selling there. He overturned the tables of the money changers and the benches of those selling doves, 16 and would not allow anyone to carry merchandise through the temple courts. 17 And as he taught them, he said, "Is it not written: 'My house will be called a house of prayer for all nations? But you have made it a den of robbers."

—Mark 11:15-17

13 When it was almost time for the Jewish Passover, Jesus went up to Jerusalem. 14 In the temple courts he found people selling cattle, sheep and doves, and others sitting at tables exchanging money. 15 So he made a whip out of cords, and drove all from the temple courts, both sheep and cattle; he scattered the coins of the money changers and overturned their tables. 16 To those who sold doves he said, "Get these out of here! Stop turning my Father's house into a market!" 17 His disciples remembered that it is written: "Zeal for your house will consume me."

—John 2: 13-17

God is very clear that He is an all-consuming fire and that we walk on dangerous ground when we make Him a commodity, especially at the expense of His children. Taking advantage of others who are desperate for the work of the Holy Spirit by charging money for it is exactly something Ruach Narcissus would inspire, as manifestly evident in the Renaissance practice of paying for indulgences in the Catholic church. This spirit always takes, takes, takes. There will never be enough. People become seen as an endless supply of, well . . . supply. Because Ruach Narcissus is a black hole, an empty void, it is always seeking supply. That supply comes in many forms, but it is always devouring someone else and their resources. This is exactly what is happening when the Bride sees image bearers as a way to make a ton of money.

This practice can happen at a local small church that expects everyone to clean out their entire purses every Sunday or at the largest churches that are begging for money to uphold these extremely extravagant and luxurious lifestyles.

I went to an event one time that asked the most absurd thing: I was in my twenties, a young mom, and had spent more than I should have to get to the event in Texas. It was four states away, and we had to have a hotel, food, and gasoline. I took my young son so the expense was even greater than just for me. Our little ministry at the time jam packed in a Ford Expedition and off to Texas we went. We drove overnight for twelve hours and arrived early the next day. We slept for a bit and then prepared for the event the next day. It was a twelve-hour fasting event. We had great expectations to meet the Lord there. It was in November, which in the South can still be warm, but it was not warm at all. It was absolutely freezing at this event, but we were committed to making it a wonderful experience and leave enriched and prepared for more ministry.

After a few hours of freezing, the absurd request came from the stage in a loud bellowing voice: "Trust God. Give everything you can. Empty out your wallets. God will take care of all your needs. If you will give everything, then God will make sure that you are taken care of." And at that . . . we were out!! We left the event immediately.

See, I think they rented an event space and had maybe a fourth of their expectations met and now they needed *all of our* money to make up for it. But if we were supposed to trust God to meet all of our needs to eat and travel, then why weren't they trusting God to do the same? Or was it that they saw us as the means by which that was supposed to happen?

Here is my issue with this kind of thinking: What if they put someone in serious financial strain making promises on God's behalf that God isn't involved in? Can God do miraculous work through us giving away our money? Absolutely. He even says we can test Him on it. The difference between some man asking for everything you have and you feeling conviction to do it is God. God may indeed ask you to bring everything you have to the "storehouse," be it your church, an event, a nonprofit. But when He calls you to it, you will know it. You will feel that deep tug on your inside that propels you to do it, and God will honor it.

6 *"I the LORD do not change. So you, the descendants of Jacob, are not destroyed.* 7 *Ever since the time of your ancestors you have turned away from my decrees and have not kept them. Return to me, and I will return to you," says the LORD Almighty.*

"But you ask, 'How are we to return?'
8 *"Will a mere mortal rob God? Yet you rob me.*
"But you ask, 'How are we robbing you?'

"In tithes and offerings. 9 You are under a curse—your whole nation—because you are robbing me. 10 Bring the whole tithe into the storehouse, that there may be food in my house. Test me in this," says the LORD Almighty, "and see if I will not throw open the floodgates of heaven and pour out so much blessing that there will not be room enough to store it. 11 I will prevent pests from devouring your crops, and the vines in your fields will not drop their fruit before it is ripe," says the LORD Almighty. 12 "Then all the nations will call you blessed, for yours will be a delightful land," says the LORD Almighty.

—Malachi 3: 6-12

But I am always super leary of people who give charge to others to give everything they have. I believe God will move within your heart if that is His will for you. Outside of God prompting you to give financially to that degree, set some healthy boundaries and do not give more than you feel prompted to.

I will often ask God what He wants me to give. Sometimes I am hesitant because the amount seems like more than I can handle, yet it has never hurt me. God does exactly what He promises and provides. God may pull you out of your comfort zone, but He is able to sustain you. If it is just people putting pressure on you, walk away. The chances are you are being used as a commodity. God will never see you or use you as merely a means of financial gain. He already owns everything.

Our Money

We are very attached to our money. Money means status and respect. The more we have the less vulnerable we are to . . . well, almost anything society throws at you. If we have enough money we can pay our way out of any situation, therefore we do not have to trust anyone.

I keep thinking to myself that one day, if people can quit being bought, our society would be so much better. People will do the most heinous things for the smallest sums of money. We will even quit seeing people as people and abuse, torture, and kill them for some money. But say that you don't think you could go to that extreme, though I challenge you that we all can do horrible things under the right conditions; we still have an ever-persistent pursuit of money that we will compromise for. When both parents work to maintain these large lifestyles, we have compromised our children. We compromise our health by working insane amounts of hours, swing shifts, night shifts—and yet most of the time it seems like we are just getting by. We compromise our integrity by gaining money in shady or morally unsound ways. Money is always a driving force for us.

Money has always had power and status attached to it. The contrast from biblical days to today is what we consider being rich. Back then it would have been land, animals, and size of family. Today it is the size of your bank account and credit score, cars, yachts, and European vacations. No matter which time frame lived in, there are perks to being rich. So many perks that it is hard to refuse or hard to give up when asked by God to let it all go. I think that we can overcome almost any temptation more easily than the desire to be rich.

Ruach Narcissus active in our lives will cause us to desire money and wealth because it represents that endless supply. Supply is what narcissists need to function. Just like we think we need an endless supply of money to function, or at least to have the respect we deserve. It is not often, probably never, that you see poor or underprivileged folks sitting at the table with the wealthy unless the wealthy are using them for show and tell, but more on that in the next section. When we see poor people as only projects because they aren't rich, we have again put money as the god.

Why would Jesus want us to give everything away? Is He so cruel and selfish that He doesn't want us to have anything? Or have anything nice anyway? Quite the contrary. Jesus' focus for us is for the eternal and not the temporal. He knows the glory that we will be able to live in forever, so He implores us not to hoard things here on Earth. When we have all the riches in heaven, the riches on Earth seem a bit worthless. But ultimately, the purpose here is to love God with our whole being and to love our neighbor as ourselves. The rest of it is vanity.

16 Just then a man came up to Jesus and asked, "Teacher, what good thing must I do to get eternal life?"
17 "Why do you ask me about what is good?" Jesus replied. "There is only One who is good. If you want to enter life, keep the commandments."
18 "Which ones?" he inquired.
Jesus replied, "'You shall not murder, you shall not commit adultery, you shall not steal, you shall not give false testimony, 19 honor your father and mother,'[a] and 'love your neighbor as yourself.']"
20 "All these I have kept," the young man said. "What do I still lack?"

21 Jesus answered, "If you want to be perfect, go, sell your possessions and give to the poor, and you will have treasure in heaven. Then come, follow me."

22 When the young man heard this, he went away sad, because he had great wealth. 23 Then Jesus said to his disciples, "Truly I tell you, it is hard for someone who is rich to enter the kingdom of heaven.

24 Again I tell you, it is easier for a camel to go through the eye of a needle than for someone who is rich to enter the kingdom of God."

—Matthew 19:16-24

There is speculation about the meaning of the phrase, "camel [going] through the eye of a needle." I have heard that it is a reference to a gate called "Needle Gate" that would have been an "after hours" entrance to the city. It would need to be small and complicated to get through so that an enemy could not easily pass through it. Therefore, a camel would definitely have quite a challenge to get through it. It could also be Jesus using hyperbole to emphasize his point by the literal meaning of a camel (a gigantic animal) trying to fit through the eye of a needle (one of the smallest holes known to man)[1]. The wealth being the great large issue, and the entrance into heaven being the smallest hole.

It is hard for us to fathom that being rich is an issue of any kind, when truly it sounds more like the answer to all of life's woes. However, greed is an insatiable state of being. There will never be enough when we are greedy. This brings to mind Ebenezer Scrooge, a fictional character in Charles Dickens' *A Christmas Carol* (1843). He was so greedy that he sacrificed every beautiful part of life for money. He forsook family, love, marriage, and life's joys all so he could make more, hoard more, and count his money. It wasn't until he was shown the error of his ways through some very colorful dreams that he began to change. Once he realized that money was not satisfying after all, he truly began to live, and his newfound generosity was evidence of that. I believe there is some of this character in all of us, which is why this story became popular and truly a classic.

So Jesus asking this man, often referred to as "the rich young ruler" in the passage in Matthew, to give everything away was an imploring to be generous. Would the man have ended up destitute doing what Jesus said? We don't know because the man wasn't willing to risk it. But knowing the character of God, this man's willingness to let it all go would have opened the door to God being able to trust him with more than he could have ever dreamed or imagined. See, the love of money prevents us from being able to trust God because we put our trust in our money instead. Money equals security, but it is unstable ground. There is no guarantee in money, therefore the constant pursuit happens.

God has used the wealth of people since the beginning of time to further His kingdom. Having money is not wrong, becoming wealthy is not wrong, but the heart that is attached to that money is where the folly can lay. If we know that it is all God's wealth to start with, and follow His commands with it, then we are glorifying God with His gift of finances. If we use it to further our glory and judge others for not having it, we are agreeing with the enemy's use of wealth. If you are questioning where you stand, start giving it all away and see what happens to your flesh meat puppet. This is a great test to see Who (meaning God) or what you trust.

When Ruach Narcissus has us fooled into thinking that our earthly wealth means something, we then will use it as a way to manipulate and exploit others. Buy offs, bribery, and other very sinful tactics may be used to keep people's mouths shut about our unsightly and sinful behaviors. We buy into the lie that we can buy other's silence. A cunning deception from the enemy of our souls. This is the most heinous use of wealth in the Church. This practice may come from an individual, or even a corporate gathering of believers who are using their wealth for evil, because they think it will cover sins.

The podded part of Ruach Narcissus will prevent the truth that sinning will never cover up sins. You can't sin your way into hiding sins. All sins have a way of revealing themselves in one way or another. Add wealth and false power to the mix and you have a recipe for disaster that has taken down many, many saints, and those who were crushed under the weight of their heavy sins. The sinner carries the heaviness of the sin upon them, but the victim carries the same heaviness of the sin on top of them. The sinner will often feel a burden, the victim of the sin will feel like they are dying from it. To think that money can buy you out of that is foolishness! Only Jesus, and the beautiful act of forgiveness, can remove a weight that is huge and cumbersome. Jesus paid a price that can never be touched with human currency to remove that weight. To access that sustaining gift requires repentance and humility, and the sinner should confess their evil act. This is the only path to redemption, because money is never enough, no matter what lie it has told you.

Money exploits the rich by confusing them into believing that they hold status. The Bride is only wealthy in her pursuit of Jesus Christ, and nothing else.

Exploit the "Story" of People

It would be interesting to see what modern day church services would be like without exploiting the stories of others. See, I think the point in "going to the ends of the Earth" should cover that the Church needs to be aware of the struggles around the world. Now don't get me wrong, I don't have a problem with making others aware of the needs of others. I have a problem with the fact that the American Church, especially, has to be convinced of how good their works are at helping people around the world. This may be a plagued mindset of much of the first world church, but we should be embarrassed that we need to be reminded of where our money was spent and who it helped. Again, please do not misunderstand me, I agree with accountability for funds. You should know exactly where and how the congregation you are a part of is spending the funds.

What I am talking about is the poor family that gets a "gift" from the church and is then put on the screens to huge applause. I am talking about the story of the kid with no education who is starving, and instead of just knowing that there are people with that issue moving us into action, we have to see them, know their story, and feel good about what we are doing for others.

This often doesn't propel us to get off our derriere and actually do anything. No. That would require effort and energy. We are able to just give money and be glad someone else is doing the hard work. We are able to exploit the story of others and feel good about ourselves, like a good narcissist, without having to be face to face with people who, frankly, we don't have time for. We are able to pat ourselves on the back for a good job well done, while we haven't even begun to touch the crises that are all throughout our world. The Bible promises that the poor will always be with us (**Matthew 26:11**). We cannot necessarily remove the plight of the poor, but we should always be propelled to engage with it. It is the call to every believer to not think more highly of ourselves than we ought (**Romans 12:3**).

I want to know how often people who meet these people once invite them into their world. How many times do they sit at a table with them and dine? How many times are they involved in the family gatherings? How many times are the "poor" welcomed past their story that is so easily exploited?

My late husband and I once had a ministry called R.I.O.T. It was an acronym for Reaching Into Our Territory. We used to go and hang out with the homeless at their camps. We would bring some camping chairs and food and sit and talk. We learned so much about their lives and believe it or not, some had jobs and bank accounts and just chose to not live in a house.

One man touched my heart in such a deep way: he had lost his wife and children in a house fire, and he said he would never have a house again. Yet, he held a job and was not on drugs. He was lucid and interesting and struggled with the loss and why God allowed such a huge devastation to happen.

I tell you these stories not to pat us on the back, this was nearly twenty years ago, but to let you know that you can get to know people and not see them as a project or a story to exploit to show how good you are, but just to see them as people. We weren't rescuing these image bearers. We were just hanging out with them. They aren't all pathetic, and not all of them need to be rescued by super Christians with super capes that swoop down with a tract and a temporary answer to a much greater issue that leaves them feeling so good about themselves. "Do-gooder syndrome" is what my hilarious and truthful friend, Jill, calls it.

For example if you give someone, who doesn't have one, a car that is a great, heroic thing to do. But what if they can't afford the insurance or the maintenance? Do they even know how to maintain it? Do they know how to take care of it? Can they afford what all comes with having a car? How long is the support that comes with that great gift of the car? Did we give the car away for them or for us? Change that scenario to a new roof, a house, or anything that requires upkeep and know-how. We can't do things just to feel good for a day.

I am not trying to discourage anyone from doing kind things, but I am trying to encourage everyone to be more like the Good Samaritan and back up our goodness with support. The Good Samaritan didn't just help the man and walk away, he promised to follow through with whatever cost was needed to help the man. This is what we should do when we do kind efforts. Back it up with follow-through.

When I became a widow with five children, I had people offer to help me with things, but at times I was left with a larger mess to manage than I expected. I get it, people are busy, life is full. But I could have used someone, or actually an army of people, who were committed to helping me with ongoing situations. I think that is more helpful. Not the temporary 'yea me' actions, but an ongoing discipleship that leads others. I had very little consistent help from the Bride past the first year, yet widowhood lasted for years. There were some amazing people who were in it for the long haul and I am forever grateful for them. I share this in my book *The Death Tsunami* (https://www.thestephaniejordan. com/product/the-death-tsunami-paperback/) if you'd like to read more of my story.

I had a conversation with a sweet fellow widow friend this last weekend about her experience with "help" from the church. She said that she felt violated by groups that came to help her as though she was a project. Widowhood is such a vulnerable position to be in already, and we know when someone is there to help genuinely and when it is a project. It isn't about the receiver being thankful or not. Of course people are usually thankful for help for work that needs to be done, but there is a feeling that is left behind. The Bride is a spiritual element, and when we are in the presence of others we either leave a feeling of a void (narcissism: all about me serving you to feel good about me) or a feeling of fullness (genuine heart of the Lord: this is about sacrificing me to make sure that your needs are met).

You can have a genuine heart and still fall into Ruach Narcissus when you can't see the people instead of the project. If there is no sacrifice to the service, then it probably is tainted with the spirit of self and less about the person in need of the service. Like I said, they are most likely thankful that you helped them with some projects, but what about the aftermath? That is when the rubber meets the road. When living, breathing families become the same as an inanimate building, this is the disconnect between God's heart and self. When the checklist on a house is marked off by one or two items, but the humans inside feel yucky, or left abandoned, or still alone at the end of it all, is when we have to be so careful. We, the Bride, will feel good about ourselves because we can lay our head down and know we did something good. But what about them? Do we continue to think about them? Do they have to impact us to a deep degree for them to ever cross our minds again? Do we check in with them again and again because we can't get over it?

I used to attend a church with "serve days." People could sign up for projects that they had a heart for or that needed to be done. I love the idea. I think the heart is good, but my issue is what is left undone. I think it would be best to have set projects that are completed all the way through, no matter how long that takes. Continued discipleship. That may not ever get a huge applause, truly, because it becomes boring. No one is cheering for the discipling of long-term project people. Is it still awesome if, years down the road, nothing has changed? Does that make the church feel good about itself? No. So we don't see those stories. They don't stroke the narcissistic ego nearly enough. They don't make us feel like we are doing enough to rescue the others, the ones who aren't like us; you know, the project people.

What if it is a marriage that needs long-term care? But you won't get any recognition for being a part of it? What if you can't fix anything and you just have to sit in the mess and mire with them? Can your ego handle that?

When image bearers become projects to stroke our own ego and not as a call to disciple, we have followed Ruach

Narcissus. The Church can't possibly overlook that there are needs, the world would shun us to the nth degree, but we can make it all about us as we "love on" and "serve" these projects. They become less image bearers, who deserve a seat at our table, and more pats on the back of the good things we have done, all in the name of Jesus, yet His heart is nowhere to be found.

THE ANTIDOTE TO INTERPERSONAL EXPLOITATIVE BEHAVIOR

The antidote for exploitive behavior is to *FEAR GOD*. Until you recognize your proneness to participate in it and how destructive it is, you will deceive yourself. Let Holy Spirit shine the light in those dark places of your heart. Exploitation is an area that we need God to redirect us from quickly. This slippery slope is so slick that just one toe dipped over the edge can suck you down quickly. The reason exploitation is so easy to fall into is because sometimes it is covered in "good." If we can make ourselves look good, like nothing bad happened or we did a good deed, then everything is fine. It is all about us, and no consideration about what the other person feels, thinks, or needs.

Why is fearing God the antidote? Because the beginning of all wisdom is the fear of the Lord. This term "fear" means utter reverence. We should shutter at the knowledge that God sees our wickedness. This fear is not about being scared, like we would be of something scary or evil, but knowing that God is greater than we are and justice is important to Him. Respecting Him and our fellow image bearers is a call we cannot overlook. We have no humility when we exploit God's image bearers blatantly and forget *WHO* God is.

> *10 The fear of the LORD is the beginning of wisdom,*
> *and knowledge of the Holy One is understanding.*
> *11 For through wisdom your days will be many,*
> *and years will be added to your life.*
> *12 If you are wise, your wisdom will reward you;*
> *if you are a mocker, you alone will suffer.*

—Proverbs 9: 10-12

He says that His arm is not too short to save. He sees what is happening in our hearts, minds, and lives. Are we so foolish to believe that He will not bring justice to us who call His name and label ourselves with His redemptive power? There should be a sense of dread that we have a just Father who does not take sin lightly.

> *1 Surely the arm of the LORD is not too short*
> *to save,*
> *nor his ear too dull to hear.*
> *2 But your iniquities have separated*
> *you from your God;*
> *your sins have hidden his face from you,*

so that he will not hear.
3 For your hands are stained with blood,
your fingers with guilt.
Your lips have spoken falsely,
and your tongue mutters wicked things.
4 No one calls for justice;
no one pleads a case with integrity.
They rely on empty arguments, they utter lies;
they conceive trouble and give birth to evil.
5 They hatch the eggs of vipers
and spin a spider's web.
Whoever eats their eggs will die,
and when one is broken, an adder is hatched.
6 Their cobwebs are useless for clothing;
they cannot cover themselves with what they make.
Their deeds are evil deeds,
and acts of violence are in their hands.
7 Their feet rush into sin;
they are swift to shed innocent blood.
They pursue evil schemes;
acts of violence mark their ways.
8 The way of peace they do not know;
there is no justice in their paths.
hey have turned them into crooked roads;
no one who walks along them will know peace.
9 So justice is far from us,
and righteousness does not reach us.
We look for light, but all is darkness;
for brightness, but we walk in deep shadows.
10 Like the blind we grope along the wall, feeling our
way like people without eyes.

At midday we stumble as if it were twilight; among
the strong, we are like the dead.
11 We all growl like bears;
we moan mournfully like doves.
We look for justice, but find none;
for deliverance, but it is far away.
12 For our offenses are many in your sight,
and our sins testify against us.
Our offenses are ever with us,
and we acknowledge our iniquities:
13 rebellion and treachery against the LORD,
turning our backs on our God,
inciting revolt and oppression,
uttering lies our hearts have conceived.
14 So justice is driven back, and righteousness stands
at a distance;
truth has stumbled in the streets,
honesty cannot enter.
15 Truth is nowhere to be found,
and whoever shuns evil becomes a prey.

—Isaiah 59:1-15

We have the ability to walk away from these behaviors.
We have the ability to do something different. We are
able to say, "No more, I won't continue on the path that
I walked in."

11 But you, man of God, flee from all this, and pursue righteousness, godliness, faith, love, endurance and gentleness.

—1 Timothy 6:11

"I will use this divine power of the Holy Spirit inside me to start a new way that honors God and doesn't exploit His children." This is a declaration that will purify your motives. We all have to dissect our motives because deception is that sneaky.

3 His divine power has given us everything we need for a godly life through our knowledge of him who called us by his own glory and goodness. 4 Through these he has given us his very great and precious promises, so that through them you may participate in the divine nature, having escaped the corruption in the world caused by evil desires.

5 For this very reason, make every effort to add to your faith goodness; and to goodness, knowledge; 6 and to knowledge, self-control; and to self-control, perseverance; and to perseverance, godliness; 7 and to godliness, mutual affection; and to mutual affection, love. 8 For if you possess these qualities in increasing measure, they will keep you from being ineffective and unproductive in your knowledge of our Lord Jesus Christ. 9 But whoever does not have them is nearsighted and blind, forgetting that they have been cleansed from their past sins.

[10] Therefore, my brothers and sisters, make every effort to confirm your calling and election. For if you do these things, you will never stumble, [11] and you will receive a rich welcome into the eternal kingdom of our Lord and Savior Jesus Christ.

—2 Peter 1:3-11

Ask yourself if you are doing the work of discipling others or are you just doing checklist projects that make you feel good? What if the other person feels overwhelmed by it? We need to be aware that others have feelings and that what may seem like a good thing to us may actually *not* be a good thing for them. Can you handle it if someone were to refuse your good deed? If they told you no unless you can help them further?

These are genuine questions and honest situations. We push our good deeds onto others and believe they should be thankful, yet never consider the weight of what we left them with. There is no end to the needs that this world will create. It is a wicked, evil, dark place. Instead of spreading ourselves wide and thin, let's be purposeful and be a deep well of living water and bring life to the ones we can. None of us is capable of doing everything for everybody, but we can impact a few deeply. Jesus picked twelve people to teach them everything He knew, and they spread like wildfire. See people. Not projects.

> *²² But the fruit of the Spirit is love, joy, peace, forbearance, kindness, goodness, faithfulness, ²³ gentleness and self-control. Against such things there is no law. ²⁴ Those who belong to Christ Jesus have crucified the flesh with its passions and desires. ²⁵ Since we live by the Spirit, let us keep in step with the Spirit.*
>
> **—Galatians 5: 22-25**

REFLECTION QUESTIONS

1. Do you love your money more than you should?

2. Do you see others as merely a means for more money?

3. Pray that God will reveal to you His fullness and that you no longer desire to harm or destroy human relationships because you see them as a means to make money.

4. Have you participated in exploiting others?

5. What creative ways can you share a message or story without exploiting others?

6. Do you understand how exploitation would be offensive to God?

7. Ask Holy Spirit to reveal the needs of others to you and ways you can become active and help logistically.

CHAPTER 9

LACK OF EMPATHY

This is the cold inability to accurately recognize how other people feel. This speaks to the narcissist's lack of emotional awareness or depth. It is not always that the narcissists don't "care" about another's feelings, it is just that they are unaware that others might even have those feelings.

Oh, how I wish I could say that the Bride has mastered empathy. I mean, seeing as all of us as Christians know that we need a Lord and Savior to save us from ourselves and our own damnation, you would think that we would offer empathy in droves. Yet, here we are in 2024 on publication of this book, full of arrogance and lack of empathy.

Kat Von D, famous for her tattooing and makeup line, publicized her baptism. I was so excited! I had quit following her or buying her products for years because of her ties to witchcraft and the occult. I didn't set a campaign against her; I didn't dislike her. As a matter of fact, it broke my heart because I actually love her style, taste, and talent. It is very similar to mine. However, I couldn't continue to ignore that her leaning toward evil misaligned with my heart for Christ. So, I prayed for her. I would touch her display when I went to Sephora and claim Christ over it. I asked Jesus to reveal Himself to her. Do I think I was a part of her coming to know Jesus? I have no idea. That would be super cool, but it isn't about me. I often pray over and for people to know Jesus because I want them to have freedom, not because of me.

Unfortunately, when she made her baptism public, which is exactly the point of baptism, she was slandered, attacked, and ridiculed by, you guessed it, CHRISTIANS!! Christians came after her in droves with all their asinine opinions on how she should "Jesus the right way," and how she "can't possibly be a Christian with how she looks," and so much other trash. IT. WAS. TRASH. Here's the kicker, this trash wasn't thrown onto Kat Von D, this trash was thrown right into the *face of Jesus*. Why? Because Jesus had already covered her in His redemptive blood and nothing anyone could say about her could land without making it to Christ first. Jesus had been working on Kat Von D for years. In His loving and summoning way, the same as He has done with all of us who call on His name, HE impacted Kat. HE taught her His love. HE redeemed her, and HE didn't ask anyone's permission to do so. Nor does she need anyone's permission to love Jesus and walk *her* walk with Him.

I would love to say that Kat is one glitchy exception to the rule of crappy Christian behavior today. But the response she got is the rule. The audacity and lack of empathy and compassion is the rule by which too many Ruach Narcissistic Christians are operating. The Bride has forgotten that she is only holy because of her Groom, not because of herself. What right does she have to boast about anything?

*¹ As for you, you were dead in your transgressions and sins, ² in which you used to live when you followed the ways of this world and of the ruler of the kingdom of the air, the spirit who is now at work in those who are disobedient. ³ All of us also lived among them at one time, gratifying the cravings of our flesh and following its desires and thoughts. Like the rest, we were by nature deserving of wrath. ⁴ But because of **his great love for us, God, who is rich in mercy, ⁵ made us alive with Christ** even when we were dead in transgressions—it is by grace you have been saved. ⁶ And God raised us up with Christ and seated us with him in the heavenly realms in Christ Jesus, ⁷ in order that in the coming ages he might show the incomparable riches of his grace, expressed in his kindness to us in Christ Jesus. ⁸ **For it is by grace you have been saved, through faith—and this is not from yourselves, it is the gift of God—**⁹ not by works, so that no one can boast. ¹⁰ For we are God's handiwork, created in*

Christ Jesus to do good works, which God prepared in advance for us to do.

—Ephesians 2:1-10 *(bold text emphasis mine)*

Oh Church! Bride! We must quit allowing Ruach Narcissus to trick us into thinking that our redemption has anything to do with us! We are merely clay in the Master's hands. We only came to understand our own wretchedness through the work of Holy Spirit. But I guess I would pose the question: Did you realize your own wretchedness? Or do you think that maybe you thought you could be "born" into Christianity through human standards? Like maybe you were just born into the right family who goes to church and that makes you a Christian? Or maybe you were born into wealth and that is your true god but you plaster the name of Jesus on the front of your idol of money because it seems more palatable? Maybe you were born Southern and in the Bible Belt and that automatically qualifies you as a Christian? Maybe you grew up and realized that what you mostly knew was trash, and then you became a Christian in title, but not in practice? Therefore, the realization that you are indeed wretched without Christ falls short on you.

Most people think they are good people. If I asked you today, "Do you think you are a good person?" What would be your response?

Kat is just one current example of how Christians show lack of empathy. A new believer, learning how to navigate her walk and journey with the Lord, and instead of blessing her and showing our light in the darkness, we just gave her more obstacles to overcome. We didn't light a path to follow, we littered hers with opinions and harsh, cruel words. Instead of welcoming her onto a smoothed-out path that Jesus made, we pushed her off into the woods and hoped that she would stumble and fall on every tree branch so she could "prove" her worthiness to find her way back to the path of Jesus. It's gross.

And she is even claiming Christianity!! What must it look like for those who don't call on the name of Jesus? I can't imagine what the lack of empathy experience is for them. We are not meant to, or expected to, judge non-believers. We should show them infinite compassion. Yes!! Even those monsters who do horrific and horrible things! Why? Because Jesus died for them too. If Jesus said that he wasn't here to condemn the world, then I am confident to say God didn't send you to condemn the world either.

17 For God did not send his Son into the world to condemn the world, but to save the world through him.

—John 3:17

When we condemn others, who do not believe what we believe, we harm them, we harm our witness, and we are treading on dangerous ground. Truly, we are in disobedience to our calling.

> 29 *"The most important one," answered Jesus, "is this: 'Hear, O Israel: The Lord our God, the Lord is one. 30 Love the Lord your God with all your heart and with all your soul and with all your mind and with all your strength.' 31 The second is this: 'Love your neighbor as yourself. There is no commandment greater than these."*
>
> **—Mark 12:29-31**

I know it may sound cliche, cheesy, or redundant, but Bride, your role is to love others well. Loving others can mean setting hard boundaries. Loving others sometimes includes having to part ways in a relationship. Loving others can look like tough love, but it doesn't ever sound like hate, malice, or cruelty.[5]

---

5 I wrote a book called *Believing in Boundaries* (https://www.thestephaniejordan.com/product/believing-in-boundaries-paperback/) that can help you learn how to set boundaries in complicated relationships. I also have an online course on my website* that will help you work through issues you may have that prevents you from loving yourself and others well. Learn more about boundaries by going to https://thestephaniejordan.com/.

Loving others doesn't include lack of empathy. Because the truth is that you and that person are not so much different. You both were on the path to the second death without Jesus. If you could see your own wretchedness, and that is what summoned you to accept Christ, then you must be able to have compassion for their wretchedness. They have yet to see the light, so show them the light. They are already saturated in darkness; no need to show them more darkness. Darkness is what they already are comfortable in; it does nothing beneficial to continue to cover them in darkness.

Jesus is the Light of the world. If you are truly a believer in Christ, you live in the light, and darkness should not be a part of your life. Your first inclination should never be to condemn others with darkness. That is following the image of the black hole of narcissism. Narcissism will consume light. It doesn't matter how bright the light is, it will continuously try to dim it until the light is barely visible or snuffed out completely. Ruach Narcissus will try to do this with your light that Jesus gives you. It will try to consume it until all you have left is judgment in your heart toward those for whom you should be nothing but a ray of hope.

12 When Jesus spoke again to the people, he said, "I am the light of the world. Whoever follows me will never walk in darkness, but will have the light of life."

—John 8:12

If we fail to see humans as image bearers of God, we will only see them as their actions and behaviors. None of us is a summation of the best or worst things we have ever done. Most of what we do here on this earth will fade away, but who we are is eternal. When we truly fall in love with our Groom, we will want to love like He loves. We will learn what that looks like. The beauty is that we are all parts of a whole, we are not all called to do exactly the same things. That is OK. But what we do will always look like a ray of hope, a light on a hill, a promise of a future, and a sacrifice. These are the ways our Groom has modeled.

JESUS AND EMPATHY

Jesus wanted to connect with us. Why? Because God loves us so much. Loving someone *requires* empathy. Empathy is vulnerability in one of its greatest forms. Jesus allowed Himself to become vulnerable for us. He left heaven, came as a baby, grew in a human body and all its limits, then died a horrific and painful death. Every one of these situations was a vulnerable situation. Satan even knew it! He tested Jesus in each of these areas just to see if Jesus would opt out. Because if Jesus opted out of having empathy and feeling our pain where we are and how we experience it, then we would have no hope to have empathy either. Satan often reminded Jesus that He could just call down the angels of Heaven to come rescue Him.

No biggie.

Just save yourself, use your resources at hand, Jesus.

No one would blame you.

You know you want to.

But Jesus, steadfast on His mission from His Father, refused to be tempted to rescue Himself. He knew there was a greater battle to defeat Death and Hades than to rescue Himself from the pains of earth. He refused to remove empathy out of His journey to rescue the human race. So we cannot remove empathy either. We cannot overlook the pain and hurt of those around us so we don't have to be uncomfortable. We must remember that we have a greater prize on the other side of this physical experience and we need to share that joy with everyone.

PITY, SYMPATHY, COMPASSION, EMPATHY

I think maybe some people do not know what empathy is. I have fallen into this category much of my life. To be honest, when I have taken spiritual gifts tests in the past, I would get a big, fat, goose egg zero on compassion and grace. They were just not characteristics that I cared about, much less practiced. I didn't even care. It didn't prompt me to seek those traits in my life. I just kept on doing what I knew and what was comfortable to me. Truth be told, it wasn't until my husband passed away that I began to even understand empathy and the need for it. It is amazing how God can use horrible things to humble us in beautiful ways.

There is a difference between pity, sympathy, compassion, and empathy. Distinguishing between them is important to understand the practice of empathy.

Pity is seeing that someone is going through a hard time or hurting and thinking, "Man! That must suck!" but we aren't interested further. Pity is the most disconnected form of recognizing suffering in others. You can pity someone for small things. Maybe you see someone yelling at their kid and you think, "Poor kid." However, the thinking about that kid doesn't pass that one thought, and it certainly does not propel one into action to help. Pity may happen when you see someone trip and fall, but you just watch them get up and everyone moves along. Pity is not a strong enough emotion to light a fire under us to help. If Jesus just had pity for us, we'd all still be going to hell.

Sympathy is when we look at someone's situation and either try to diminish it by comparing it to a better or worse situation or feel bad but do not feel compelled to act. This is a very disconnected feeling from the other person. I would say the Bride practices sympathy toward others more than compassion or empathy. Sympathy might compel you to give the homeless guy you pass everyday a dollar or two. It will definitely have you saying, "I'll pray for you," but you don't do that or anything else for the person. It might spark you to act kindly toward someone who is clearly having a bad day. Sympathy is what we see in the Bible in the story of the Good Samaritan. The second passerby takes sympathy on the wounded man, but still leaves him in the place of hurt. Sympathy is useless in the practice of Christianity unless it spirals into compassion, and then to empathy. Sympathy can be the diving board that you jump off of, but empathy must be the deep end of the pool that you land in.

Compassion is when we care about someone else's situation, but it doesn't really compel us to be fully engaged. We may do some kind things for them, and even check up on them a little. Compassion is a sweet thing, but it is not a life-changing behavior typically. Compassion would be similar to the law that God gave in the Old Testament. With the law came a recognition of what we are even doing wrong and gives us the ability to change it. So having compassion for someone gives us the ability to see that something is wrong in someone's life, and we can maybe help them change the situation by acts of kindness. We are still a bit disconnected. Compassion can make us feel good about ourselves because we are "helping" the person in need, but we still aren't feeling the need ourselves.

Empathy is a catalyst to get into the situation with someone else. Empathy compels you to take a deep dive into the hurt and pain and all the messiness that comes along with life. This behavior is what the Good Samaritan practiced and why we named the story after him. He mattered because of his empathy. He changed the trajectory of the person's full experience by getting into the mess of the beaten man's life. That is what

Jesus did for us. He deep dove into humanity and all the messiness that came with it. He felt it for us. He felt it with us. He felt it to share and heal others. His compassion often would move into empathy as he healed the sick, cast out demons, and defeated Death.

The modern-day inability of much of the American Church to get into the mess with others is a devastating bruise on the Bride. I don't just mean the homeless, poor, or obvious people whom we can exploit, but I mean the average marriage that needs some support, or a new mom who needs support. We are "too busy" filling our calendars with junk like football, sports, dance class, music class, choir, scouts, and all the time takers that make us feel important and like "good parents/people," while we overlook how that time could be better spent. Better yet, we never even ask God if we should be doing any of those things. We never give Him our calendars and say, "God, you put whatever/whoever You want into this space because I am not concerned for anything more than what You would have me do."

Our lack of empathy shows up to the world as a body disconnected from each other—lonely people, overlooked people, and our "head up our asses" syndrome. We aren't fooling the world with our plastic smiles and fake everything. People can see through the Bride like she is shattered glass with holes everywhere.

I am going to share a story about my friend, the hilarious and truthful one, Jill. Her mother is elderly, we will call her Sue. Sue was pretty much knocking on

Death's doorstep in fall of 2023, but miraculously survived. At Christmas, this *compassionate* lady, we will call her Rose, brought Jill's mom a Christmas tree. It nearly filled an entire corner of the tiny room. When Jill came to visit her mother, she asked where the tree had come from. Jill, and the other caretakers, had already decided with Sue that she didn't have space for a Christmas tree and would forgo one that year. So naturally, Jill was rather perturbed that this cumbersome tree was now something she would have to manage along with Sue. This seems a bit trivial, right? I mean, it was a nice thing to do to get the little ol' lady in the assisted living home a pretty tree. You're right. It was compassion, but it wasn't empathy. Why? Because the family was never even considered when the action was taken. The *compassionate* lady, Rose, didn't *empathize* with the situation of the entire family, and what this action may mean for them. The tree was impractical and became a nuisance.

Another example is that there were some elderly friends at Jill's mom's church who wanted to come and take her to church on Sunday. That sounds so kind. It is *compassionate*. The mom loves her church. So what is the problem? The problem becomes the *lack of empathy* for the entirety of the situation. The mother is no longer self-sufficient. Jill has to take care of her, which can make Jill's full life complicated when disaster strikes, like if Sue falls and breaks a part of her body, and she has to manage it. Instead of asking Jill if it was OK to get her mom and take her to church, these people were just making plans around Jill. The issue: If there is an emergency, Jill is the one who is expected to drop everything and run to solve, redeem, and fix the problems. If mom falls and ends up in the ER, it is Jill who is expected to drop the million balls she is juggling and come help. It is best for everyone if mom goes with Jill to church, so she knows that the proper support her mother needs is taken care of. Empathy in this situation would have included thinking about Jill before an offer was made to her mom. Having empathy would mean being able to see that mom is no longer capable of taking care of herself and that now the burden falls on Jill, so honoring Jill by asking for her permission and making proper plans to be responsible for her mother in these people's care would be empathy.

For example saying to Jill, "Hey Jill, we would love to be able to spend some time with your mom on Sunday and take her to church. We have made plans to make sure she will be safe and protected, and we also have plans if something were to happen to her, so that you are not put into an emergency situation. Please leave us with her insurance cards, and any number we need if you are not available. We will feed her lunch after the service and then return her to her home and let you know when she has arrived safely."

This is empathy. It sees deeper into a situation than compassion. Being kind is not the same as being considerate. Jill recognizes that these people are being kind, but she knows the burden falls into her lap, and she isn't able to take the risk of someone else's potential misstep.

Maybe with these scenarios you can see the difference between compassion and lack of empathy, and how it can hurt others. Jill has had to pour a lot of emotional energy into situations and circumstances that she wouldn't have had to manage if others had been more empathetic and considered the full weight of the situation at hand. The "Do-Gooder Syndrome" strikes again, and leaves nothing but frustration in its wake. This syndrome is a symptom of Ruach Narcissus.

THE SICK

There are a few different types of "sick" we will talk about. There is the sick meaning the infirm and the sick meaning the unsaved. We are called to the sick, both kinds. However, I see a lot of Christians protesting in front of abortions clinics but none standing in front of emergency rooms praying for healing. I see a lot of Christians protesting other churches and their beliefs, but I don't see many Christians at the local bar ministering to people. Goodness how foolish we have become in our lack of empathy. We want to regulate morals and behaviors when people are so sick in their hearts and souls. We have forgotten that Jesus came and rescued us from ourselves, but we don't think He can do that for others. We think we need to step in and do it for Him. You know why? Ruach Narcissus. We are so arrogant to think that they need us to be their lord and savior because Jesus isn't powerful enough to be their Lord and Savior.

THE INFIRMARY

14 Is anyone among you sick? Let them call the elders of the church to pray over them and anoint them with oil in the name of the Lord.

—James 5:14

There is so much sickness in today's world, more than ever before, at least in my lifetime. Ever since 2020 and the Covid-19 issue, there is an insane increase in viruses, diseases, and cancer. Feel free to google the statistics, because it is heartbreaking how much the increase is in cancer, disease, and deaths. People who have always been healthy are dropping dead and fighting illnesses. Yet, we hear little to nothing about the Bride doing anything about it. The Church is sitting back and doing the funerals without ever interceding prior to that or speaking against illnesses and sickness.

Ruach Narcissus has deceived us into thinking that we can't or shouldn't intervene because we no longer have empathy. We have the Great Physician living inside of us, but we aren't able or willing to share Him with the world. Why? I truly believe it's because we don't believe that He can . . . or will. Which would make us look foolish!! We would look like utter fools going to hospitals and praying for the sick for years and not a single person healed. Our egos would be trashed and we might even be made fun of by everyone around.

"Look at that fool! He/She has prayed here for years and nothing happens."

"Why don't you just give up already? Nothing you pray about ever works."

"Why do you keep coming here? Isn't it a waste of your time?"

All blows to our ego. All moments where Satan is saying, "Why don't you just rescue yourself?" All the moments when we can't handle God not serving us and making us the hero. We can't fix it, control it, or protest it into submission, and therefore it isn't worth pouring our energy into. Yet, all throughout the gospels, Jesus is doing healing ministry. What if . . . what if one day, three years into your praying-and-nothing-happening, the anointing of the Lord falls on you and for the next forty years everyone you pray for gets healed? Would it have been worth the three years of looking foolish to gain forty years of miracle healings? What if it is vice versa? You pray for forty years and nothing happens, but then that one day the anointing falls, and you raise the dead. Would it have been worth the forty years? Even just for one life to be raised again?

Can we look at time in God's way? Can we look at people in God's way? Can we look at the hope we have and not get lost in our ego? Can we humble ourselves before the Lord for just one miracle? Can we take others under our wings and lead them to believe that with us even if we never see it happen while we are still alive? What if it is your protégé who is the one who sees the promise? Can you still take the journey? Can you step out?

You are meant to do greater things than what Jesus did!

12 Very truly I tell you, whoever believes in me will do the works I have been doing, and they will do even greater things than these, because I am going to the Father. 13 And I will do whatever you ask in my name, so that the Father may be glorified in the Son. 14 You may ask me for anything in my name, and I will do it.

—John 14:12-14

Maybe you tried it once and you felt foolish because it didn't work. Bust your ego to pieces and go again. When Noah built the ark, no one had ever seen rain before. He built this gigantic boat for a flood that was inconceivable. It took a really long time to build the boat. Yet he plugged away at it, just trusting God and not having to know all the outcomes, and he saved his entire family and humanity along with it. You can thank old uncle Noah for your very existence.

You may not see the miracle in the moment, but what if in all those years you thought nothing was happening, every single person was actually healed of their infirmity and you just never knew? What if they all survived against impossible odds because you kept at it? We don't know how we play into God's glory story, but if we will learn to empathize and get into the mess and trust God's promises, we will have such a rich experience.

23 Jesus went throughout Galilee, teaching in their synagogues, proclaiming the good news of the kingdom, and healing every disease and sickness among the people. 24 News about him spread all over Syria, and people brought to him all who were ill with various diseases, those suffering severe pain, the demon-possessed, those having seizures, and the paralyzed; and he healed them.

—Matthew 4:23-24

5 These twelve Jesus sent out with the following instructions: "Do not go among the Gentiles or enter any town of the Samaritans. 6 Go rather to the lost sheep of Israel. 7 As you go, proclaim this message: 'The kingdom of heaven has come near.' 8 Heal the sick, raise the dead, cleanse those who have leprosy, drive out demons. Freely you have received; freely give.

—Matthew 10:5-8

38 Jesus left the synagogue and went to the home of Simon. Now Simon's mother-in-law was suffering from a high fever, and they asked Jesus to help her. 39 So he bent over her and rebuked the fever, and it left her. She got up at once and began to wait on them. 40 At sunset, the people brought to Jesus all who had various kinds of sickness, and laying his hands on each one, he healed them. 41 Moreover, demons came out of many people, shouting, "You are the Son of God!" But he rebuked them and would not allow them to speak, because they knew he was the Messiah.

—Luke 4:38-41

I get it, the first thing people will say in a rebuttal is, "But I'm not Jesus." Nope, you are right. But once you have accepted Him as Lord and Savior, you have the same resurrection power living inside of you. He told us that we would do greater things than He did. Is it that you don't trust that you are filled with the Holy Spirit? Because that is an entirely different story. If we don't understand *who* we are as believers, then learning our identity will be the first step in beginning to walk an incredible faith journey with God. This book is not about our identity in Christ, but how to be the Bride of the Christ. Learning to be the Bride that the Bible describes will definitely help you on your journey to understand your identity in Christ, but there are many books about it. Research and find one to help you understand that you have infinite power through the Holy Spirit to perform all sorts of miracles for God's glory! He **wants** us to impact this world!

SPIRITUALLY SICK

17 On hearing this, Jesus said to them, "It is not the healthy who need a doctor, but the sick. I have not come to call the righteous, but sinners."

—Mark 2:17

¹² On hearing this, Jesus said, "It is not the healthy who need a doctor, but the sick. ¹³ But go and learn what this means: 'I desire mercy, not sacrifice.' For I have not come to call the righteous, but sinners."

—Matthew 9:12-13

We have the unique directive to heal the spiritually sick as well as the physically sick. This is an incredible gift because many only recognize the physical and struggle with realizing that the spiritual side of themselves is the eternal and most real side.

What I mean by 'most real' is that these physical meat puppets (my late husband coined that phrase and I think it is so fitting for these bodies we reside in) are temporary dwellings. We are only in these bodies for a blink of an eye of our existence. If we are lucky, we will see eighty years old, but that isn't a guarantee. So the physical presence we experience in being physically ill is only until our flesh passes away, or as believers, we fall asleep. (Note: Believers are only referred to as falling asleep in the New Testament because a Believer in Christ cannot die. Our physical body returns to dust, but our spirit and souls are awake and in the presence of Jesus!) So as cool as it is that we can do miracles of healing with the physical body, the fact that we can lead others to know Jesus and have true genuine spirit awakening soul healing is an incredible miracle!

I asked God last year, "Why aren't we seeing you part the Red Sea and knocking down the walls of Jericho anymore? Those things are really cool!"

He said, "Creation *has* to submit to Me. The miracles I am doing are in the hearts of men, because they do not have to submit to Me."

Mind. Blown!

Yes Lord! Indeed! Moving in the hearts of men (of course you are included in that ladies!) is a miracle! I know how stubborn I am . . . and to get me to submit is certainly a feat only a super loving and infinitely patient Father could accomplish. God designed me with fire in my soul. He has always known how to harness it; it was I who was ignorant of how to control it.

I thought burning everything down around me with my abrasive attitude was beneficial. At least I wasn't having to deal with it! But I learned that I was spiritually sick, and I needed a doctor. I needed someone to teach me how to harness this fire before it destroyed everything around me, including me. God started with the music I was listening to.

He would ask me, "Does this glorify me? Does your heart align with this?"

"Well, now that you mention it, God, nope, it sure doesn't."

I threw quite a few cassette tapes out of the window! Then it was CDs. Now it is playlists. Sometimes I'll think fondly of a band I used to love and think that I should add that to my playlist. Then I will remember why I don't listen to them anymore. Because sickness is contagious, including spiritual sickness, so I have to prevent myself from being exposed to it. It doesn't mean I don't still love the way the music sounds, it's just that I know that it doesn't feed my life. I am built for life, specifically life in Jesus Christ. I am not made to be spiritually sick, but to be well and teach others to be well too.

Truly, if I were still the same person I was in my twenties, there is no way I would be writing, or could write, this book. I would have never been able to wear the bridal clothing that I can now as God has continued to pursue a relationship with me, and I have allowed him to purify my heart and mind. I am on this journey along with you all. I am continuing to learn how to love and live like my Groom. I am glad that you are willing to take this journey with me!

God shifting and working in the hearts of men and women all around the world is such an incredible spectacle to watch. I see people coming to the truth in Christ almost daily, and it excites my spirit. God is revealing Himself in beautiful ways and people are taking off the blinders and getting healed spiritually.

Know this: It is *NOT* your responsibility to save anyone. It is through Holy Spirit revelation that one comes to know Jesus. The Spirit of Truth will summon hearts and penetrate into hearts with wisdom only from God.

6 This is the one who came by water and blood— Jesus Christ. He did not come by water only, but by water and blood. And it is the Spirit who testifies, because the Spirit is the truth.

7 For there are three that testify: 8 the Spirit, the water and the blood; and the three are in agreement. 9 We accept human testimony, but God's testimony is greater because it is the testimony of God, which he has given about his Son. 10 Whoever believes in the Son of God accepts this testimony. Whoever does not believe God has made him out to be a liar, because they have not believed the testimony God has given about his Son.

—1 John 5:6-10

40 For my Father's will is that everyone who looks to the Son and believes in him shall have eternal life, and I will raise them up at the last day." 44 "No one can come to me unless the Father who sent me draws them, and I will raise them up at the last day.

—John 6:40 & 44

12 What we have received is not the spirit of the world, but the Spirit who is from God, so that we may understand what God has freely given us. 13 This is what we speak, not in words taught us by human wisdom but in words taught by the Spirit, explaining spiritual realities with Spirit-taught words.

14 The person without the Spirit does not accept the things that come from the Spirit of God but considers them foolishness, and cannot understand them because they are discerned only through the Spirit.

—1 Corinthians 2:12-14

Your responsibility is to share the truth about Jesus Christ and share your testimony. What is your testimony? It is your story with God. How did you meet Him? What has He done in your life? This is a beautiful freedom given to us. We don't have to win anyone to the Lord, our Trinity takes care of that. We just have to be faithful with the gift of our faith story and tell others the story.

11 They triumphed over him
by the blood of the Lamb
and by the word of their testimony;
they did not love their lives so much
as to shrink from death.

—Revelations 12:11

This is how we overcome Satan and his tactics. We share the story to any and all who will listen. We give them the information and then trust Holy Spirit to do the revelation.

I had a conversation about this recently, and I gave this analogy: I love to ride my Harley Davidson Sportster 48. She is so much fun! I will often tell people how much fun it is to ride a motorcycle and they respond that they are too scared of motorcycles. I will go into details about how the scenery, the wind, the curves, and the thrill are unmatched, yet they are not swayed any further to ride a motorcycle. See, I just gave my testimony about motorcycles. I explained why I love to ride and my experience. I didn't try to force them onto a motorcycle. I just encouraged them by sharing my experience. Some people may begin to get curious and decide to try it themselves. Some will always think I am crazy for riding a motorcycle. Some will have already fallen in love with the ride, and we can share that experience together.

This is similar to sharing our testimony with non-believers. You do not have to regulate their actions and behaviors. You do not have to convince someone that you are right and that they are wrong. The Ruach Narcissus will make you think that you do because it is ego-driven. If *you* save them, then you have done a good deed and are winning. If you don't save them, worse, they reject you, you have lost. This is ego-driven. You want to win the person and ultimately prove that you are right and they are wrong. But the Bible says that the words we say will seem like foolishness, and we have to be OK with that. Our egos have to take a back seat to the glory of God. We get the honor to plant seeds and then we can pray for them to be watered, but we may not see the fruit on this side of heaven.

18 For the message of the cross is foolishness to those who are perishing, but to us who are being saved it is the power of God.

—1 Corinthians 1:18

Ruach Narcissus will continuously pull your ego to front and center and have you worship the ego. Remember, this spirit is incapable of loving and being loved, so empathy will not even be on the radar if you are allowing that spirit to control any part of your relationship with Christ. This is when you will need to pray to the

Holy Spirit and beg for the light from the Spirit of Truth to shine into your heart and reveal any darkness. Ask where and when your ego might have stolen your empathy. The Lord will want to reveal any unwell spots in your heart.

Empathy is an indwelling in the pain of others around us. We must be able to get comfortable with pain. Jesus was a man of many sorrows (**Isaiah 53:3**). He knew that the world was sick and needed Him for healing. All the evil and pain that we experience is close to Jesus' heart. He had empathy and came from heaven to heal us in his greatest love story for His Bride.

THE ANTIDOTE TO LACK OF EMPATHY

The antidote is to begin to practice sitting with others in pain, even when it makes you uncomfortable. This is the very heart of Jesus that we can mimic to others in a real form and real time. You may even find that others ask why you are still there. Why didn't you leave? And you can answer: Jesus. He didn't leave me in my mess, and I am not leaving you in your mess. I will be here, leaning on the Lord. I can't fix your situation, but I can be here with you and praying to a good, good Father that can help you through this.

There are some seasons that will be particularly challenging, like when you have small children. There is grace in these seasons. The premise is that you do what you can do to the best of your ability to get into the mix with your fellow brothers and sisters and love them well.

Do you still think you are a good person? I hope you can genuinely answer: No. I need Jesus desperately to show me the areas I am weak in. I hope that you can see your areas of weakness in faith and in empathy so you can begin to heal and change your ways. We all need a Lord and Savior named Jesus Christ. We are not capable of having true empathy without Him.

Sure, there are some people who are naturally prone to be more empathetic than others. That is a beautiful gift that we are all different. You may feel like you are always practicing empathy and don't know what to do about it.

Boundaries are important with empathy. We must be healthy in our empathy and not allow codependent behaviors to become the *modus operandi*. Boundaries allow us to get into the mess but not become convoluted in someone else's mess. We are able to keep our focus and remain a stabilizing force in the situation, without feeling like their situation has become ours personally.

Sometimes we may start with empathy and realize that we have found ourselves in a very unhealthy and even potentially dangerous situation, and we now need to separate ourselves a little more. This is healthy recognition. You are not saying that you can't/won't continue to help, but you are setting healthy boundaries about how much help you are able to give. Sometimes people seem healthier than they are. We get in a little deep with them and realize that they are trying to drown us along with them, and that is not healthy for anyone. You cannot feel guilty if someone refuses to take the help that you are able to offer. Likewise, you are not supposed to be manipulating or exploiting with your help, so it will come from a genuine heart.

Setting healthy boundaries will not prevent you from helping, but it will prevent others from taking advantage of your help. This makes the relationship with empathy so much healthier. Boundaries are a God-designed feature and they are important for us to learn. Boundaries are how we are able to remain healthy in relationships. [6]

Getting into the mess with others will be too messy unless you set healthy boundaries and verbally express those boundaries. I had a ministry years ago that loved on exotic dancers. We would go to the clubs once a month and talk with the dancers and share the love of Jesus with them. We took them toiletries and some nice little gifts because it opened the door to conversation. One of our boundaries to respect them was we would not hug any of the ladies unless they offered or requested a hug. We wanted to honor their personal autonomy. That is a boundary. It created safety for the ladies not to have their personal space invaded, and it kept us from being overly friendly with a lady who may not find that to be loving.

Another example is when I did mentorship at a rehabilitation house. My mentee was a young mom, and so was I. We would go to lunch once a week and I would buy her lunch. We talked about life and struggles. We shared hardship and I would encourage her to make the next right decision. She was only responsible for the next

---

[6] My book *Believing in Boundaries* is a great place to start to learn how to set boundaries.

right thing. She ended up leaving the rehabilitation house and called me for money. I told her that I wasn't able to give her any money. That was my boundary. I never wanted her to see me as a bank account, but as a friend. She didn't invest in our friendship. She quit calling after I refused to give her money. I knew she was in a relapse, and I wasn't going to allow her to manipulate me into feeling guilty about her bad decisions. Boundaries.

Sometimes when someone is angry with you for not being able to manipulate you, they will revert to using guilt. Both manipulation and guilt are lies from the Devil and you mustn't give into those feelings. Having empathy and getting into someone's mess is a beautiful gift, but if you know you have to remove yourself because they are destructive and potentially dangerous, that is wisdom. Wisdom is also a God-given gift. Use wisdom as your leader to know when empathy is the best path and how to set healthy boundaries around it.

Just getting messy with people is not what Jesus exemplified. He came to our mess and healed us. That is the goal of practicing empathy. You may not be able to change the circumstances, but you can make as much impact as you can. Take Holy Spirit with you and pray diligently. Jesus didn't become tainted by joining our mess, and if that is your experience, that is not empathy, that is codependency. If we allow someone else's mess to begin to define us, or our lives, we are acting out of codependency. Codependency and empathy can be confused easily. If we have unhealed codependent issues, we will struggle to maintain empathy with someone else and convolute our lives with theirs. We need to be clear on our intentions before we ever start stepping into the mess with others.

The Good Samaritan could make an impact on that beaten man without it harming him in the process. He not only got him to a safe place to heal, but offered to pay for the stay and whatever needs the man had. This is an empathetic impact with healthy boundaries. Seeing people's needs without assuming you know what needs they have or that you can make everything in their lives better is wise empathy.

Ruach Narcissus will quickly have you living in codependency and make a mess out of you and the people you are trying to help. Everyone loses in this scenario. Use wisdom and boundaries, along with empathy and make an impact.

REFLECTIVE QUESTIONS

1. Have you been unfairly judgmental against others?

2. If so, list particular times that you have practiced judgmental behaviors and ask for forgiveness.

3. Ask Holy Spirit to reveal the root of your heart that has created a judgmental heart.

4. Do you practice empathy?

5. If you have just learned the difference between pity, sympathy, compassion and empathy, what is your revelation?

6. How can you begin to put empathy into practice in 3 practical ways?

7. Do you understand the difference between helping someone and codependency?

CHAPTER 10

ENVY OF OTHERS OR BELIEF THAT OTHERS ARE ENVIOUS OF HIM/HER

This describes the narcissist's constant comparison of themselves to others, wishing for themselves the success others experience, and the false belief that everyone else is envious of them. That's how they keep their egos intact. Being perceived as "normal" or "subpar" would represent an ego wound they could not handle.

Envy is like the pulse of the blood of Ruach Narcissus. Churches being envious of each other and in competition as though we aren't all trying to operate in the same way. Believers are living in comparison land with others over money, lifestyle, gifts, talents, positions, and all sorts of things. It has turned the blood of Jesus' Bride into a black goop of toxic behaviors. We are supposed to be covered in the healing blood of Jesus, but have traded it for this counterfeit, toxic, envious black goop that is nasty.

Crazier is when we think the world is jealous of this hot mess we've become. Remember, we are a collective whole. When one of us operates out of envy, we are all struggling with it. The world looks in and sees a bunch of immature, infantile adults who are fighting each other like they are toddlers. I am not sure how we think that anyone would want to emulate us when we are so vicious to each other, but we do. We think the whole world wants to be like us.

One of the very first issues once sin arrived is envy. Where does it lead? Let's take a look.

2b Now Abel kept flocks, and Cain worked the soil. 3 In the course of time Cain brought some of the fruits of the soil as an offering to the LORD. 4 And Abel also brought an offering—fat portions from some of the firstborn of his flock. The LORD looked with favor on Abel and his offering, 5 but on Cain and his offering he did not look with favor. So Cain was very angry, and his face was downcast.

6 Then the LORD said to Cain, "Why are you angry? Why is your face downcast? 7 If you do what is right, will you not be accepted? But if you do not do what is right, sin is crouching at your door; it desires to have you, but you must rule over it."

8 Now Cain said to his brother Abel, "Let's go out to the field." While they were in the field, Cain attacked his brother Abel and killed him.

—Genesis 4: 2b-8

Abel was a shepherd and Cain a gardener. God looked favorably on Abel's offering, but not Cain's. I think the key to knowing why God was partial to Abel's gift is that it was from the firstborn of his flock, but it doesn't say that Cain brought any first fruits. God cannot be fooled, and when we just bring him leftovers, some of what we have to offer, or even worse try to consume as much of Him as we can without giving, He is disinterested in our offering of fruits. They will not be looked upon favorably.

What does this response from God spark in Cain? Vicious envy and jealousy. So God asked him why he was having these feelings. Interestingly, we don't get Cain's response because God speaks directly to his heart, which is God's specialty. Knowing exactly what we need to hear, but may not want to hear. God told him to do what is right, bring his firsts. Then God gives Cain a warning. "If you do not do what is right, sin is crouching at your door. It desires to have you, but you must rule over it." God was trying to tell Cain to settle down, reign his envy and hate in, because this was going to destroy him and even go beyond him. Sin never stops with the initial thought or action. Sin is a ripple effect kinetic action. It spreads far and wide, even to far greater reaches than we can understand.

Cain couldn't reign himself in. Sin had taken hold, envy had done its brutal work of leading to hate, hate bred its physical result of murder. Now everything was a mess, and there was no going back. Envy won the rest of Cain's life.

How many times has envy won your life? Has it cost you friends, family, positions and, most importantly, a submitted heart to the Lord? Envy is sneaky. This story is a great example. It wasn't like Cain didn't bring anything. I mean, Cain tried, right?! Couldn't God have given Cain credit, maybe a bone? See, God doesn't have to be the one who gives, or bends His standards, because we are made for Him and His glory. He was not made for us. Cain knew the rules, he just wanted to bend them . . . hoping God wouldn't mind. It was Cain's arrogance that opened the door to envy. Pride is always a propeller of envy, like fuel to the flame inside of our sinful heart.

The Bride is so full of pride, it is no wonder envy has made its way through the blood vessels into every crevice.

Let's define envy. Maybe you don't even know what it means. Merriam-Webster.com defines envy as: *painful or resentful awareness of an advantage enjoyed by another joined with a desire to possess the same advantage.*[1] Envy and jealousy are similar words, but not the same exactly. You can have feelings of jealousy that do not give you envy. Jealousy will not always propel you to act out toward a person or situation. Jealousy is a feeling, but envy is more of a potentially action-based adjective. Envy creates a desire to possess, which compels an envious person to act on their feelings instead of just merely feel them. Envy is one of the seven deadly sins according to Catholics. Typically envy will always incite some form of jealousy. Envy is a perfect word for what Cain experienced. Painfulness caused the downcast face. Resentment and deception led to asking his brother to go to the field. Murder was his answer to solving these issues.

The Bride tends to operate with envy in a few areas, especially spiritual gifts, positions within the church, and with our fellow brothers and sisters.

SPIRITUAL GIFTS

The reality of spiritual gifts seems to be that they are either fully accepted or completely rejected by the various extant denominations. There is mysticism in the spiritual gifts that is hard for us to grasp. Since we have an obsession with controlling everything, *especially* things we don't understand, we will either embrace them or shun them. Some people try to fence-walk and say they are OK with one or two of them, but the others are false. This is silly because if the Bible speaks about them, how can someone say that one is correct and the other a lie? Either the Bible is true or it isn't. It can't kind of be true and we are able to put our full faith into it.

Ruach Narcissus needs to retain control. If you've ever experienced a relationship with a narcissist, once you have left the relationship and healed, you can see how they used all types of tactics to remain in control. They will question everything about you, sometimes overtly and sometimes covertly. Instead of being forthright and saying, "I don't like the way that shirt looks on you, do you mind changing for our date?" They would say, "Are you sure you want to wear that shirt?" or "Do you have a different shirt?"

"What is the difference between these sets of questions?" you may think. The difference is how the recipient processes the information. The first question takes ownership of the asker's feelings. They openly state that they don't like the shirt. This is genuine and forthright communication. Often people confuse honest communication with being rude, but being genuine is loving, not rude. No one is having to navigate deeper to figure out if they mean something else. This is loving and kind. Forthrightness doesn't equate being mean when it is used with gentleness and care.

The second set of questions makes the receiver of the question need to navigate their choices and the feelings of the other person. It may look like this is their head:

"Did I make the wrong choice?"

"What is wrong with my shirt?"

"Do I look bad?"

"Do they not like me?"

"Do they think I look ugly?"

"Are they mad at me?"

All this happens in a few milliseconds in our brain, but it is enough to plant doubt. When this behavior is repeated over and over again, for years upon years, the one receiving these interrogations will eventually question everything about what is true and what isn't. It becomes extremely confusing and frustrating and makes one not be able to trust themselves. This is underhanded cruel behavior.

Whereas if the question asker had just stated that they didn't like the shirt, well, that is the reason for the request to change. The receiver of the question can then choose whether they want to honor the request, or not, but they aren't trying to figure out what is happening in the situation.

How this applies to the gifts of the spirit is that Ruach Narcissus will ask you, "Isn't that too weird?"

"Doesn't that scare you?"

"Aren't those people weird?"

"You can't do that. You'll look like you're out of control."

"Does the Bible *really* say that?"

The purpose of these questions is to make you feel the need to trust yourself and not God. If you are questioning yourself all the time, and don't trust yourself to know that you can, should, and are meant to experience the fullness of God, including through your spiritual gifts, then you will shy away from even trying. Ruach Narcissus has been successful in the Church in creating these exact kinds of doubts.

We want to remain in control because God might make us too far out of control for our own good. I mean, creating distrust in God is the same thing the serpent did to Eve in the Garden of Eden. It made her doubt God and His goodness toward her. Since Ruach Narcissus is an evil spirit, it also operates in similar fashions as Satan. Satan is referred to as the Father of Lies (**John 8:44**), and lying is certainly one of the narcissist's strongest traits.

So we bash people who are operating in the gifts of the spirit and insult people who aren't. And then we, again, wonder why the world doesn't want to be like us! We can't even get ourselves on the same page in the same book we are reading! In fact, neither the Catholic church nor the mainline Protestant denominations, a large fraction of Christendom, recognize these spiritual gifts.

How did we miss it? Because we are afraid of it, and especially if it causes us to be out of control.

Maybe some people don't know that the spiritual gifts are listed in the Bible. We begin to see that the disciples operate out of spiritual gifts in Acts when Holy Spirit first comes to reside with us. Jesus told us during the majority of His time on earth that it was important for Him to leave earth so the "Helper" could come. The Helper is Holy Spirit, who empowers us to do with the will of our Father.

The gifts of the spirit are:

4 There are different kinds of gifts, but the same Spirit distributes them. 5 There are different kinds of service, but the same Lord. 6 There are different kinds of working, but in all of them and in everyone it is the same God at work.

*7 Now to **each one the manifestation of the Spirit** is given for the common good. 8 To one there is given through the Spirit a **message of wisdom**, to another a **message of knowledge** by means of the **same Spirit**, 9 to another **faith by the same Spirit**, to **another gifts of healing by that one Spirit**, 10 to another **miraculous powers**, to another **prophecy**, to another **distinguishing between spirits**, to another **speaking in different kinds of tongues**, and to still another* the **interpretation of tongues**. [11] *All these are the work of **one and the same Spirit**, and he distributes them to each one, just as he determines.*

—**1 Corinthians 12:4-11** *(bold emphasis mine)*

Let's recap:

We are given different kinds of gifts, service, and work.

Manifestation of the Spirit: Wisdom, Knowledge, Healing, Miraculous Powers, Prophecy, Distinguishing (Discernment) of Spirits, Different kinds of Tongues, Interpretation of Tongues.

None of these gifts are human, but they are manifestations of the Spirit in us. OOOOOO! Creeeeepy! This is where people, including whole denominations, leave the conversation because here comes the spooky stuff. Here is my question: What makes it spooky? The fact that you don't control it? Or that you don't understand it? When the term 'manifestation' is used, we think of witchcraft so fast. But isn't that a perfect way for you to be deceived to not acquire in fullness what the Lord has for you? You fall into all those questions I mentioned above and doubt has taken over. Your mind is reeling for a satisfactory answer, and all it gets is more confusion.

Let me put your mind at rest. *You do not have to understand why or how it occurs. You just need to be open to the beauty of God and the working of Holy Spirit.*

We cannot keep fighting and/or bickering about these things and show the world ourselves as the Bride. The Bride is not divided about Who she loves. She is not concerned whether anyone else sees how beautiful and amazing He is. She is going to operate in a way that honors Him.

Think about a blushing bride who is about to marry a total disaster. Have you ever experienced that? I had a friend who got engaged, and the moment she told me, I was like, "NOOOOOO! Don't do it!!" I just knew this guy had ulterior motives and was a nightmare waiting for divorce. I tried to warn her without outright telling her that she was making the one of the biggest mistakes of her life. I did say something to that effect, just in nicer words. (If you know me, you know that is still forthright.) My friend did exactly what I expected her to do, defend him. She told me how awesome it was going to be and how much she loved him and she couldn't believe her luck. He was her dream guy. (Smack my forehead!) Guess what? They divorced. I know that surprises you. (Sarcasm noted.) The marriage went down in horribly burning flames. But there was nothing that I could say that would have prevented her from marrying this total disaster of a man!

So why is it that we don't have the same loyalty to our healthy loving Groom, Jesus, as we do to toxic humans? Because we think we can control humans, and we know we can't control what is bigger than us. Our relationship with Christ causes us to forego ourselves and trust him. It forces us to lay down our own thinking and follow Him.

The scripture that comes before the one I listed above is important because it encourages us to know that anyone who calls on Jesus as Lord has to be from Holy Spirit. They may say that Jesus is anything else: teacher, prophet, good guy, saint, any other term. But *only* by Holy Spirit can one claim Jesus is Lord.

> *1 Now about the gifts of the Spirit, brothers and sisters, I do not want you to be uninformed. 2 You know that when you were pagans, somehow or other you were influenced and led astray to mute idols. 3 Therefore I want you to know that no one who is speaking by the Spirit of God says, "Jesus be cursed," and no one can say, "Jesus is Lord," except by the Holy Spirit.*

—1 Corinthians 12:1-3

If someone claims that Jesus is Lord, then maybe just remove judgment and say, "Whatever God has in full is great!" Move on with your day. Ruach Narcissus will have you judging that person like they should answer to you in court. If good things are happening to the people around us, why are we so skeptical?

A devotion on the Bible app called Revelation Explained inspired me as I started writing this section of the book and I think is applicable here. It was talking about the church in Sardis in Revelation 3.

1 "To the angel of the church in Sardis write:

These are the words of him who holds the seven spirits of God and the seven stars. I know your deeds; you have a reputation of being alive, but you are dead. 2 Wake up! Strengthen what remains and is about to die, for I have found your deeds unfinished in the sight of my God. 3 Remember, therefore, what you have received and heard; hold it fast, and repent. But if you do not wake up, I will come like a thief, and you will not know at what time I will come to you.

4 Yet you have a few people in Sardis who have not soiled their clothes. They will walk with me, dressed in white, for they are worthy. 5 The one who is victorious will, like them, be dressed in white. I will never blot out the name of that person from the book of life, but will acknowledge that name before my Father and his angels. 6 Whoever has ears, let them hear what the Spirit says to the churches.

—Revelation 3:1-6

Some beautiful truth here is that though we are a collective whole, Jesus acknowledges that some stand out and haven't soiled their clothes. He won't leave those of us who are willing to have the fullness of God, who refuse to be dead on our insides, and who passionately seek Him, even if those around us remain stubborn. This is an encouraging promise in light of how divided the denominational churches are on this.

I would be remiss to not touch on the topic of handling snakes here since it is a conversation in the Church, primarily in the southeastern United States. The handling of snakes is one of the topics I find to be a secondary issue and not one that falls in line with the fruits or gifts of the spirit or aligned with the entire message of the Bible. Snake handling is a dangerous concept of building a whole belief system off onesie twosie scripture picking (picking out one or two scriptures to fit a narrative). It is mentioned one time in the Bible and not an accurate translation of the original language into English. I do not think that if you want to handle snakes as some form of worship that you are doing anything wrong. By all means, you are free to do anything unto the Lord. The Bible says that all things are permissible but not all things are beneficial (**1 Corinthians 10:23**). However, it is an incontrovertible truth that it is not necessary to show any sort of proof or support that one operates in the spirit by handling snakes. Truly, this poor translation of the original language has caused unfortunate confusion and an unnecessary struggle for people raised in these churches. If you look up this scripture in *Strong's Concordance*, you will see that the translation into English is an inaccurate representation of what the original words mean in Greek. The scripture is:

> *18 they will pick up serpents, and if they drink any deadly poison, it will not hurt them; they will lay hands on the sick, and they will recover."*
>
> **—Mark 16:18** *(NASB)*

The Greek word for "pick up" is *airo* (ah'ee-ro)[7] The primary verb tense is "to lift," which is the term that the translator chose to use for this scripture. However, it has a figurative tense "to raise" (like your voice) and "keep in suspense" (like your mind). Ultimately translating to the Hebraic word that means to "expiate sin, remove or take away."

Then we have the term for snake, again a poor translation. The Greek word is *ophis* (of'-is),[8] which means a figurative snake, like sly cunning or an artful, malicious person. Following this word further in the *Strong's Concordance*, the Greek term is *optanomai optomai* (op-tan'-om-ahee op'-tom-ahee),[9] which means "to gaze

---

[7]Strong's reference G142
[8] Strong's Reference G3789
[9] Strong's reference G3700

with wide eyes at something remarkable" or "watching from a distance.'[2]

So this verse would be better translated[10] as: *They will keep people in suspense and lift away or remove any sin from sly, cunning, and malicious people.*

I know that some people, especially those who have been raised in a particular mindset, may have a hard time with this new concept of studying the original words to understand scripture better. Sometimes the English translations are not great at expressing the depths of what the Greek, Aramaic, and Hebrew words mean. For many generations using the term "snake" might have been sufficient for the culture and they understood that it meant a sly, cunning, malicious person. But somewhere along the way it became too literal and people started handling actual live serpents. Remember we do not earn salvation, it is freely given. We do not have to prove our spiritual aptness because it is all in Jesus Christ that we have salvation. He has proven everything that ever needs to be proven. But I think the scripture referring to the hearts of terrible men not being able to hurt us is definitely more in line with the heart of God and His purpose for us here than to hold snakes in hopes that we can prove a spiritual superiority and not be harmed.

---

[10] My translation based on the definitions in the Strong's Concordance

A few versions say: "take up in their hands," but I cannot find those words in King James, New King James, NASB (1995) or other versions and there is no reference to those words in the *Strong's Concordance*, leaving me to believe they were added to help make the concept of "taking up snakes" make more sense. Again, an edit that was poor to start with and didn't need the added words. I know. I know. The thought of the Bible being edited freaks people out, but can we all agree that Matthew, Mark, Luke, and John were not the names of the authors of the gospels. Those would have been the most English Hebrews on the planet. The translators edited their names to be acceptable English names for Hebrews. So the Bible has some edits, but that does not take away from the message of God to save His children through Jesus Christ. There is no violation of the inerrant truth of scripture because of poor translation. The divine inspiration for the author still stands, which is why learning the original wording is so important. The original intention for this passage is perfectly in line with the entirety of God's word, but the translation has left many scratching their heads in confusion. The Bible is always for us and it is the greatest love story of all time. Everything the Bible is telling us is that God is searching our hearts and wants a relationship with us through the redemption of Jesus Christ. That is the standard that we should use when reading all of scripture. Studying scripture for yourself and becoming educated is a very important part of having a genuine relationship with God so that you are not led astray by men and their belief systems. If you hang onto traditions over truth, or religion over relationship, Ruach Narcissus has done its deceptive work on your mind and heart. We are designed for a relationship with and truth in Christ.

"Poison" is also not listed in *Strong's Concordance* in the following section of the scripture that says, "if they drink any deadly poison." The word translated as "poison" is a pronoun that can mean person or thing, similar to our English "it." This part isn't as poorly translated, but it could mean an extension of the prior part of the sentence that if the malicious person "snake" tries to harm, "poison," them, there will not be any success—supporting the scripture that "no weapon formed against me will prosper" (**Isaiah 54:17**). You could probably extend the meaning of the verse to say, *"They will keep people in suspense and lift away or remove any sin from sly, cunning, and malicious people who may offer to have a drink with you."*[11] A concept like if a sly, cunning, malicious person was to offer to have a beer with you, they would not succeed in being able to harm you because you would be able to discern their motives and call out their evil intention.

---

[11] My extended translation of the original verse **Mark 16:18**

Denominations and Positions within the Church

How did we get to a place where we have denominations? Maybe envy. Maybe jealousy. Maybe arrogance. Maybe pride. Maybe control. Maybe just the inability to agree. Whatever got us here, we have seen a steady decline backing out of the denominational pigeon-holes for nearly the last fifty years. We see more nondenominational churches, community, and "unaffiliated" churches than ever before. I believe this is a good thing. It opens the door to breaking free of denominational theology and walking into the fullness of what God has to offer. Hopefully soon the days of rules and regulations weighing the church down will be gone. Her Groom came to set her free, and it was for freedom that He died.

I don't know if I can say that denominations are envious of each other, but I definitely think that people within certain denominations think that others are envious of them. There is sometimes a distorted sense of having bragging rights because one attends a certain church or certain denomination. My brother says, "Episcopalians carry a certain disdain for those ignorant Baptists, and Baptists clearly see no benefit in adopting 'Whiskey-palianism.'"

The envious feelings get even more potent when we talk about positions within the Church. Man oh man! I don't know how the Church became a corporate ladder to climb, but it has, and it is ugly. People being viciously cruel to someone who "took their position" or "isn't right for the job." Ruach Narcissus will deceive someone into total character assassination of another believer if they have taken what the person thinks is rightfully theirs.

I am not one to yield. I don't like yielding. But I am having to learn. I find the inability to yield is one of the primary issues that will open the door to Ruach Narcissus. Why does yielding matter? Because it reminds you that you are not as important as you think you are. You are not first. And in this "me first" society, yielding looks a lot like Jesus.

However, in this corporate church culture, there can't be yielding and climbing. If you are climbing and try to yield, you may be knocked off, and you will most likely lose your place.

I had a friend share with me one of her stories in ministry. I'm going to use her words, but promised I would keep it anonymous.

> "This was just my experience. There's a celebrity-type status that comes with a [leadership] position in a mega church, maybe even [in] small ones [churches] too. I'll admit, I wanted to be that person. I felt like they were SUPER important and I wanted to feel needed and important. So I did everything in my power to make it to the top. It's all about who you know.

Everyone seems to be striving for power and influence. When someone is picked for a position over someone who has been there longer, there is a jealousy and envy that is tangible. I literally had someone call me after I got hired on and said she was angry that I got her position. I was shocked. She left the ministry, but others had a chip on their shoulders for a while. Instead of being joyous and happy, some were jealous and catty. The sneakiest tactic of the enemy is this! It stops movement in the ministry. It breeds rivalry, competition, covetousness, territorialism, and resentment. It assaults relationships, and eventually breaks the church down. It was so sad to see."

My friend left the ministry.

What if the people around her had yielded? What if she had had support because the people around her weren't fighting for the same space, because they knew that heaven is big enough for everyone, because they recognized that the church's primary role is to BE IN LOVE WITH JESUS, HER GROOM? What if she had had light-bearers to help her shine, instead of black-hole-Bride narcissists tear her down. I am not saying the people themselves are narcissists. I am talking about the spirit they are operating out of. We don't know any of the answers to these questions because it didn't happen.

What we do know is that there was so much destruction that the ministry lost two great lovers of Jesus.

What does yielding look like? I am going to give a physical example that we can all relate to, driving. When someone is clogging up the left lane, they have like ten cars behind them, but no intention of moving over. The rule is that if someone wants to pass you, it is your responsibility to move over to the right. This driver is willing to just frustrate, irritate, and sit in entitlement. This is a picture of not yielding and the danger and damage that this can create. Then we have right-hand turns. If no one yielded when they made right hand turns, there would be constant wrecks. If people just pulled out onto the road because they had the right of way regardless of the other traffic, this would create a mess. But most people will yield at a right-hand turn and wait until it is their turn without any negative feelings involved. If we could learn to yield in life like we are taking right-hand turns, waiting for our turn, we would show the world Jesus.

Our ego will get mixed up in the middle of everything, and the more independent our society is, and the less we can depend on each other, the more it creates an environment of "me, myself, and I." But we need each other. The Bride needs all the other parts to support her life. There is enough Jesus, enough ministry, and enough heaven to go around. We do not need to focus on feeding our ego and climbing the corporate ladder of the church. It is a lie.

I hope you can see that this section compiles a lot of the previous sections into a tangle of emotions. Envy is an emotion built off of ego, pride, arrogance, and all of the other personality traits that Ruach Narcissus operates in regularly. Being envious of others will always bring out the ugliest attributes in you. Comparison, feeling like someone has taken something you deserve, and coveting what others have is devastating behavior that will lead to destruction of relationships. The very goal as a believer is to establish relationships, but we cannot do that if we are stuck in envy and jealousy. I believe that is why the Ten Commandments speak to this issue. It is so inherent in humans that God had to put His foot down against it.

17 "You shall not covet your neighbor's house. You shall not covet your neighbor's wife, or his male or female servant, his ox or donkey, or anything that belongs to your neighbor."

—Exodus 20:17

This pretty much sums up everything that you can possibly be envious of. We need to make sure that we pay attention to our hearts as we journey through our days if we want to keep Ruach Narcissus at bay.

THE ANTIDOTE TO ENVY

The antidote to envy is being led by Holy Spirit in a close relationship. The reason that this will help defend you from envy is because the Spirit will remind you that you have a significant and sole purpose and you are not left behind or forgotten. The gifts of the spirit partner with the fruits of the spirit in amazing ways. The fruit only comes once we are firmly rooted in Jesus Christ. When we know how incredibly loved we are, we will mature in our walk, and begin to bear fruit in our lives.

The fruits of the spirit are:

> [22] *But the fruit of the Spirit is love, joy, peace, forbearance (patience), kindness, goodness, faithfulness,* [23] *gentleness and self-control. Against such things there is no law.*
>
> **—Galatians 5:22-23**

When we live out the fruits of the spirit, we have the ability to have grace for the gifts of the spirit. You may not always understand the call of another believer, but if you are willing to live in joy, seek peace, have some fortitude and tolerance (forbearance, also stated as patience in some translations), be kind, know that it is good, be faithful in your walk, be gentle with your thoughts, judgments, and criticism, and have self-control to decipher if you should engage in any way, then you may find how surprised you are at the level of being quiet and how open you are able to practice.

I am struggling right now with a friend who I think has lost his footing a bit in his Christian walk. I am not envious of his situation; it actually makes me a little bit sad. I considered messaging him, but my first response was to chastise him for his foolishness. Thank-fully, I didn't respond out of my first reaction, but I am able to sit on my thoughts and allow myself to process with Holy Spirit and reckon with my own feelings. Before I message him, I will ask myself if I am operating out of these fruits vs. coming at him in a way that will make him recoil. Even if I am right, am I winning if I destroy relationships with my arrogance and suppositions?

He was in a leadership position in a Christian organization. After he stepped down from the main leadership role, he began to post a lot of questionable and unfortunate posts on his social media pages. These posts were not behaviors of a leader, nor of a Christian. I waited. I prayed. I finally told him that he is a child of the Most-High God and that he needs to come back to his first love. I encouraged him that men of God are in desperate need these days and that his example matters. He assured me that he was in good standing with God and thanked me. Though I don't know if my message touched him, I hope that it at least got him thinking. But ultimately, it is between him and God. I am OK with that, but I knew that God was encouraging me to speak to him. I am thankful that I waited and didn't attack him because it would have been a fruitless conversation. I spoke the truth. He will make his own choices, but I am thankful to have retained the relationship.

So when we are envious, even if it is valid, maybe we need to process through and bring every thought we may have captive and ask Holy Spirit to work in us first. Let's take my girlfriend's scenario above and work through this little exercise.

The lady who called and told her she took her job might ask herself:

1. Am I showing love with this phone call?

2. Will this bring joy to the person I am calling and myself? (both parties matter)

3. Am I practicing tolerance and fortitude (mental and emotional strength)?

4. Is this phone call kind?

5. Will we both see goodness at the end of this conversation?

6. Am I being faithful to God and my purpose?

7. Is this call showing my ability to be gentle?

8. If I make this phone call, am I practicing self-control?

9. Will this phone call bring me peace, her peace, and peace to this situation?

I bet if the lady had even asked herself the first three to four questions, she would have never made that phone call. But certainly if she had made it to question 9, she would have put the phone down and moved on with her day. She could have taken that time to praise God for His wisdom and patience.

See God is so good that He doesn't just let us do whatever we want and then say, "It is OK." He has standards for us. Standards for our good. But we allow Ruach Narcissus to operate and dominate our hearts because that is the spirit that lurks among us that we feed. I bet some of you, even if you have gotten this far in the book (thank you!), are thinking that all this sounds crazy. You think to yourself that no one spends that much time with God that they would ask those questions. But there are a bunch of lovers of Jesus, who call themselves the Bride of Christ, that do spend so much time seeking relationship with God, Holy Spirit, and Jesus because they know that without that close connection, every-thing becomes a disaster. Maybe you haven't made a total mess of your life, but you know that you feel deep envy for others. You are always wanting more, wanting better, and nothing ever satisfies. There is a void that only God can fill.

Now back to my friend; she could ask herself:

1. Am I showing love in my response to this lady?

2. If I continue this conversation, will it bring joy to her and myself?

3. Am I practicing tolerance and fortitude by engaging in this conversation?

4. Is this phone call kind?

5. Will we both see goodness at the end of this conversation?

6. Am I being faithful to God and my purpose?

7. Is this call showing my ability to be gentle?

8. Am I practicing self-control by being on this call?

9. Am I creating peace for me, for her, or for this situation?

There are just a few subtle differences in these questions. The reason is my friend was the receiver of the call. She needs to decide if she is going to have a conversation with the upset lady or if she needs to set boundaries in place that prevent this conversation from taking place. If someone is attacking us out of envy, we do not have to let the conversation happen. It is not our responsibility to pacify someone else's anger and envious feelings.

As a matter of fact, it would have been within a safe boundary limit for my friend to pause the conversation and guide the lady through her nine questions before she proceeded. This might have been a great way to avoid receiving someone else's venom and protect herself.

So next time you find yourself in a conversation with someone who is operating out of envy, or of whom you are being envious, try asking yourself, or them, these nine questions before you proceed. If we can learn to pause, and not be so quick to respond, we may be able to break out of poor relational patterns and begin to have better relationships in our lives. This is God's goal! The very thing Ruach Narcissus will seek to destroy is healthy relationships.

Another way to defeat envy in your life is to desire God's fullness for you. Whatever that looks like and however scary it may be. So often fear and control steal our ability to let go and let God just have His way with us. We want to *know* what is happening and more safely control what is happening. What if we just don't think something is for us . . . but that is the very thing that

God has in store? It is the key to our freedom in Christ that we haven't tapped into. Can we trust that God is good? Can we trust that what He has for us is better than we can ever imagine, even if we don't understand it?

Years ago, I told God, if it is in the Bible, I want it if it is something You have for me. I have lived by that ever since. I make mistakes, I take back the reins of control, I get discouraged, but I will always correct my direction to go towards God. I know that He is capable of making things happen that I can't even begin to imagine, but He will withhold if He can't trust me with it. Not because He isn't good, but because only a fool would give someone something valuable when they are not trustworthy with it. Often God works in the stages of building. He starts with small things and puts them into place, and as the faithfulness of those small things are honored, He is able to give us more and more. So be faithful in the little things, don't let envy steal those seeds. That phone call made to my girlfriend was a stolen seed. The lady couldn't see that maybe God had something bigger or better for her. Maybe it was smaller, but it was better! The loss of what the lady thought was hers, always belonged to God. She couldn't see that she might have been tested to see if she could handle this loss. Ministry is the hardest job on the planet. It is relentless and comes with a lot of disappointment, rejection, frustration, and sadness. Why would anyone do it, really? Because the compulsion to share the Gospel of Jesus Christ is ingrained in the fabric of the believer.

The heart should always remain focused on God and not on man. When we begin to focus on man, that is when envy will have its way with us. If we can't handle the rejection of a job, how in the world can we handle the rejection of nonbelievers? If we can't handle the disappointment that we didn't climb another rung on the corporate church ladder, how can we handle the disappointment a very broken and fallen world is definitely going to give us? We must learn to operate in all the gifts of the spirit, so the fruits can flow freely, and most importantly, we can remain a light in a very dark world. God must be able to trust us with His image bearers, and to do that, we have to quit looking at ourselves and pitying ourselves for what we do not have.

We are a holy people. Set apart for the ways of God. We cannot be distracted by silly, and even not so silly, feelings of envy. When you can see yourself as a priest of God, you may begin to see your status differently. You have all of heaven at your disposal. You are a fellow heir of Jesus Christ. What do you have to be envious of? You are meant to experience power and authority to build God's kingdom. You are part of a holy nation. You are not desperate, even at your worst! You are able to shift things in this life with your words and your prayers.

1 Therefore, rid yourselves of all malice and all deceit, hypocrisy, envy, and slander of every kind. 2 Like newborn babies, crave pure spiritual milk, so that by it you may grow up in your salvation, 3 now that you have tasted that the Lord is good.

The Living Stone and a Chosen People

4 As you come to him, the living Stone—rejected by humans but chosen by God and precious to him—5 you also, like living stones, are being built into a spiritual house to be a holy priesthood, offering spiritual sacrifices acceptable to God through Jesus Christ. 6 For in Scripture it says:

> *"See, I lay a stone in Zion,*
> *a chosen and precious cornerstone,*
> *and the one who trusts in him*
> *will never be put to shame."*

7 Now to you who believe, this stone is precious. But to those who do not believe,

> *"The stone the builders rejected*
> *has become the cornerstone," 8 and,*

> *"A stone that causes people to stumble*
>
> *and a rock that makes them fall."*

They stumble because they disobey the message— which is also what they were destined for.

9 But you are a chosen people, a royal priesthood, a holy nation, God's special possession, that you may declare the praises of him who called you out of darkness into his wonderful light. 10 Once you were not a people, but now you are the people of God; once you had not received mercy, but now you have received mercy.

11 Dear friends, I urge you, as foreigners and exiles, to abstain from sinful desires, which wage war against your soul. 12 Live such good lives among the pagans that, though they accuse you of doing wrong, they may see your good deeds and glorify God on the day he visits us.

—1 Peter 2:1-12

When we can't or won't trust God, we are truly acting as nonbelievers. When we allow envy to be our trait that people see, we are acting like nonbelievers. This is the deception of Ruach Narcissus and why we must defy it. We must defy the spirit that is leading us to destruction and go toward the path of life. That requires sacrificing ourselves and our wants, knowing that God sees. He will give you the best for you, if you can just learn to trust Him.

God knows we struggle in this area, and if we are honest with Him, He is so faithful to walk us through the steps to rid envy from our lives. You may feel it sometimes, but you don't have to operate out of it. You may have moments when you are struggling, but you will let the Lord minister to your heart. Envy can be so deeply ingrained into our psyche that we don't recognize it until we bring it under the self-reflecting light of the fruits of the spirit. Practice the pause. Pause and question yourself if you think you may be struggling, there is nothing to lose by pausing, but you have everything to gain. Your story may even become one of your greatest testimonies.

REFLECTION QUESTIONS

1. Do I feel like others are envious of me? What propels this thinking?

2. Am I envious of others?

3. Have I hurt others by being envious?

4. Do I understand spiritual gifts?

5. What did I learn about spiritual gifts to help me know God better?

6. Do I trust God to give me His fullness, whatever that looks like?

CHAPTER 11

DEMONSTRATION OF ARROGANT AND HAUGHTY BEHAVIORS OR ATTITUDES

Arrogance and conceit are traits that are often noticed first in narcissists. This is evidenced by disrespect for the positions or rights of others and the narcissist's willingness to demand and expect that others will bend to their will. Like exploitative behavior, this behavior can be easily noticed without the narcissist having to say a word. They break in lines, use patronizing tones, and act as if they have every right to take away what is rightfully someone else's.

I think if you asked the majority of nonbelievers in the United States of America how they would describe most Christians, "arrogant" would be in the top three adjectives. So far from the heart of Jesus![12]

---

[12] *Note from author:* I started writing this chapter and decided to ask my Facebook page what people thought when it comes to

THE JESUS BUFFET

¹ But mark this: There will be terrible times in the last days. ² People will be lovers of themselves, lovers of money, boastful, proud, abusive, disobedient to their parents, ungrateful, unholy, ³ without love, unforgiving, slanderous, without self-control, brutal, not lovers of the good, ⁴ treacherous, rash, conceited, lovers of pleasure rather than lovers of God—⁵ having a form of godliness but denying its power. Have nothing to do with such people.

—2 Timothy 3:1-5

Second Timothy tells us not to have anything to do with such people, but we are those people. The Bride is a lover of herself first, not of her Groom. We boast a story that we do not live out.

Ruach Narcissus is the reason that we could be described as arrogant. We chase the world and its passions. We think we can congregate into our church buildings and ignore the world around us. I would love to see a church walk out the door one Sunday and do something cool like collectively go eat at a restaurant

---

Christians being arrogant. Though the answers didn't shock me, and every one is covered in this book, I have to admit that my heart sank in sadness at how much pain sometimes is carried for image bearers when they hear the very name that means "little Christ." So far from the heart of our Trinity is right! We must do better!

and just bless the socks off the wait staff. Defy the issue we talked about earlier where wait staff dreads seeing "the church people" come. Instead, we show up with entitled and arrogant attitudes, and everyone is repelled right after we just got our "fill" of Jesus. Consumers of Christ . . . maybe we should just start calling the church buildings "Jesus Buffet: All you can consume of Jesus. Come empty, leave entitled."

Is this every church everywhere? Of course not. We aren't expressing hyperbole to lose the point. The goal of becoming aware of yourself, the Bride, and how we affect others is to change what needs to be changed. Encourage the best out of ourselves, other believers, and summon those who don't believe to know the incredible freeing love of Jesus Christ.

¹ The Spirit clearly says that in later times some will abandon the faith and follow deceiving spirits and things taught by demons. ² Such teachings come through hypocritical liars, whose consciences have been seared as with a hot iron.

—1 Timothy 4:1-2

We cannot deny that we are being warned about how awful we can be. The Bible is a mirror if nothing else. We should reflect it as it shows us Jesus. When we have abandoned our faith in Jesus because we need something that is more palatable, or a little less . . . searing to our desires, we are aligning with evil. Just because you *can* justify it in your mind does not make it accurate with scripture. Again, do not misunderstand. I am not talking about onesie twosying[13] scripture to distort the purpose and story of God. God's themes stand cover to cover.

Misrepresenting, not being able to agree, and just wanting to remove things all together because we don't like them has created a mess. Mix that with arrogance, and boy, the narcissistic traits will become a vast black hole that many unsuspecting souls will fall in and desperately try to save themselves from.

A narcissist's arrogance can show in different ways. An overt narcissist will be showy, flashy, dominant, and potentially very in-your-face. You might be a bit captivated at first, until you are in an intimate relation-ship with that narcissist and find that the charismatic show that sucked you in is now sucking the life out of you. I find that megachurches fall into this category. They put on great shows but lack the ability to support their people. This is also where we most often see the "corporate ladder climb" experience.

A covert narcissist is going to be much more subtle. Their arrogance is never seen from the outside. As a matter of fact, often they look very humble and kind. How can this be? Because this spirit is so cunning! But

---

[13] picking out one or two scriptures to fit a narrative

the person in the interpersonal relationship will consistently be berated with comments, underhanded insults, backhanded compliments, and slights that are extremely painful and leave the other person feeling horrible about themselves. It takes an incredibly strong person to survive narcissistic abuse. I believe that small-to medium-sized churches are where you are most likely going to find this behavior. They do not have the same amount of people and may be more cunning so that people don't catch on as quickly. Covert narcissists tend to stay in long-term relationships more than overt because the abuse is so subtle that it may take the victim a quarter-century or more to figure out what is happening to them. If someone has been in a covert situation at a church, they may not even realize how they have been trampled on in subtle ways for a long time, but when they do, they will be crushed by the devastation.

I believe this is why we have so much 'church hurt.' Church hurt is a commonly used term for when people have experienced negative situations in their congregation and typically have to leave that particular group to protect themselves from further pain. Church hurt is a perfect example of fallout from the narcissistic Bride of Christ. There are plenty of social media pages about it. Go look some up. Study the situations. Study the pain. Not to become more cunning to confuse others, but to begin to self-reflect as the Bride and ask Jesus, "Do I reflect Ruach Narcissus instead of You? Is this how people experience me?"

I am going through a refining process myself right now. I am in a situation that I don't always love. I love the people, not particularly the environment. I wanted to leave. I have continued to be a hair stylist while writing my books. I have a lot of items because I owned a large store front for over seven years. It is very hard to slim down from 1750 square feet into a single booth, so I have a lot of stuff that needs space to be used. Some passive-aggressive behaviors started happening in the salon, and I asked to have a meeting about it. I was denied a meeting, but informed of where I had folly. This surely caused me to begin to rebel in my heart against the whole situation. I had an appointment set up to go and visit another salon space, with the hopes to move fairly quickly. But I felt the Lord tell me to stay put. Guess what one of His questions to me was? He said, "Did you ever think you are the one in the wrong?" Uh. Uuuuuuh. (Insert shoulder shrug.) Well dang it! So, I am learning that maybe it is me. Now it is my responsibility to ask myself every time I am faced with one of these situations, "Is it you, Stephanie?" My second question, once I confirm that it is indeed my poor attitude or arrogance, "What can you do to change, to yield to this situation?"

So I have started to yield. I am not taking responsibility in areas that are not mine to take but practicing boundaries, so that I do not get irritated. I posted a visual to remind me that I can be loud when I talk, a glitch most of us speakers can probably appreciate. When you spend a lot of time learning to project your voice, it is hard to stop when you are talking to someone, especially in a loud environment like a salon. I am doing better than I would have ever done in any other time in my life. It may not be spot on every day, but the fact that I am even trying is a huge win. Rebellion sits deep in my heart. Rebellion and arrogance are like best friends. They hang out together a lot. I am having to learn to recognize when I am hanging out with rebellion and arrogance.

Some days I still stumble through my progress. It is not my natural tendency or my favorite thing to yield, but I am learning there is fruit there. This place of yielding, not for the sake of pacifism, but for the sake of God, has some incredible fruit that I have never experienced before. Remember, I told you that my heart is that if God offers it, I want it. Sometimes He is calling me into new gardens, but they require a different kind of entrance.

STANDING FIRM IN THE FAITH

One comment that I have gotten regularly when asking about arrogance is that people are offended that we believe that there is a hell and that people who don't believe in Jesus are going there. I disagree that there is any form of arrogance here, but quite the opposite. I think it may be the way that it is presented that is where the damage is done.

Are we presenting the concept of hell as a celebration of punishment that they are wrong and we are right? Or are we presenting the concept of hell as a place we are all heading without Jesus as well? When we remember that we stumble, trip, and fall short of His glory, we tend to be able to represent the message of the gospel more accurately.

What is your concept of people going to hell? I can't tell you how many times I have heard silly things that have had eternal impacts on others. Things that WILL NOT send you to hell:

- How you dress
- What you look like
- Tattoos
- Piercings
- Drinking, Smoking, Drugs
- Having non-Christians as friends
- Having a rough past
- Being sexually assaulted
- Divorce
- Remarriage
- Mistakes
- Foolish decisions
- Poor money management
- The music you listen to
- Riding motorcycles
- Being unique
- Being artsy
- Crass language

- Struggling with yourself
- Mental struggles
- Suicide
- and many other things...

What WILL send you to hell: not allowing Jesus to pay the debt to Death for your sins. Sin creates a debt to Death. Death is coming for all humanity now that it has access. We can either choose to let Jesus pay the debt for us, or we can pay for it ourselves. The only difference between someone who isn't going to hell and someone who is, is who paid the debt. But what I need you to see is that you *had* debt! The same amount of debt as everyone else. Maybe more! You just chose to allow Jesus to pay it, and His work removed it, not your work. There is literally no way that you could have paid the amount of debt.

Let's think of it like the financial hot mess of our government. We are going into more and more debt every day. We are 30+ trillion dollars in debt at this point, supposedly that we can't possibly pay. We gain more every day at an astonishing rate. What if all the countries we owe money to were just kind enough to say, "OK. It's paid in full. You owe nothing." WOW! We would all have a huge sigh of relief and feel secure and celebrate. We would also want to share the good news! We no longer have debt! Now, let's bring that down more personally. What about your house? That is typically people's largest debt. What if the bank just called you up and told you that you didn't have another mortgage payment and that everything was paid off. You would celebrate. Maybe even take a vacation because now you have extra money!

This excitement is what we need to have spiritually. If you *knew* that you could tell your neighbor how to not have any debt to the bank, you would certainly tell them how. It wouldn't be a, "Look at me, I don't owe the bank, and you do! Na nanny boo boo!" situation. Or if it is, this book is absolutely perfect for you because that is a horrible way to see a great gift. You would want to help your neighbor. We should always approach the situation of hell as one in which we are rescuing people from a debt they cannot pay. There is no place for arrogance in this situation.

One thing I really respect about homeless people is their generosity, especially with other homeless people. I have known quite a few homeless people as friends, even family. When they get anything, they will usually give most of it away. If someone is generous and shares a meal with them, they will often save leftovers or only eat a small amount so they can share it with their friends. It is such a beautiful part of a very hard life. We are the same spiritually. We are all homeless, poor, and wretched, and then Jesus comes along and lavishes us with His richness. It is all his, all we need to do is share it with all of our friends. We don't have to figure out who is and who isn't going to hell. That is so far above our pay grade! We cannot even begin to fathom what that knowledge requires, so why do we need to focus on it?

If you think someone is going to hell, then share with them the greatest appetite-satiating meal or debt-canceling, mortgage-freeing gift you have ever experienced, JESUS! Tell them how He can love them and rescue them. They just need to repent, which is a fancy word to turn around and go a new direction. But for the love, do not tell them that they are going to hell for things that you just may not agree with.

There are absolutely some behaviors that the Bible specifically lists that we need to be aware of.

9 Or do you not know that wrongdoers will not inherit the kingdom of God? Do not be deceived: Neither the sexually immoral nor idolaters nor adulterers nor men who have sex with men 10 nor thieves nor the greedy nor drunkards nor slanderers nor swindlers will inherit the kingdom of God. 11 And that is what some of you were. But you were washed, you were sanctified, you were justified in the name of the Lord Jesus Christ and by the Spirit of our God.

—1 Corinthians 6:9-11

19 The acts of the flesh are obvious: sexual immorality, impurity and debauchery; 20 idolatry and witchcraft; hatred, discord, jealousy, fits of rage, selfish ambition, dissensions, factions 21 and envy; drunkenness, orgies, and the like. I warn you, as I did before, that those who live like this will not inherit the kingdom of God.

—Galatians 5:19-21

I see quite a few things on this list that are addressed in this book as behaviors that the Bride participates in, and this is the primary reason that others may find the idea that we think others are going to hell arrogant. Hypocrites they say. Are they wrong?

THE FALSE PROPHET HIGH HORSE THAT PEOPLE ARE ON

12 Therefore, as God's chosen people, holy and dearly loved, clothe yourselves with compassion, kindness, humility, gentleness and patience.

—Colossians 3:12

Out of nowhere, like I've never seen before, there seems to be a plethora of people who feel the need to stand against and "call out" every teacher, preacher, or pastor that they don't agree with. I can't figure out what gives them that kind of authority, but nonetheless, it has become quite the Great Salem Witch Trials for many pastors and teachers. Now, I understand not agreeing with everything that people say or do, and sometimes specific things need to be called out because they are damaging and hurtful to the message of Jesus Christ. However, if that teacher/pastor doesn't look at your social media feed, how do you think you are giving them the message that they need to receive?

I believe that social media attacks against fellow believers are much like autoimmune disorders inside the human body. When the autoimmune system feels the need to attack an invader in the body but can't identify exactly what the enemy is, it just starts attacking everything. This wreaks havoc in the human body. If you have ever struggled with autoimmune issues or helped a loved one with them, you will be familiar with the havoc I am referring to. It is awful to see what can happen—from rashes, sores, fatigue, skin issues, organ malfunctioning, to paralysis. Autoimmune issues are extremely damaging, and the person suffering from them is usually somewhat miserable.

I share all of this to help you see how attacking other parts of the body of Jesus is hurtful and wreaking havoc within the Bride. We begin the attack with what is a pure heart to maybe call out a teaching that we disagree with, but soon our arrogance gets fueled by just how right we are and just how wrong they are, then we find ourselves hell-bent on tearing that teacher/pastor down. The hope is to destroy their ministry, make them seem irrelevant, and harm their reputation. This type of behavior usually hurts the person doing the attacking more than the person being attacked, but ego will prevent that reality from being acknowledged.

I have a friend that I have known for quite a while. I care about him, but unfortunately, he has decided to take the path of attack. He has become an autoimmune disorder in the Bride. I had to block him on social media because of his relentless disrespectful attacks. I tried to engage in private messages to encourage him to quit. I offered to sit with him and watch some teachings that he thinks are anti-biblical so we could dissect them together. Nothing. No response. He just kept sending me random onesie twosie[14] scriptures that didn't even make sense and were taken somewhat out of context. After a bit of time trying to reason with him, I decided that his ego and arrogance had settled in to the point that there was no use in trying to continue a reasonable conversation with him. I am willing to have an in-person conversation with him. I am willing to have genuine discussions, but I am done trying to penetrate the shell of arrogance that he has chosen to be encapsulated in. We can break open

---

[14] picking out one or two scriptures to fit a narrative

the pod. We aren't bound to it; we choose to allow it to operate.

The podded spirit of narcissism will encapsulate you to the point that there is no ability for penetration to your heart if you allow it. You can break the pod open yourself by pushing back against it. It will be one of the most difficult tasks because you must first even realize that you are practicing the behaviors. Asking yourself some good, honest questions will begin to help, but even better is to get that one friend who is super honest and ask them what they think.

So many people say that they value an honest friend until they actually have one who will call them out on their mess. Typically people will then avoid that person as much as possible because the honest friend is willing to break through the facade. These are pod-breaking friends and they are extremely valuable! Allow them to do some refining work for you. When we are podded up in our arrogance, it will take a pod-breaker to help us see that we are in a mess. Arrogance is such a powerful deceiver that we rarely can see it when we are in active practice. We end up being the greatest liars to ourselves.

*44 You belong to your father, the devil, and you want
to carry out your father's desires. He was a murderer
from the beginning, not holding to the truth, for there
is no truth in him. When he lies, he speaks his native
language, for he is a liar and the father of lies.*

—John 8:44

Remember that Narcissus was encouraged not to get to
know himself. When we lie to ourselves, we refuse to see
ourselves for who we truly are. We refuse to get to know
ourselves. It is uncomfortable to get to know our ugly
sides. We are so much more comfortable with pointing
out what is wrong with everyone else that to see it
within ourselves is very difficult.

*22 Do not merely listen to the word, and so deceive
yourselves. Do what it says. 23 Anyone who listens to
the word but does not do what it says is like someone
who looks at his face in a mirror 24 and, after looking
at himself, goes away and immediately forgets what
he looks like. 25 But whoever looks intently into the
perfect law that gives freedom, and continues in it—
not forgetting what they have heard, but doing it—
they will be blessed in what they do.*

—James 1:22-25

James encourages us not to deceive ourselves by only hearing and not living out what the word says, but then he goes on to use a deeper meaning in the next verse. He says that we are like someone who looks in the mirror, goes away, and then forgets what we look like. Remember in Narcissus' story that when he looked at himself, he realized that he could never love himself because of his curse, and he was warned never to get to know himself. When we look at ourselves in the mirror, which is the Word of God, but do not let it penetrate into us, we are operating out of Ruach Narcissus. Then even worse, we look in the mirror but turn away and completely forget who we are. We forget our imperfect traits that need a savior. We forget our dark sides and encapsulate them in arrogance so they are then impenetrable from those who love us enough to call us out on our mess. The only way to freedom is to look intently at Jesus and allow him to operate through us.

The Bride must remain enamored with the image of Christ, even to the point of losing herself in it, where there is nothing left of her but her love and ability to reflect Jesus. This is the only option to carry forward the call the Bride has to ready herself for her Groom.

THE gOD OF COMFORT

I am using a little "g" in the title of this section on purpose. I refuse to give a capital letter recognition to any god other than God our Father. Comfort, the god of our time that craves our worship is the most sneaky idol in our society because we love it and it feels good to the masses. We crave comfort, we desire comfort, we sacrifice everything for comfort. We will sacrifice our walk with and calling from God to remain comfortable.

What do I mean by comfortable? I mean making sure that we are not having to sacrifice more than we are comfortable with and avoid breaking out of our thinking patterns enough to see what comfort for us means to God. Getting uncomfortable for God may be stopping that drink you take at the end of a long workday to relax, or maybe it is stopping all the sports your kids are involved in so you have time for ministry, or maybe it is selling everything you own and moving to another country. Truly, with God, there are no limits on what He might call you to do according to His purpose in your life. But are you willing to get uncomfortable?

Out of all the people I know, there are only a handful that have truly gotten uncomfortable to follow God. Granted, there may be others and I don't know their intimate story, but the majority of people I know prefer comfort. They are willing to step out so far, but not to the point of their lives looking more like a cross than a couch.

This couch-style-of-living reaches into nearly every aspect of our lives when we are operating out of Ruach Narcissus. The spirit lures us into a deep sleep with the god of comforts and when we threaten to awaken, it lulls us back into our dulled senses with more pleasure. The Bride moves around often in a sedated state, so when our Groom is calling the voice is muffled and unclear. Can't you hear this conversation?

Jesus says, "My Bride, you are so beautiful. Come walk with me and tell others how much I love them so they can join us at our marriage feast."

The Bride, with her eyes barely open, lounging backward on a sofa, in the same clothes she's been wearing for days, her messy top knot in her hair, slurs in answer, "But I am so comfortable here. I don't want to move right now. Can't we do this later?"

Jesus implores, "My Darling, the time is now. Our wedding is coming soon and the table will be empty if you don't get out today and meet the family."

The Bride, unmoved from her same position, eyes now rolling back in her head as she has rested it again against the sofa, falling back into her state of slumber, replies dully, "I just don't think that you pushing me is what I want to do. I think that I would rather just wait here and rest longer, so I can be ready for the feast myself."

Jesus roars, as He pulls the Bride to her feet and says, "Wake up, sleeper! You are wasting time. We have a mission before our feast so get up on your feet and share the good news of our wedding feast that all may join us!"

This conversation is fictional, but reflective of what this book is sharing about Ruach Narcissus creating an indifferent heart toward our Groom and the letters from **Revelation** that we visit in **chapter 12**.

God is trustworthy. We must believe that to the core of our being. It is what will propel us up off of the couch and say, "Whatever You want for me, God, is all I want. I will lose it all to gain my relationship with You." And honestly, He could call you to do that very thing, like He did with the rich young ruler. If we want to be married to our Groom, acquire His inheritance, and take His name, we must be willing to do whatever that looks like.

I have done bridal hair for a very long time. From start to finish, the bride does not hesitate to do a myriad of uncomfortable things for her wedding day. I have seen brides practically starve themselves to lose weight, go into serious debt to buy goodies, have nearly complete meltdowns wanting every detail to be perfect, willingly wear extremely uncomfortable clothing items to tuck in, hoist, or hide imperfections their dress might otherwise show. Boy! I have seen so much willingness to become uncomfortable and do whatever it takes to be "perfect" on the wedding day. Rarely will most brides wait for the day of their wedding to get their hair done. They want to have at least one trial run, if not multiple ones, so that when the day arrives, they are prepared. These bridal hair appointments can be extremely costly for the amount of time they take, but I haven't had a bride yet that wasn't willing to pay for whatever needed to be done. The wedding, in her eyes, was always the razor-sharp focus and goal, and like a trained athlete, she intends to be prepared. I always gently remind these brides that the goal is marriage and no matter what happens on the day of the wedding, if they are married at the end of it, the goal is accomplished and all is wonderful . . . and oh yes, don't forget to eat! Many of these brides are prepping for years, though some are brave to fit it all in within a few months.

Here's the kicker, never once have I had one tell me their groom had to force them to get uncomfortable. Their willingness comes from the eager anticipation of one of the most important days of their lives, and they desire to make it as wonderful as they can. They want their groom to be fawning when he takes his first gander at his soon-to-be wife. His pleasure and pride in her is her primary goal of the wedding day. I have never seen a single bride in all my years of working with them who was indifferent to her groom. Not one. The hope that the groom was in awe of her, her beauty, and her preparation of the day is always a primary conversation with a bride.

We should be this way with Jesus. Diligent, willing to sacrifice, passionate, and indomitably pursuing whatever God has called us to do as the Bride, no matter the amount of cost or discomfort that it may cause us. When we break down our arrogance and cling to Him like our life depends on it, we will live like we have never lived before. We will change the world for Him, so He can change our world for us.

THE ANTIDOTE FOR ARROGANT BEHAVIORS

The only antidote to arrogance is becoming authentic, genuine, and fully submitting your will to that of our Father's will. We must decrease so that He can increase.

29 The bride belongs to the bridegroom. The friend who attends the bridegroom waits and listens for him, and is full of joy when he hears the bridegroom's voice. That joy is mine, and it is now complete. 30 He must become greater; I must become less."

—John 3:29-30

John the Baptist is a great example for us to follow. He knew that he was attending the Bridegroom of Jesus. He came to encourage the Bride in anticipation of her Groom. He wasn't trying to steal the show! He wasn't trying to talk the Bride into falling in love with him or hoping to distract her in any way. John was so loyal to his friend, and kept focus on what was important, which was not himself.

This is exactly how we will have to operate to break arrogance from deceiving us. I was talking to a friend today about work. He said that they were behind and when they were trying to encourage one of the coworkers to move a bit faster, his answer was, "I have one speed, and I am going it." There was no attempt to go faster or ask for help if he wasn't sure how to do something well. His arrogance was the first response. "I am doing all I am willing to do. I will not yield. I will not bend. This is me. This is who I am. Love it or leave it." Of course he didn't use that many words, but the premise is the same. This is often our attitude toward any type of correction. We feel the need to increase for self-protection, but truly we are harming ourselves and others.

We cannot continue to be consumers of Jesus. His example was to pour himself out, and we must do the same. We must be willing to be the fool or be taken advantage of. We must be willing to submit our will, sacrifice ourselves, and become the least version of us. I struggle with this. I have, by no means, accomplished this. However, I am farther along today than I was even a year ago. I am aware of my response to puff up and stand in arrogance first. Now that I recognize it, I am able to take a minute to pause, rethink, reassess, and try again. Sometimes, trying again comes with an apology.

38 "You have heard that it was said, 'Eye for eye, and tooth for tooth.' 39 But I tell you, do not resist an evil person. If anyone slaps you on the right cheek, turn them the other cheek also. 40 And if anyone wants to sue you and take your shirt, hand over your coat as well. 41 If anyone forces you to go one mile, go with them two miles. 42 Give to the one who asks you, and do not turn away from the one who wants to borrow from you.

—Matthew 5:38-42

There have been more times than not in my life that I wasn't willing to give my coat or go the extra mile. As a matter of fact, I would certainly dig my heels in not to do those things. I can't possibly count how many times throughout my life that my arrogance was way more obvious than humility. I wasn't considering Jesus. I wasn't paying any attention at all. I didn't even care. I was completely indifferent to Jesus.

Have you ever found yourself looking around you to the people that are close to you, and think, "They really don't know me at all?" If so, you have allowed the pod to fully encapsulate you. You must do the hard work of breaking it open. It is the only way to become authentic and genuine and remove the wrinkles and blemishes that have been obvious in your bridal gown.

Our bridal clothing is all we have to offer someone else. We remove our garments, place it on others to protect them, and show them that they can have the garment through the work of the cross. We must be able to stand firm in our faith, but have enough love for others that they understand the reason we believe in hell is not because we want to punish them, but because Death wants what it sees as being owed. Death and Hades operate together, much like God and heaven. So when we talk about hell, we can't be self-righteous in any way, we must be so very humble. Let's teach others how to cancel their debt! Show them that Jesus has already paid everything they will ever owe, if they will just accept it.

As a spiritual Bride with Jesus, we should be like all human brides. Diligent, willing to sacrifice, passionate, and indomitably pursuing whatever God has called us to do as the Bride, no matter the amount of cost or discomfort that it may cause us. When we break down our arrogance and cling to Him like our life depends on it, we will live like we have never lived before. We will change the world for Him, so He can change our world for us.

I can promise, only because the Bible does, that if we are willing to decrease, so that Jesus can increase, we will reap the greatest rewards ever given. It may not feel like it on this side of heaven, but our eternal spot is secured and it will be so worth it. We will be able to sit with our Lord and Savior and talk about how much we loved who

He loved and what a glorious, radiant, stunningly gorgeous Bride we will be!

REFLECTION QUESTIONS

1. Do you see arrogance in your behaviors?

2. Have you been a consumer of Jesus more than a contributor to building His kingdom?

3. Do you understand that you have/had debt to Death?

4. Have you let Jesus pay that debt?

5. If so, how do you share that good news with others?

6. Do you seek comfort over your God-given calling?

7. How can you begin to seek God first above anything else? List 3 practical behaviors that will help you.

8. Can you be a beacon for others who may think the Church is arrogant by being kind, loving, and showing them Jesus?

CHAPTER 12

THE CHURCHES OF REVELATION

I believe the seven letters to the seven churches in Revelation will help us understand what is happening today in the modern Ekklesia.

CHURCH IN EPHESUS

¹ *"To the angel of the church in Ephesus write:*

These are the words of him who holds the seven stars in his right hand and walks among the seven golden lampstands. ² I know your deeds, your hard work and your perseverance. I know that you cannot tolerate wicked people, that you have tested those who claim to be apostles but are not, and have found them false. ³ You have persevered and have endured hardships for my name, and have not grown weary.

⁴ Yet I hold this against you: You have forsaken the love you had at first. ⁵ Consider how far you have fallen! Repent and do the things you did at first. If you do not repent, I will come to you and remove your lampstand from its place. 6 But you have this in your favor: You hate the practices of the Nicolaitans, which I also hate.

7 Whoever has ears, let them hear what the Spirit says to the churches. To the one who is victorious, I will give the right to eat from the tree of life, which is in the paradise of God.

—Revelation 2:1-7

This letter is written to the Ephesians in Ephesus. They were doing so many amazing things. Jesus says that He recognizes their hard work and perseverance. The church isn't tolerating evil. These are great things and exactly what we should be doing. But they forgot to pursue His love. **First Corinthians 13** tells us that without love, there is absolutely nothing. When we forget to love Jesus first, have a relationship with Him and let everything else flow from that love, we need to repent. We need to turn back to that love for our Groom. Pursue Him with everything in us. This is what will lead us to eat from the tree of life.

The church that looks like the church of Ephesus might be very rules based and push works. They will have a sense of expected purity, but without love, the experience would feel very judgmental. It would be very hard to find Jesus here above rules and regulations.

CHURCH IN SMYRNA

8 "To the angel of the church in Smyrna write:

These are the words of him who is the First and the Last, who died and came to life again. 9 I know your afflictions and your poverty—yet you are rich! I know about the slander of those who say they are Jews and are not, but are a synagogue of Satan. 10 Do not be afraid of what you are about to suffer. I tell you, the devil will put some of you in prison to test you, and you will suffer persecution for ten days. Be faithful, even to the point of death, and I will give you life as your victor's crown.

11 Whoever has ears, let them hear what the Spirit says to the churches. The one who is victorious will not be hurt at all by the second death.

—Revelation 2:8-11

Easter Sunday of 2024, preferably called Resurrection Day, since Easter is actually completely pagan, is the day I got to write about this particular letter. I can't think of a better letter to approach on this day. What a beautiful promise the Lord is giving in this letter. Jesus so beautifully saved and rescued us from the second death with His complete work of the cross. But the world is against this message, and it will cost us. We may face things we never expected, like poverty, hard circumstances, and various afflictions. How can this be considered rich? That is almost absurd in a culture that idolizes wealth, happiness, and comfort, none of which are listed here. This church is rich because it has weighed the cost of following Jesus and chose to stay steadfast. Each member of this church will receive life as a victor's crown!

Life is Jesus' specialty. It is what He came to give us. He never could have accessed Death because He is Life. Sin creates debt to Death. Death always comes to collect its debt. Jesus had no debt to Death, so He took all of our sin, past, present, and future on Himself, so that Death would come for Him. And boy did it! Darkness hovered for three hours! The battle of all eternity ensued for the next three days. All of heaven, in the form of Jesus Christ, went to defeat Death and Hades. It took God three days, but He came back as the victor, holding the keys. He absolutely has the authority to give anyone Life as a victor's crown, just like He wore when He was resurrected.

The devil hates us because we are made in God's image. He will use anyone and anything he can to make us feel like we are defeated. The church at Smyrna realizes that there is no defeat as long as they stand in the promise of who Jesus is. He is the First and the Last, who died and came to life again. The very celebration of this glorious day, Easter Sunday/Resurrection Day. This church has a promise never to experience any part of the second death, which is when Hades will come to collect its people for Death. This is what we talked about in the last section about hell. The Church in Smyrna may suffer from physical death, but that is the only form of Death they will ever encounter. Such a beautiful gift and promise.

CHURCH IN PERGAMUM

12 *"To the angel of the church in Pergamum write:*

These are the words of him who has the sharp, double-edged sword. 13 *I know where you live— where Satan has his throne. Yet you remain true to my name. You did not renounce your faith in me, not even in the days of Antipas, my faithful witness, who was put to death in your city—where Satan lives.*

14 *Nevertheless, I have a few things against you: There are some among you who hold to the teaching of Balaam, who taught Balak to entice the Israelites to sin so that they ate food sacrificed to idols and committed sexual immorality.* 15 *Likewise, you also have those who hold to the teaching of the Nicolaitans.* 16 *Repent therefore! Otherwise, I will*

soon come to you and will fight against them with the sword of my mouth.

17 Whoever has ears, let them hear what the Spirit says to the churches. To the one who is victorious, I will give some of the hidden manna. I will also give that person a white stone with a new name written on it, known only to the one who receives it.

—Revelation 2:12-17

Thanks to *Strong's Concordance*,[1] this letter gets spicy quickly! I love using *Strong's Concordance* to help understand the original language. So let's dissect this letter. The sharp, double-edged sword is a representation of the Word of God. Jesus is talking about God's Word in this passage. The Word of God is what we as Christians use to defeat Satan and his schemes. That is why Jesus is pointing out that He recognizes we are living where Satan has his throne. If we didn't have the Word, we would struggle to battle without a sharpened sword.

So my mind was blown when I looked up Antipas. The way this sentence is structured, it sounds like a man. He is a man, and if you just want to look at this passage for face value, it may retain its blandness without moving you to your core. If you will go deeper into living water with me and allow me to baptize you into the depths of a more complex meaning, I want to reveal how powerful this passage about words is.

But alas, my friends, it is a preposition! A part of speech!! A preposition is a word that shows direction, location, or time of the noun or noun phrase to follow. I know you may be struggling with this English grammar lesson, but it is important to understand the breakdown of this word. This word "Antipas" would better be defined as "for the Father's cause." The prefix "anti" (antee) is a primary particle (does not change with inflection) and preposition that has various meanings, and the suffix "pas" means father.

"My faithful witness," also translated as "martyr" in some translations, is talking about how the Word is being sacrificed. It is being murdered in our cities. It is being killed off for a "better version" that is accepted where Satan lives. This is also a reflection of the cross. The Word of God (Jesus) was martyred in a city where Satan lives (which would represent Pharisees and all those who wanted Him crucified). So it would read: You did not renounce your faith in me, not even in the days of the Father's cause, where I was martyred and put to death in the city where Satan lives.

But the things Jesus has against this ekklesia (ek-klay-see-ah) is all about the Word! Holding fast to the teaching of Balaam, who was a Mesopotamian false teacher and represents false teachings, even for the modern age. Jesus is specifically talking about following false teaching and how destructive it is. We must be quick to point out false teaching, but we cannot be arrogant in our pursuit to do so. If we become arrogant and think that because someone says something we don't like or disagree with it is equivalent to false teaching, we begin to hurt ourselves and our own testimony.

I had an experience recently with a guy I have known for a long time. He has a vendetta toward some teachers. The problem is he isn't even solving anything, just spouting hateful rhetoric. Instead of making an impact, he has become another recipient of the "block" option on social media. He might have had some valid points, but you couldn't hear them through the noise. I even offered to sit down with him and dissect together some teachings that he was claiming were false. I was truly interested in hearing his perspective. Unfortunately, he didn't have perspective, he only had accusations.

Following Jesus' prompt to call out false teaching is so important, but if we do it without love, humility, or authenticity, we become a clanging cymbal and no one is listening. It is a duty, a responsibility, to call false teaching what it is, but we need people to listen when we say it. The best way to do that is when we are not looking like a bunch of narcissistic hypocrites.

False teaching always creates double the sons of hell (**Matthew 23:15**). This even goes for a Christian who is living in narcissistic tendencies. If you are raising other people to be a narcissistic Bride representative, they will be twice as bad as you are with all the characteristics listed in this book. We, the Bride, are currently in great danger of facing this rebuke from Jesus. We have allowed a spirit to come in and corrupt our stance on the Word of God. It is still a double-edged sword, sharp enough to separate bone and marrow.

Balak follows the false teaching; this is where you see the "double the sons of hell" principle begin to take shape. Balak, a Moabite, then begins to entice the Israelites (insert Bride, children of God, you, here) to sin. Convincing them that it is no big deal to sin and that doing what they want to do is up to them. Entice is a simplistic translation of what this should say. Scandal is the definition of the root word used here, *skandalon* (skan-dal-on). The translation should read: to throw scandals at the Israelites by having them eat food sacrificed to idols and practice sexual immorality. Scandals are exactly what we are finding ourselves in over and over. What a mess!!

Sexual immorality always follows false teaching that goes against God. Why? Because we were created and designed for sex. It is God-designed, God-established, and outside of that design, utterly destructive to us. So when we are succumbing to false teaching that leads us into sexual immorality and participating in scandals, we are in direct opposition to the cause of the Father.

Next we have the teachings of the Nicolaitans. You could translate this to mean: teaching to conquer the people in heresy. Let's meet the Nicolaitians. Nicolas from

Antioch was chosen to help establish the Church (**Acts 6:5**). He was a large influence in the early establishment of the Church. Unfortunately, his influence was determined to be evil and heretical. He encouraged the new followers not to worry about eating food sacrificed to idols, practicing sexual immorality, or including pagan practices in their lives. Does this sound familiar? These went against specific instructions in the letter he was given in **Acts 15:23-29**.

Do you know how many of our "Christian" holidays are pagan celebrations and rituals? Nearly every single one! Rabbits, colored eggs, decorated trees, stockings and so many others are representations that Jesus would have never participated in. I had conviction about this so many years ago and have struggled to fight the cultural tidal wave as a mom of five. My late husband and I had decided we were no longer going to celebrate any of these holidays, but focus on what Jesus celebrated. I am still working on incorporating that, but I am much farther along than I used to be. Can you do it? Can you stop the vortex of the Nicolaitian way and stay true to the Father's cause? Let's celebrate His victories! We can allow our pride and arrogance to dig our heels in, discredit it, and make it out like it isn't a big deal, but the next bit will tell us that we are lying to ourselves to think this way.

Jesus says he is coming with the sword of His mouth, which is the Word of God. Jesus is the Word, and He is razor sharp. None of the excuses you are telling yourself now will matter when it is facing that sword. Any amount of arrogance that you would like to have in your stance will literally be shredded like the finest paper shredder you have ever seen. Not a single letter will be able to stand, so heed Jesus' rebuke and begin today. Take one step in a new direction. Repent and let the Lord teach you His ways!

17 Whoever has ears, let them hear what the Spirit says to the churches. To the one who is victorious, I will give some of the hidden manna. I will also give that person a white stone with a new name written on it, known only to the one who receives it.

—Revelation 2:17

Oh the promise Jesus makes to those who have ears to hear this letter! He promises hidden manna, which literally means a secret manna. This is the provision God gave the Israelites in their deliverance journey from Egypt. This is a divine provision that will never be explainable.

He will "give," meaning deliver, a white stone. Let's talk about this white stone; again the translation doesn't seem spectacular, but when you get to the root words, they will excite you. The word "white" is also "light" and "stone" means "a pebble worn smooth by handling, to be used as a ballot or verdict acquittal, or ticket, that will be sung as a psalm."

So I am going to retranslate this to help you understand what is being said: Whoever has ears, let him hear what the Spirit says to the churches. To the one who is *victorious and conquer*s, I will give them *secret* manna (*provision*). I will also *give that person a light shining pebble that I have rubbed smooth to use as a verdict acquittal that will be sung as a psalm* that has been given a *new surname* that no *man, woman, or thing* will know it, except for the one who receives it.

I did not embellish this. It is all in the *Strong's Concordance* and by all means, take the time to look it up. But I believe my translation will help you to understand what the translation we are reading is trying to say. Sometimes reading the Bible on a surface level, OK, pretty much all the time, will not help you to understand complex or wordy passages. It is best to get to the root of the words. Jesus is all about words! *Jesus is The Word.*

I am going to rewrite this scripture with the more in-depth understanding that I share in this section so that you can see how beautiful it would be written in language that we can understand.

12 These are the words of Jesus who is the Word of God.

13 I know where you live—where Satan has his throne. Yet you remain true to my name. You did not renounce your faith in me, not even in the days of the Father's cause, where I was martyred and put to death in the city where Satan lives.

14 Nevertheless, I have a few things against you: There are some among you who are creating scandals by teaching my children to sin so that they ate food sacrificed to idols and committed sexual immorality. 15 Likewise, you also have those who hold to the teaching of the pagans and follow their ways, going against the teachings I gave. 16 Repent therefore! Otherwise, I will soon come to you and will fight against them with the sword of my mouth (Word of God).

17 Whoever has ears, let them hear what the Spirit says to the churches. To the one who is victorious, I will give some of the hidden manna (provision). I will also give that person a light shining pebble that I have rubbed smooth to use as a verdict acquittal that will be sung as a psalm that has been given a new surname that no man, woman, or thing will know it, except for the one who receives it.

*—***Revelation 2:12-17** *(my edited version using the Strong's definitions)*

Church in Thyatira

18 "To the angel of the church in Thyatira write:

These are the words of the Son of God, whose eyes are like blazing fire and whose feet are like burnished bronze. 19 I know your deeds, your love and faith, your service and perseverance, and that you are now doing more than you did at first. 20 Nevertheless, I have this against you: You tolerate that woman Jezebel, who calls herself a prophet. By her teaching she misleads my servants into sexual immorality and the eating of food sacrificed to idols. 21 I have given her time to repent of her immorality, but she is unwilling. 22 So I will cast her on a bed of suffering, and I will make those who commit adultery with her suffer intensely, unless they repent of her ways. 23 I will strike her children dead. Then all the churches will know that I am he who searches hearts and minds, and I will repay each of you according to your deeds.

24 Now I say to the rest of you in Thyatira, to you who do not hold to her teaching and have not learned Satan's so-called deep secrets, 'I will not impose any other burden on you, 25 except to hold on to what you have until I come.' 26 To the one who is victorious and does my will to the end, I will give authority over the nations—27 that one 'will rule them with an iron scepter and will dash them to pieces like pottery'— just as I have received authority from my Father. 28 I

will also give that one the morning star. ²⁹ Whoever has ears, let them hear what the Spirit says to the churches.

—Revelation 2:18-29

Oh Jezebel. What a terrible legacy to have! Her story is in **1st and 2nd Kings**. She was married to King Ahab, who ruled Israel. She encouraged Ahab to turn away from God and worship Baal, a god of nature. She put to death many of the prophets of God and threatened to kill Elijah and Elisha, great prophets of the Most-High God. She dined and spent her time with the many prophets of Baal. This brought all sorts of debauchery and evil into Israel, which was set apart for God's people. It was an utter slap in the face for her to not only support the worship of Baal, but to bring that worship into the rulership of Israel.

God is very particular about what is acceptable in His presence. We cannot worship Him and take residence with Jezebel's ways. The Bride of Christ must rebuke and resist the temptation of Jezebel. She is very cunning and very seductive. It is easy to fall into her ways without much reserve or hesitation. Sensual desires are a part of our makeup, but they are meant to be managed with boundaries and limits.

Just recently there was a men's conference called Stronger Men. For some entertainment, they had a male performer dancing around a pole, shirtless, and he was swallowing a sword as another part of his act. Only one single pastor stood against it. Only one of the men in the whole audience said something. Guess what? He was asked to leave. His rebuke was so gentle, so heartfelt, and so true. Yet, instead of taking the rebuke, realizing the truth in his words, the lead organizing pastor asked him to leave.

Oh how Jezebel has done her powerful and fantastic work of luring us to sleep by drawing our sensual senses to her gods. We can watch the world burn around us, souls walking right into the gates of hell like zombies, and be completely unmoved because we have forgotten that we are called to diligently fight evil. We cannot allow ourselves to become gorged on her delicacies. We are suffering as a body, just like this passage promises, because we have committed adultery with her. As long as we remain in her adulterous bed, we will continue to have more and more issues with ourselves, our children, and all that come in contact with this toxic behavior of the Bride.

I was in Las Vegas on a salon business trip. My staff and I had a blast. As I was sitting on the balcony of the Bellagio, overlooking the dancing water fountain, I heard the Lord say to me, "Beware of the king's delicacies." Immediately I knew that I needed to be on alert. I could have easily been sucked into the fun and party of it all and lose myself. Forget who I am. Who I am called to be. My senses were overwhelmed by evil and could have lured me to indulge in what felt good. Sin isn't always overt. Sometimes it looks like eating a good meal that was sacrificed to another god. You may be completely unaware of the tempering of your fire at first, but soon you will be in place wondering how you got there. In a place like Las Vegas, you can see how easily accessible the temptation of sexual sin is. Mostly naked women everywhere, selling themselves for a peek at their supposed beauty. Don't you think God knew exactly what He was doing when He created the female form? He knew that the female body was irresistibly beautiful. It is meant to be fully enjoyed in the context of safety and marriage. The female, a daughter of the Most-High God, is not to be cheapened by being bought with money and power, corrupted by being stared at by a man who doesn't invest in her heart, or tainted by an unquenchable desire for her to satisfy others who wish to consume her.

Pornography, casual sex, soft porn books and movies, and a myriad of other sexually pleasing experiences, outside of the marriage bed, is plaguing the Bride of Christ. We look more like the harlot in Hosea, the metaphor for Israel at the time, than an unblemished, pure bride. Pornography and its hold on the Ekklesia is a perfect example of how Jezebel has done her dirty work. Pastors are succumbing to the temptation of easy, cheap, and simple sex thrills. They are doing it by hiding their behaviors and destroying their marriages and families. Instead of making the dramatic steps to prevent it like a warrior should, their arrogance and pride protects the sin.

When someone is in a war, they don't laze around when they know the enemy is imminent. They are on high alert ready to fight and defend themselves and others. The description of Jesus in this passage "whose eyes are burning fire and feet of burnished bronze," sounds like someone you don't want to mess with. As image bearers, this is exactly what we should look like when we are presented with the Jezebel spirit operating around us. Sticking with the warrior heart, Jesus says that those in the church who stick to their righteous ways will "rule with them with an iron scepter and dash them like pottery."

We are very disconnected from the concept of an iron scepter in America. We have never had monarchy rule for over 200 years, so we don't understand the fear, respect, and awe that would come with the iron scepter. The promise here to rule with sovereignty those who aren't lured in by Jezebel's temptation is such an incredible honor. To "dash them like pottery" means to completely crush them back to earthen clay. Jesus is giving the church of Thyatira quite a powerful position when they have conquered themselves and defeated the Jezebel spirit.

CHURCH IN SARDIS

1 "To the angel of the church in Sardis write:

These are the words of him who holds the seven spirits of God and the seven stars. I know your deeds; you have a reputation of being alive, but you are dead. 2 Wake up! Strengthen what remains and is about to die, for I have found your deeds unfinished in the sight of my God. 3 Remember, therefore, what you have received and heard; hold it fast, and repent. But if you do not wake up, I will come like a thief, and you will not know at what time I will come to you.

4 Yet you have a few people in Sardis who have not soiled their clothes. They will walk with me, dressed in white, for they are worthy. 5 The one who is victorious will, like them, be dressed in white. I will never blot out the name of that person from the book of life, but will acknowledge that name before my Father and his angels. 6 Whoever has ears, let them hear what the Spirit says to the churches.

—Revelation 3:1-6

A reputation. I am not sure that is necessarily a flattering word. We often are very concerned about our reputation, but usually it is merely an image, gathered by inconclusive evidence. You may have a reputation of being an awesome person, yet the people closest to you think you are a monster. You could have a reputation of being a floozy (a person who has frivolous sexual immorality), yet you don't act that way at all. Reputations are not always true. In this letter, we see that being the case. It says, "You have a reputation of being alive, but you are dead."

What might this look like in a modern-day church? What does a dead church look like? Seeing that Jesus came and sacrificed His life, so that we can live, being dead is a huge slap in the face. Spiritually dead are truly the anti-Christ of the church body. Jesus blotting out the names makes sense, though that opens an entirely new can of worms that I am not digging into here. Let's just say this: Do not find yourself in the position to be dead, and you have nothing to worry about. Repent. Turn from the ways you have previously walked, and allow Him to dress you in white. A dead church means one where there is no interaction with Holy Spirit. They may gather under a guise of godliness, but Holy Spirit is not there. They may talk a good talk, say the right things, but you will not experience the Spirit of God move in any way.

Sardis was known for its wealth and there was a lot of affluence and influence for the surrounding areas. This church would look busy and active, but not be changing lives or summoning hearts to submit to Jesus. I believe that you would find it void of Holy Spirit. A church that denies that Holy Spirit is a required part of being active with the Trinity is a dangerous church indeed. There are many churches that are afraid of the supernatural workings of Holy Spirit. We can't truly comprehend the importance of living through this incredible power until we experience it. But for that to happen, we must lay down our pride and ego. A church that is dead will be thick with pride and ego; even though they are attractive to the world, they will not be powerful in the genuine way that God has set it to operate.

We may have affluence and influence, but what is the value of any of that if relationship with Jesus is not the prize?

CHURCH IN PHILADELPHIA

7 *"To the angel of the church in Philadelphia write:*

These are the words of him who is holy and true, who holds the key of David. What he opens no one can shut, and what he shuts no one can open. 8 I know your deeds. See, I have placed before you an open door that no one can shut. I know that you have little strength, yet you have kept my word and have not denied my name. 9 I will make those who are of the synagogue of Satan, who claim to be Jews though they are not, but are liars—I will make them come and fall down at your feet and acknowledge that I have loved you. 10 Since you have kept my command to endure patiently, I will also keep you from the hour of trial that is going to come on the whole world to test the inhabitants of the earth.

¹¹ I am coming soon. Hold on to what you have, so that no one will take your crown. ¹² The one who is victorious I will make a pillar in the temple of my God. Never again will they leave it. I will write on them the name of my God and the name of the city of my God, the new Jerusalem, which is coming down out of heaven from my God; and I will also write on them my new name. ¹³ Whoever has ears, let them hear what the Spirit says to the churches.

—Revelation 3:7-13

This letter has so much compassion and love throughout it. Philadelphia means "brotherly love." This church is going to be operating in love in the name of Jesus. The Lord will be operating closely with this church with consistent guidance of opened and closed doors. Even when they feel beat down, broken, and out of energy, they have stayed faithful and never denied Christ and His life-giving work.

What an incredible promise this church has! All who have come against this church will be falling at their feet and have to acknowledge how loved they are. The ones who looked down on them will be at their feet. Submission is a requirement from God. We can either choose it now or He will force it later, but it is coming. This church will experience the power of having submitted here on Earth. He goes on to encourage them to hold on to what they have so that no one can take their crown. The promise to be kept from the hour of trial is a safety net. We know based on the rest of Revelation that this trial will be seriously hardcore. Like a father scooping us his child in danger, God will be scooping up this church to prevent it from experiencing suffering because it already submitted. They will become a pillar in the temple. What an incredible honor!

It doesn't end there! This church is going to get honor upon honor because of their brotherly love. They tapped into the beauty of love and submission, knowing their reward is in heaven and, boy, is Jesus showing how glorious that reward is! They will *never leave* the temple of God. He will write the name of God, the name of the city, and His own new name on them. They will be fully marked for God and be pillars for Him. Oh that we may all desire to pursue this incredible church!

I don't think that people are specifically placed in any of these churches, but like our human experience, we choose which one we want to be a part of. We can always choose to look at their descriptions, promises, and warnings that come with them and choose which we would like to be. Remember, this is not about a physical location, these are spiritual churches. These churches are in our heart, and we operate out of the spirit elements attached to them. May you break through Ruach Narcissus and have ears to hear so that repentance is your story. Through submission God can lift us.

Church in Laodicea

14 *"To the angel of the church in Laodicea write:*

These are the words of the Amen, the faithful and true witness, the ruler of God's creation. 15 *I know your deeds, that you are neither cold nor hot. I wish you were either one or the other!* 16 *So, because you are lukewarm—neither hot nor cold—I am about to spit you out of my mouth.* 17 *You say, 'I am rich; I have acquired wealth and do not need a thing.' But you do not realize that you are wretched, pitiful, poor, blind and naked.* 18 *I counsel you to buy from me gold refined in the fire, so you can become rich; and white clothes to wear, so you can cover your shameful nakedness; and salve to put on your eyes, so you can see.*

19 *Those whom I love I rebuke and discipline. So be earnest and repent.* 20 *Here I am! I stand at the door and knock. If anyone hears my voice and opens the door, I will come in and eat with that person, and they with me.*

²¹ To the one who is victorious, I will give the right to sit with me on my throne, just as I was victorious and sat down with my Father on his throne. ²² Whoever has ears, let them hear what the Spirit says to the churches."

—Revelation 3:14-22

Man oh man, the title of this letter could easily be "Church in America." Amen means approval, and it is a declaration. This is the declaration of the faithful and true witness of Jesus Christ, the very Word of creation. Creation wasn't kind of created. There was no semi-tree made or semi-human. We were made in complete form and in wholeness. Sin, of course, corrupted this. This is when the concept of lukewarm entered into existence. This isn't just the temperature of food. This is a complete emotional state of being. An utter indifference to a call of our Savior. If this *ekklesia* was hot, it would be on fire with passion. If the church was cold, it would be fully against God. Either of those, hot or cold, are more palatable than lukewarm indifference. Both hot and cold are definitive states of being and can be dealt with accordingly, but indifference is the opposite of love, and must be expelled.

If you have ever been in a relationship with a narcissist, the concept of lukewarm will be quite familiar to you. They are the epitome of indifference. It is sickening and leaves such a distaste in your mouth that you want to spit it all out. Removing every single ounce of existence from memory and casting away every bit of thought when you are able to get away from their indifferent and obscenely gross lack of relational behaviors is all you can think about once you are free. Relationships with narcissists are so empty that when you try to share anything real, they leave you with a feeling of emptiness. They don't celebrate with you; as a matter of fact, they will make anything about anyone else all about themselves. They don't care about what you say, think, or feel.

In my case, I would stare at his back. It didn't matter what the conversation was about, he would turn his back to me or walk right out of the room. No acknowledgement whatsoever about what I was talking about or expressing. This is what Jesus is describing here. He is expressing a declaration about what He called the Ekklesia to do, go, and make disciples. To spit this church out of His mouth could be visually seen as almost a volatile vomit, a reaction to utter disgust, like the harshest food poisoning vomit you can imagine. Expelling every single bit of its existence away from Himself.

Because of the illusion of wealth, the heart of this church thinks that they don't need anything. They may not "need" anything physically, but Jesus cares little about our physical comforts; but He cares a lot about our heart posture. He describes this ekklesia as:

wretched, pitiful, poor, blind, and naked. These are extremely intense adjectives.

Wretched

24 What a wretched man I am! Who will rescue me from this body that is subject to death? 25 Thanks be to God, who delivers me through Jesus Christ our Lord! So then, I myself in my mind am a slave to God's law, but in my sinful nature a slave to the law of sin.

—Romans 7:24-25

Until we realize our wretchedness, and how much it desires sin, which is debt to Death, we will continue to live as slaves to sin. This is the antithesis of Jesus and why he uses this term toward this church. They are wealthy and refuse to acknowledge their own wretchedness. They think they are clean because they have the ability to be put together in the natural world, but their hearts are arrogant and full of sin.

Pitiful

¹⁹ If only for this life we have hope in Christ, we are of all people most to be pitied.

—1 Corinthians 15:19

When we are pitiful, we refuse to see the larger picture of what Jesus has done for us. This church isn't looking into eternity, they are content and taken care of. They have forgotten they are going to face a holy God. If anyone thinks that Jesus is merely for this life, that we can pretend that what comes after doesn't matter, we are certainly pitiful. It is easy to think you are a god in your world when you have wealth and the means to manipulate things in your favor. But one day, all that will burn, and you will be standing there, with nothing to show, because all you have attained is pitiful waste.

Poor

⁹ For you know the grace of our Lord Jesus Christ, that though he was rich, yet for your sake he became poor, so that you through his poverty might become rich.

—2 Corinthians 8:9

Jesus' example to us is that He didn't hang on to the riches of heaven, but sacrificed it all to be here with us. Ironically, this church is poor though they think they are rich. They are not willing to sacrifice their money, and become financially poor, so they can be spiritually rich. Again, Jesus cares very little about our physical wealth that creates a poor heart. He is all about sacrificing our wealth so we become rich in the area that matters most, our spiritual heart. This body of believers is so poor they can't possibly buy anything worth having, like the gold refined in fire.

In refineries, they melt down metals in crucibles and only the purest part makes it to the pour. All the metal, including any impurities, is put into a smelter. The smelter is heated until super hot, and then the metal begins to melt and the impurities rise to the surface. The "slag" or waste material is scraped off the top and discarded. Gold refined in fire will be the purest form. Jesus is looking for the purest hearts that hold to his declarative call to "go make disciples." Jesus is the refining fire and smelter; we will not be able to bring our impurities into our relationship with Him. He will melt us down, clean off the slag, and only accept what remains. Nothing in the physical world will be of any account to Him.

BLIND

17b I am sending you to them 18 to open their eyes and turn them from darkness to light, and from the power of Satan to God, so that they may receive forgiveness of sins and a place among those who are sanctified by faith in me.'

—Act 26:17b-18

This passage is referring to when Jesus is talking to Paul and giving him the declaration of his call. He is to open their eyes and turn them from darkness to light. The Church of Laodicea does not submit to this call, for they are so blind themselves. They are under the power of Satan, saturated in sins, leading them to death. They cover sexual sins and exploitations in the Bride, covering her white garments in blood of evil. They are willing to turn a "blind eye" to all sorts of corruption. The blindness is so obvious, yet they can't see it at all, and when called out they will trip and fall over themselves to avoid accountability.

God gave me a vision for this the other day. I could see people stumbling around, not being able to see anything. Literally blinded by the darkness around them and having blindfolds covering their eyes. Think about how many times you walk around your bedroom every day. Yet, there is that one night, blinded by darkness and sleepiness, when you stump your toe, and you stand there paused in pain, unable to continue. That is what the people in this vision were experiencing. Utter confusion because they are too blind to see what is around them. That is the kind of blindness Jesus is referring to in this letter. They have physical eyes that see their ease, their comforts, and their lack of need, but they are so blind spiritually that they are stumbling around. Spiritual salve will help heal the blindness so that this church can see.

NAKED

² Meanwhile we groan, longing to be clothed instead with our heavenly dwelling, ³ because when we are clothed, we will not be found naked.

—2 Corinthians 5:2-3

Jesus is imploring this ekklesia to see past their physical luxuries and truly see their depravity. To be naked in the spirit is shameful, and we should be seeking to be clothed in Jesus' righteousness. Clearly you cannot put on an actual garment of righteousness, but it is a spiritual principle. Just like the armor is described in **Ephesians 6**, helmet of salvation, sword of the spirit, breastplate of righteousness, belt of truth, shield of faith, and the shoes of peace. Not a single one of these items are actual physical garments, but they are spiritual principles that we cover our spiritual bodies with. Our spiritual bodies should be our leading bodies and the soul and flesh align behind it. We are spiritual beings having a physical experience, but until our eyes are open, and the blindness has ceased, we only see what is right in front of us.

Our nakedness should be covered in white bridal attire, unwrinkled, and blemish free. We cannot do that work ourselves, it is the work of Jesus on the cross that we wear. It is the blood that makes us white as snow. I know. I know. How does that even make sense, Stephanie? How can one be covered in blood and be white as snow? The same way that you can put on a breastplate of righteousness. Have you ever seen, touched, or held a breastplate? They are incredibly heavy. They are made from extremely tempered and strong metal to make them nearly impenetrable. The concept of a breastplate being made of righteousness is absurd, except that in the spirit, our righteousness also comes from the work of the cross. It is impossible for us to be righteous without Jesus.

The blood cleanses us of all impurities. Jesus' blood flows over us and takes away all the sin, paying Death our debt. See, blood is an extremely powerful source of life. Nothing in the natural can live without it, but blood is also spiritual. Death has a hunger for blood because Death is void of life. Like a narcissist seeking supply. Supply is the term used for a life-sustaining, emotionally healthy, enthusiastic person who the narcissist feeds off of because they don't have the life-giving source of love and emotions themselves. Ruach Narcissus has drained them of all of their own. Death wants to drain all of our life-sustaining blood because it is a void that can never consume enough. Jesus, one hundred percent God and one hundred percent man, possesses the only blood strong enough to pay the debt. As it flows over us, washing us white as snow, our debt removed, we are no longer valuable to Death. Death cannot feed on purity, only blood. Our nakedness offers us as ripe-for-the-picking, blood-filled victims whom Death is ready to prey upon and fairly easy blinded targets.

Jesus offers such a beautiful grace in this passage. He is standing at the door and knocking. He is calling to our hearts, as the Amen, declaring that his rebuke and discipline are out of love, and if we are willing to accept it, change our ways, and open that door to Him, He will come and dine with us. What a beautiful and gracious gift! We can fight Ruach Narcissus and open the pod, open the door, and allow Jesus to come in. I know it is scary, and maybe even intimidating to have Him knocking. You may be afraid because it all seems so scary, and trusting in your money, wealth, what you see and can control, seems so much safer. But I promise you that you cannot land in better hands than the ones of our Loving Father. Jesus will take you right to Him. The Trinity is so loving! God, Holy Spirit, and Jesus will not leave you in fear and distress, but you must follow. You cannot remain in the same place you were found. After you have dined with Jesus, follow him.

CHAPTER 13

IDENTITY, SELF-DIRECTION, EMPATHY, AND INTIMACY

If you are learning about NPD or dealing with someone who is narcissistic, you will experience how corrupt these four secondary areas are. The human who is podded by the spirit lacks each of these areas in such great amounts that the void is undeniable. There may be a varied level for each one; for example, they may seem to have a solid form of identity, but no concept of empathy. The truth is they don't really have either; one is just more noticeably void than the other. They have mirrored you or someone else, so that becomes their identity.

INTIMACY

We see this same thing in the current modern Bride of Christ. We are terrified of intimacy with Jesus. I am going to start with intimacy because it is the crux to the rest of these issues. Intimacy is being able to be authentic, raw, real, and genuine with someone else. No hiding. No faking it til we make it. No keeping the ugly parts of us hidden. We are just out there, all of us, splayed open. It is terrifying for most people, but it is the only way to have a relationship with a Groom that already knows our thoughts, actions, and everything we do. We lie, or fool ourselves, to think anything differently. We are not fooling Him. Intimacy is a requirement of an authentic relationship.

When we attempt to remove intimacy, we remove our understanding of how intimate God is with us from the very beginning. We trick ourselves. We aren't actually hiding anything from an omniscient and omnipresent God. But when we submit ourselves to Him, willfully give Him full access to us, there is beautiful freedom there. It will require us to change because a holy God cannot reside in a sinful body, but He gives us the purification that we need to get where He wants us. It is a journey that starts with redemption through the work of the cross and then a consistent walk following Jesus. There is no such thing as doing it all the right way, but it is a journey worth pursuing. Sometimes you may feel like you are going to die before the infection of the sinful life wound He is healing is fully removed, but if you will just trust Him, He will be able to clean it, heal it, and then you will never deal with it again.

We come to him really beat up. We are blind people walking around in the dark before we meet Jesus. Sin will do its work of beating us up badly. When the light is shone, we are squinting our eyes at first, and then we begin to see all the wounds that need tending. Some of these wounds are deep, gaping, infected wounds that have been harming us for so long. Thankfully, Jesus usually doesn't try to mend those first because we couldn't handle it. But giving Him intimate access allows us to begin the healing process. If we continue to refuse intimacy, we can never have the healing we are meant for. Jesus is a gentleman, and a gentle man, and He will never force Himself onto us. We must choose Him. We must choose to open up to Him. If we start the process and then rescind, we can still press in again. He will meet us wherever we let Him, but if we try to hide, He will keep calling us. Hopefully this book has been a calling to you to keep pressing into intimacy with Jesus. Keep going deeper. Keep seeking more and more intimacy with Him.

IDENTITY

Our identity as Christians must be solely in Jesus Christ, but when we are operating out of Ruach Narcissus, we have lost the ability to have identity. We look so much like the world and the people around us who are lost that no one is interested in following us. We are lost. We don't know what we stand for, so we fall for anything. Identity is an incredibly important concept for Christians to understand, but once we attain the knowledge, living it out is way more important.

Knowing and not doing is one of the major deceptions that Ruach Narcissus gives us. We are supposed to know who we are in Christ when we begin to follow Him. Our pursuit of identity should reflect what the scriptures say, but we often follow the human next to us, or one that we think is doing it the right way, then all of a sudden, we are as lost as they are.

We must make sure that when we follow someone, they understand their identity in Christ and are living what they say they believe. If we are looking to follow Christians who live against what the Word of God says, we are looking for someone to give us our identity because we are the god we are looking for. But if we want to have identity in Christ, we are going to have to look at Jesus and His ways. There is no shortcut or easy route to take. Repentance. That is the only way to start the journey to live out the identity in Christ.

Practicing intimacy will give us the ability to understand our identity in Christ. We are incapable of understanding an identity that we won't be intimate with. For example: You marry your husband and take his last name, but you don't live, have sex, or do life with him in any way. You will have absolutely no attachment to his name, nor will you even feel like his wife. You will be so indifferent to his name, his family legacy, and why you even have his name. Taking on an identity without intimacy is pointless.

Narcissists do not know their identity. They only mirror what they have seen in others. They are not capable of being intimate enough with anyone to acquire an identity that becomes theirs. They do not feel attached or grounded to their parents, which is how most people attain their identity to begin with. They will possibly have some sense of family association, but they will not have the understanding of creating a legacy through their family. Men will not be strong leaders with integrity to give their wives comfort in who they are, and the wives may not even take the last name because there is no sense of strong identity or intimacy. A woman will be indifferent to creating a legacy for her husband because she did not have any understanding of the importance of legacy from her own family. These people will have merely mirrored what you say you want and do what you do long enough to convince you that they are going to be a solid choice to build life with, then once they feel like they have trapped you, the pod starts to spin, the mask falls, and the next thing you know, you realize that you never knew them at all.

Identity matters. We cannot retain our identity as sinful people and adopt the identity of Christ. Taking on the identity in Christ is only possible if the sinful part of us dies. We must be born again into a new person.

SELF DIRECTION

The operative word here is "self." Because a narcissist cannot self-reflect or love themselves, they are incapable of self-direction. They may hold a good job, they may even make a lot of money, but they are not capable of self-directing. Their success will usually be on the back, or coattails, of someone else. To initiate something would mean that you are accountable to whatever you started and the last thing on the planet a narcissist wants to be is accountable to anything or anyone.

Becoming counterculture to the current church culture would be the beginning of self-directing the Bride away from calamity. We have to be willing to allow God to show us a new way. We can't continue riding on the coattails of the world and end up in the desired place next to Jesus. We must collectively hold ourselves accountable to keeping our eyes on the prize. We are not meant to be focused on self-direction, as in focusing on ourselves, but we need to be choosing to follow Jesus. We are active participants in choosing the direction that we go. We are accountable and responsible for choosing to follow Jesus with our self-direction.

There seems to be a lot of "self-focus" today everywhere you look. Advice to look out for yourself and follow your heart. Do you, Boo. Trust no one but yourself. This is not the same as self-direction. Being inwardly focused is a detriment outside of taking time to heal from traumas. If you have a period of time when God takes you into an intimate, quiet place of solitude to heal you, this is a very important process. Take your time with Him. But He won't leave you there because sharing your message is the goal. Whatever that message is deep down inside you, custom to you, is the self-direction that you will need to take to follow Jesus.

EMPATHY

We talked about empathy throughout this book. It is an area that narcissists are known for not possessing at all. Lack of empathy is the marker of a narcissist. There is a snarky saying, "That no one falls in love as quickly as a narcissist that needs a place to live." Because narcissism is predatory, the human is incapable of putting themselves in the shoes of anyone else. They will prey on others without ever considering how their actions and behaviors affect anyone else. But what I have found to be very disappointing in dealing with a narcissist is that though he was practically a homeless person, he looked down on others who struggle to survive. His only true support was at the expense of someone else. He didn't support himself, yet he was so very quick to make harsh judgements about others. It always made my heart so sad when I would try to get him to see that he was similar to the people he was casting stones at, but he never could see it. Because narcissists can't self-reflect, and they lack empathy, they will always think of themselves better than others, even if they are in the same sinking boat.

The Bride has become so similar to this. We watch the world burn around us, people dying in their sin, and yet, we are acting like we aren't on the same burning boat because we have Jesus. Well, that would be true IF we actually had Jesus. As a narcissistic bride, He is nowhere to be found, but He is waiting on us to pull ourselves together and turn back toward Him. He tells us that many will call on His name, even have done amazing things in His name, but He never knew them. Remember, the power lies in the name of Jesus, not us. We can do many things because Jesus' name harnesses His power from heaven, but if we don't have a relationship with Him, know Him, intimately, then He is not obligated to know us either.

I explained the importance of empathy in chapter 9, but I wanted to touch on it here again in this list of secondary issues as well. Notice that empathy is the only trait repeated in both sections. Lack of it is the marker of toxic narcissistic behavior.

CHAPTER 14

HEALTHY CONFLICT RESOLUTION

If you have made it this far into my book, thank you! I know that you may be feeling like you have been on an intense ride of learning unhealthy behaviors along the way. Conflict happens. It is part of the human experience and sin nature. How we handle it is up to us, and some of us may need to step up to the plate and try things a different way. Typically Christians handle conflict with getting angry and either using retaliation or just leaving the relationship altogether. We rarely practice biblical conflict resolution and therefore, we have a very shattered bride. Grace and forgiveness are rarely at the center of the resolution, but we can find a lot of pride and ego.

When someone brings up an issue with us, defending ourselves becomes the first response, and proving them wrong is typically our second. Ruach Narcissus is often the leading force behind both of these responses. Our ego takes a blow and instead of being able to love and care for the person who is trying to have a genuine relationship, we stay inside of our pod, locking them out. Much like we do with Jesus when He is standing at the door knocking and we refuse to answer or acknowledge it. We must allow space for others' feelings and their attempts to be relational with us if we ever want to have real relationships. This is such a scary place to be in a world where Ruach Narcissus is so prevalent and trusting others has become increasingly scary and difficult. But a great way to measure who is genuine and safe is to see who models conflict resolution biblically.

23 "Therefore, if you are offering your gift at the altar and there remember that your brother or sister has something against you, 24 leave your gift there in front of the altar. First go and be reconciled to them; then come and offer your gift.

—Matthew 5:23-24

Jesus wants us to come with a pure heart. When we know that others have issues against us, we need to do our best to reconcile them. Now, some things are not reconcilable and some people are not safe. That is not what this scripture is talking about. We are talking about basic quarrels and disagreements. This is not about abuse.

(If you are in an abusive relationship, or a dangerous situation, get safe immediately. You do not have to

make any big decisions. God is not a supporter of abuse of any kind. Please make a plan to get safe if you are in danger. Contact 1-800-799-SAFE (7233) if you are in a domestic violence situation. There may come a time when conflict resolution will apply, but not while you are in danger.)

RESOLUTION #1

> 15 *"If your brother or sister sins, go and point out their fault, just between the two of you. If they listen to you, you have won them over.*

—Matthew 18:15

The first step is to approach the person who you are having conflict with. Take some time to pull your thoughts together before you approach this situation, if needed. Sometimes when we are angry, we need to filter the *who* and *what* about our feelings. Anger can be a bit like a strong wind and muddle all of our feelings together. We need to decipher what responsibility the other person had in the conflict and what was our responsibility.

An example in my own life was a vacation from hell. I had rented a cabin in the mountains for my family's Christmas present. Without going into a long story, the cabin did not come through with their end of the deal. Our vacation was ruined and ended up being extremely stressful and miserable. It took me about three months to filter through what was their responsibility and what wasn't. It wasn't their responsibility that this was my Christmas present to my family. It wasn't their responsibility that this was the first full family trip we had taken in many years. It was not their responsibility that the whole town became flooded with vacationers, and we could no longer make phone calls and barely send texts. It was their responsibility to have better customer service. It was their responsibility to make sure that we could access and get into the cabin. It was their responsibility to not try and trap me into the contract because they couldn't guarantee that I could get to the cabin. After one night in a hotel, they told me that if I canceled, they wouldn't refund me for the rest of my booked stay, though I was in town and it was not my fault I couldn't get to the cabin. Before I left a review, I gave myself time to filter through these emotions so I could only speak to the part they were responsible for.

If we take time to filter through our emotions, we may find that the other person we need to talk to has less or more responsibility for the quarrel. Practicing this will help us approach situations without convoluting the entire emotional blow that a quarrel can produce. If you are blindsided by an issue, and there is a heated moment, attempt to remove yourself from the situation and take a moment to calm down. If it is possible, just listen to what the person has to say, and ask for a chance to think through the issue. If you must respond immediately, always take the lesser seat.

I truly can't even believe that sentence is being typed by my hand. I have lived my whole life without wanting anyone to have the upper hand. I can't trust others to have the upper hand and it is a terrifying place for me. I am learning to yield and take the path of being less if needed. Trusting that God has me covered and that He will defend me in a time of need. Learning to take the place of the lesser seat, especially for those of us who are naturally aggressive, is a noble pursuit.

After you have taken the time to sort out your emotions, ask the person to meet, preferably in a private setting. A phone call may be appropriate, but typically in person is ideal. Less confusion happens when people can see each other's expressions and apply the tone of voice at the same time. This helps people connect, even in a difficult situation like conflict resolution.

RESOLUTION #2

16 But if they will not listen, take one or two others along, so that every matter may be established by the testimony of two or three witnesses.

—Matthew 18:16

Now, this resolution can get a little tricky. Again, the reason relationships are important is because to have safe people to take along with you, you need someone you trust. It is ideal to have someone who has both parties' best interest in mind. If that is not possible, the second-best option is to have someone who isn't going to feed off the drama or try to spread rumors. You need to be wise when you are dealing with conflict resolution. The operative word is to resolve the problem, not create more or a bigger one.

I had a very unfortunate situation happen at a church. I love this church and I love the leadership, but there was a situation that was handled very poorly. I was in charge of the women's ministry. A lady that had a Bible study at the church was teaching a concept that I disagreed with then, and still do. She and I had already had a very lengthy conversation about our perspectives. I asked one of my women's team leaders how I should handle the situation and she said I should talk with the pastor. I asked the pastor to ask the lady leading the Bible study to not teach that particular concept in the church or to move her study to her house if she was going to continue to teach it. Next thing I knew, I received an email with *fifty* people on it! You read that right, *fifty*! I only knew of four people who knew anything about the situation. Where the forty-six other people became involved is still a mystery to this day for me. However, it created an issue much greater and much larger than I ever anticipated. There was a lot of hurt. I was so disappointed because for once, I thought I had done things the right way, and it ended up a mess anyway.

I am only responsible for my part. I did the right thing. I went by these resolution steps. There was no resolution, and sometimes that may be exactly what happens. When that happens, forgiveness is often your best next step. Even if you have to separate yourself from the relationship, finding forgiveness is key. I eventually stepped down from my leadership position because I realized that I wasn't leading well. The situation eventually died down and went away. This is why you want people you can trust to be involved, so that the blaze of drama doesn't burn down the relationship that you are trying to resolve.

When you bring others with you to approach a situation, make sure that each person has the heart of restoration. This will help them give you wisdom and balance as you discuss the issues. You will also have honest witnesses to stand with you if there is a reason to need them.

RESOLUTION #3

17 If they still refuse to listen, tell it to the church; and if they refuse to listen even to the church, treat them as you would a pagan or a tax collector.

—Matthew 18:17

Taking an issue before the church seems to be a lost art. I don't know what it looked like back when this was written. I don't know what it looked like in the Acts church, but I can almost guarantee that today it would look a lot like the Salem Witch Trials. The amount of drama and conflict would be astounding. I believe the reason we would experience all of that is the same reason I am writing this book, Ruach Narcissus. The blinding, gaping, void, black hole spirit that has done so much damage to the church, would prevent us from being able to operate in this resolution properly.

Resolution #3 seems nearly an impossibility in today's church culture. We are not wanting to turn the church into a courthouse, nor pastors into judges. So what does this even mean? How is this behavior even possible?

Well, I believe megachurches and large church gatherings are often the problem for this resolution. There is not a single example in the Bible of these types of gatherings. The only way to operate this out in today's culture would be in a small group environment, but the problem with that is most people rotate small groups. They do not stay with the same people year after year to have true accountability. We can easily hide in church today. We do not have to get into a true community with others that will call us to the table on our behavior. Our individual-idealization culture fights this resolution.

We use the dismissive attitude of the terms, "You can't judge me" and "Why do I have to listen to you?" We dig our heels into pride and remove relationships or the people pleasers will bend over backward trying to make things right with people who do not have their best interest in mind. People pleasers will also operate out of pride if they are called out for behaviors, but it usually looks like a lack of boundaries, and they don't know how to make things better without feeling like a victim of others. Both of these responses are based in pride.

So what is the solution Stephanie? Good question. If we want resolution #3 to operate well, we must be able to break off Ruach Narcissus and learn to: Trust. Each other! We must be willing to drop our egos, destroy our pride, humble ourselves, and seek the love of Christ so that we can have true resolution with fellow brothers and sisters. It is critical that we get back to being able to operate in this resolution step as the Bride. We are not meant to be lone sheep out among wolves, and we are definitely not meant to be the wolves to each other. People are flawed. There is no way to get around that truth, but we can operate together to hold each other accountable and make an impact on a very sad and broken world.

We can learn to practice forgiveness for ourselves and others. We can make a difference and make a large impact with others when we practice all three of these resolutions. I have seen resolution #1 and #2 being practiced at times, but until we are operating out of all three, we lose a large part of accountability. We have so many families falling apart, marriages in disaster, and people spinning out of control because they do not have support and accountability from fellow brothers and sisters. Many of these situations could be deterred if we could go before our family, ekklesia, and find the resolutions that are God-given.

Ruach Narcissus will prevent us from wanting to let others speak into us or challenge us when we are in a mess. Narcissism refuses to self-reflect or allow others to love the person well, so when we are saturated in narcissism, we will not accept any of these resolutions with a heart of humility. We must break off the spirit with the name of Jesus Christ and fall in love with our first love again. Jesus will defend us and protect us against this corrosive spirit so that we can have authentic relationships again. That is the heart behind the love of our Groom.

FINAL ENCOURAGEMENT

A basic judge of where your heart is with others is how you drive. I know I used this analogy earlier, because so many people experience this daily. Did you know that it is your responsibility to move to the right if someone wants to pass you? Yep, even if you are in the middle lane. If you are just cruising along the speed limit, it is still your responsibility to move. But wholly cannoli! If we look at how drivers are today, we can tell that our pride and ego are steering. You can't tell the difference between a Christian and non-Christian on the road. What if we collectively started there? You don't even have to talk to people. You just have to follow the guidelines and be willing to yield to others. Hard, right? I know.

I struggle with it too. Especially if I feel like someone is messing with me on the road, you can believe I get aggressive. All logic and reason fly out the window, pride and ego step in, and now it is "the strong who survive" mentality. I have had to ask for forgiveness so many times on the road. I am currently working through what inside me makes me feel like I am in a race when I hit the interstate. It is a "me" issue. Literally no one else cares what I am doing or where I am going. I must take responsibility for how I allow this situation to affect me and how I show up each day on the road.

This is a simple exercise in heart condition. When our heart is submitted to Jesus as Lord and Savior, things like our ego in driving become gross to us. We will be able to feel it rise up in us. If our cars are so expensive that we value them over people, they make us feel important, they "brand" us as cool, then we are more focused on Ruach Narcissus and wooing that spirit. The majority of us drive or have some mode of transportation, so this can apply anytime you are in charge of transportation of any kind. It is all about the heart experience, not the physical. I hope that you have gathered that by this section in the book. The physical realm is meant to mirror the spiritual realm, and the farther away we are from the heart of our Father, the harder it is to love others well.

We are all a part of this journey. I am not judging or casting stones at anyone with the content of this book. I am walking along with you, hand in hand, as a fellow member of the body of Christ. I have learned so much writing this book and I am forever grateful for the lessons God has given me and trusted me to share with you. Walking out my own faith journey has excited me even more to share this content. The amazing hope we have in Jesus to restore us to our rightful place with Him blesses my soul. I want you to wake up everyday and feel how very loved you are by our Groom. The awful Ruach Narcissus will steal all of that from us, but only if we let it happen.

Every single exposure you have to a narcissist will set you back into the crazy making cycle. You may find yourself in a full spin after you have been touched again by someone covered in this tornadic spirit. You will have cyclical and obsessive thinking that will leave you so confused. You will feel hurt deep inside, even if you weren't that close to the person. They will often request that you trust them because they need your trust to prey upon you. This is why it is important to completely rid yourself of Ruach Narcissus. Jesus, our Groom, will not suffer any of these experiences. He will simply spit us out and then we will face the consequences of our passion for corruption. Taking the time to let the Bible be our mirror, which we consistently self-reflect, is the greatest weapon against deception. We can defeat this spirit! We are victors! We have victory in Jesus, but we must have intimacy with Him to experience it. We are not the defeated foe, we are children of the Most-High God. Let's get intimate, learn our identity, operate out of empathy, and practice self-direction toward spiritual growth. This is how we bring life back to the Bride and fall in love with our Groom.

Let Holy Spirit penetrate the darkest places of your heart and heal you. We need you. The Bride is not complete without you! Jesus is passionately in love with you!

----

12 Therefore, as God's chosen people, holy and dearly loved, clothe yourselves with compassion, kindness, humility, gentleness and patience.

—Colossians 3:12

HOW TO HEAL FROM NARCISSISTIC ABUSE

I am not licensed in any way to give you counseling or clinical help for healing from narcissistic abuse, but I can share with you what Holy Spirit revealed to me to help me heal after my own experience. I would be remiss to not share this section with you. I came out of that relationship feeling so hurt, so confused, so devastated, so bitter, so angry, and the worst for me was being completely unchosen. How could someone tell me that they loved me and be so utterly indifferent?! I had never experienced anything like it before. I didn't know a human could be so void of emotions and so neglectful in their care. I have experienced domestic violence and addiction in past relationships, but this monster, the spirit of narcissism, was something else entirely. My light had been sucked into a black hole, and I was fighting like heaven against hell to get out. I came out dimmer. I came out feeling hopeless. But I did come out!

It was like a tornado had passed through my heart, leaving damage in a specific path. My daughter has validated me many times with the kind words, "Mom, I was there. He became a different person." Oh! How I needed to hear those words; salve to my aching heart. I don't consider myself a victim, but a survivor. Though I still am restabilizing extreme trust issues, lasting effects from gaslighting, future faking, and all the incredible amount of lies, I am continuing to look to God for healing and wisdom from Holy Spirit. I trust the Trinity, even when I don't trust myself. Here are the ways Holy Spirit has healed my heart from this devastating experience, and I hope it helps you. Can I encourage you to know that God can and will use any situation for His good? Even if it leaves you a mess in the middle, He can and will redeem it. He is using my painful experience to write this book, share with you everything He has taught me, and change the trajectory of the Bride.

I want what I share in this section to help heal those who have experienced a relationship with a human with Ruach Narcissus (aka NPD). Don't be afraid to look at yourself, see your reflection in the mirror of the word of God. Jesus has come to break the power of sin, and Holy Spirit is here with us to give us the ability to walk in the ways of Father. When we love Him, we will keep His commands (**John 14:15**). If we have experienced the devastating effects of narcissism, we should understand how devastating it is for the Bride to operate out of these behaviors, and why God is warning us to change. Here are the five steps to healing from narcissistic abuse that has nothing to do with the narcissist...for once:

STEP 1: ACKNOWLEDGE

We must first acknowledge that we will never under-stand *why* they do the things that they do. I talked about this a bit previously in chapter two, but this is the first step to healing. When you are emotionally healthy, the behaviors like gaslighting, manipulation, emotional disconnect, lack of empathy, and lack of care will never make sense. Trying to understand them only leads to more crazy making.

Let go of the need to try to reason out what happened to you. The reason it happened is because the person has the spirit of narcissism (Ruach Narcissus) and is emotionally unhealthy. They are incapable of recognizing or even caring why they did those awful things to you. You will not get a genuine apology. You must move on without them ever acknowledging or taking ownership. I hoped an apology would come. Certainly he could recognize the pain that he brought by being unavailable. I tried to talk to him about how messy our relationship had become, hoping that he would see it too. I begged and pleaded. My last words were, "I can't beg you to love me anymore." I had to acknowledge that that is what I was doing. Begging. So much begging to be seen, heard, cared for, only for it all to fall into a black hole void. I had to acknowledge that I was never going to understand what was happening.

You must be the one to acknowledge, and then you must lay it at the feet of Jesus. It is okay to let go of a person and situation without fully understanding how you ended up in such a hurtful place. Healing can begin with surrender. Letting go will free you up for step two.

Step 2: Accept

You must accept your role in the relationship. All relationships take two people, so we must accept our role in a very unhealthy one. What did you justify, overlook, and accept from the narcissist? I know that I can recall things in my dating period that made me question the relationship, but I thought I had found a unicorn, so I overlooked them.

One night, he had a major confession time with me. He told me some very important things that he had withheld from me for the two months we were dating. He chose a very inopportune time for me, but a perfect opportunity for him. I was out of town, with sleeping children, and it was very late at night. He opened with the sentence, "Please don't leave me..." and then proceeded with the confessions. I should have woken my kids up and left, putting myself in a neutral situation to contemplate everything I had been told. But I didn't. I stayed, did as he asked, and didn't leave him. I compromised. I overlooked it. This was all on me.

There were other similar situations that I overlooked, or accepted, because I loved him. I wanted to work things out, and ultimately, my codependency thought that I could love him into living out all of his potential. See, I probably fell in love with his unactualized potential more than I did with him as a person. One of my biggest flaws, so I had to accept that I had gotten myself into this situation.

Justifying is making excuses for them when you notice something is off or there is questionable behavior. We justify to prevent ourselves from having to accept that something is off because we want that person to be "the one."

Overlooking is choosing not to be aware of something so we don't have to address it. We often overlook their behaviors because confronting them may cost us the relationship. When we have our eyes set on someone, and maybe they don't seem as great as we thought, we have to accept that we are overlooking those behaviors.

Accepting is allowing behaviors that we absolutely know are not okay, but we allow it anyway. We accept crossed boundaries or questionable behaviors because we would rather accept them than to have to sever the relationship. The idea of severing a relationship is painful. When we accept behaviors that we don't agree with to prevent the pain, we often create a greater pain for ourselves when the relationship is severed in a much harsher way and with more time and heart investment.

We cannot control others; we can only control ourselves. Taking ownership of our actions, thoughts, and behaviors is critical for our own healing. You will never understand what they did, but you can learn why you did what you did. Was it your codependency that led you to justify, overlook, and accept the unacceptable? Learning your behaviors will lead you into healing step three.

STEP 3: ALLOW

Allow yourself to grieve the hurt and pain caused by the relationship. A poor heart investment will leave us broken and feeling empty, but it can heal. Processing your emotions in the moment is beneficial for healing. When you feel it, acknowledge it. If you feel betrayed, say to yourself, "I feel betrayed because _____ (fill in the blank with whatever the experience was)." Then process it by telling God that you are struggling and need Him to minister to that situation. If you feel angry, take the same steps. The worst thing you can do is to try to shove your feelings down like it isn't happening because your heart is hurting. Each emotion that surfaces, if dealt with, will encourage your heart, so allow yourself the time to do so. Jumping into a new relationship to try and stop the spin out that is happening in your mind from the narcissistic relationship will not help you get to a better place emotionally. It will only cause more chaos, and you will look more like the narcissist to the new person. You must allow yourself time to heal.

Sometimes the victim leaves the narcissist first, but because of cognitive dissonance and trauma bonding, he/she may have a hard time staying away. If you have left and you are now questioning yourself, give yourself a year before you attempt to rekindle any relationship. This allows the time for your brain to break patterns of addiction to the person. Most likely, if you are dealing with a narcissist, you will not have any desire to repair the relationship after the year of separation. Time is often your friend when escaping a narcissistic relationship.

Allowing yourself time to grieve the heartbreak gives your heart time to be restored. There is no way to exit a relationship with someone you love and care about without pain. Often with a narcissist, you are the one that is being discarded. It feels like being thrown away like trash. This is extremely painful. It is a gift in the long run, but in the moment it feels like you were tossed out of a tornado and hit a tree. You feel so beat up, but if you allow yourself the time to rebalance and nurture your wounds, healing will come. You will be better for giving yourself the grace of time to get yourself into a more emotionally healthy mindset. Taking the time to heal will lead you into step four.

STEP 4: BELIEFS

Now that you have experienced cognitive dissonance and broken trust, you will need to work on your belief system. This will be important for all future relationships that you will have after the narcissist. Your belief system will need to be as healthy as possible before you begin a new relationship. You cannot punish a future person because of a past relationship. Take your time to develop this healed belief system. It may take months, or even years, to heal and process through all the neglect and abuse.

Break your codependent patterns and work on what you believe. Codependency is a ripe field of thinking processes that allows you to be picked by a narcissist. I have an online course that helps to heal this behavior. We will continue to repeat behaviors that we refuse to recognize in ourselves.

Ask yourself these questions:

1. What do I believe about myself?

2. What do I believe about love?

3. What do I believe about relationships?

Take some time to really filter through your mind and heart about these questions. I had to really dig into these questions with God. I needed Him to speak into these areas for me, so that I could answer them from His perspective and not my broken one. Once I allowed Him to guide me, I had a better understanding of my beliefs.

For example, I felt completely unchosen by my narcissistic relationship. So I questioned myself, and felt like I didn't deserve to be chosen. I mean, I was thrown away like a piece of trash after all. I was talking to God and pouring out my heart, explaining to Him how unchosen I felt, and God said to me, "But I choose you. I have always chosen you." For the first time in my life, that was enough. The fact that the God of the Universe has chosen me, requires me to change my belief that I wasn't worthy to be chosen. I also had to allow God to heal my beliefs about these other areas.

Changing my beliefs has given me hope for myself and excitement for future relationships. I originally had a lot of fear, reservation, and hesitation about even considering new relationships. Not just romantic relationships either, but the entire human race felt untrustworthy. God helping me realize that His Truth and His love are trustworthy makes me open to new possibilities in others. Healing in this capacity leads to step five.

Step 5: Boundaries

Narcissists never respect boundaries. If they did, they wouldn't be in control. Controlling the relationship is the primary need and goal of a narcissist. Similar to how the Bride is acting with Jesus, instead of Him being the leader, she is trying to usurp Him and be in control of the relationship. God has extremely healthy boundaries that we will not be able to cross. He requires repentance, a change of our ways, to access Him. We cannot come to God except through the redemptive work of Jesus on the cross, and we cannot access that redemption except through acknowledging our sin and turning away from it. These God-established boundaries will never change, and your boundaries shouldn't either.

Setting boundaries is your first line of defense from abusive behaviors. Boundaries are never about controlling others. Boundaries are for you and your safety. They create the safest environment by establishing what is comfortable for you emotionally, physically, mentally, and spiritually. Setting healthy boundaries will require you to do some healing; otherwise you will set boundaries in an attempt to control others' behaviors, which will backfire. Boundaries are always meant to help you set parameters around your belief system, so that you have good relationships.

Setting boundaries is important but holding them is where the rubber meets the road. Just like God will not budge on His boundaries for relationships, we should not either. Holding your boundaries can be a challenge, especially if you are dealing with codependency. Setting and holding your boundaries will help you move forward into healthier relationships.

These five steps are how I have healed and moved forward after a relationship with a narcissist. I hope that they help you navigate through the heartache and pain. Blessings to you as you heal.

REFERENCES

Entire Book

1. Bible. *New International Version (NIV)* Holy Bible. https://www.biblegateway.com/

Chapter 2

1. Dictionary.com Unabridged Based on the Random House Unabridged Dictionary, Random House, Inc. 2024. https://www.dictionary.com/browse/narcissist
2. Degges-White, Suzanne. "Lifetime Connections: Narcissism—The 13 Traits of a Narcissist: What Do the Clinical Signs of Narcissism Look Like in Everyday Life?" *Psychology Today,* October 25, 2021.https://www.psychologytoday.com/us/blog/lifetime-connections/202110/the-13-traits-narcissist.
3. Duncan, Ryan. "10 Warning Signs of a Spiritual Narcissist." Crosswalk.com, November 14, 2023. https://www.crosswalk.com/faith/spiritual-life/10-warning-signs-of-a-spiritual-narcissist.html. Accessed August 3, 2024.
4. Wikipedia. "Narcissus (mythology)." Wikipedia. https://en.wikipedia.org/wiki/Narcissus_(mythology) Accessed Jan 2024.

Chapter 4

1. Pastoral Care, Inc. n.d. "Statistics in the Ministry." https://www.pastoralcareinc.com/statistics/. Accessed June 27, 2024.

Chapter 6

1. Stewart, Don. "Why Is Satan Sometimes Called Lucifer?" Blue Letter Bible. https://www.blueletterbible.org/faq/don_stewart/don_stewart_79.cfm. Accessed February 8, 2024.
2. Bible. *English Standard Version (ESV).* "100 verses we were were created to worship and praise" Open Bible Info. (https://www.openbible.info/topics/we_were_created_to_worship_and_praise) Accessed March 2024.
3. BibleStudyTools Staff. "The Top Bible Verses about Confession." BibleStudyTools.com, September 19, 2019. https://www.biblestudytools.com/topical-verses/bible-verses-about-confession/. Accessed May 13, 2024.

Chapter 8

1. GotQuestions Ministries. "What Did Jesus Mean When He Said It Is Easier for a Camel to Go Through the Eye of a Needle?" January 4, 2022. https://

www.gotquestions.org/camel-eye-needle.html.
Accessed April 10,2024.

Chapter 10

1. *"Envy."* Merriam-Webster.com Dictionary, Merriam-Webster, https://www.merriam-webster.com/dictionary/envy. Accessed March 21, 2024.
2. Preacherboy Production. *Strong's Concordance.* Apple App Store, Vers 70.0 (2024) https://apps.apple.com/us/app/strongs-concordance/id1425215177 Accessed on June 29,2024.

Chapter 12

1. *Strong's Concordance.* Danny Carlton copyright 2022. https://strongsconcordance.org Accessed April 2, 2024.

ABOUT THE AUTHOR

Stephanie Jordan is an author, teacher, speaker, passionate Jesus follower, and mom to five amazing children. Birmingham, AL is called home. Sharing her journey of God's faithfulness in the face of trials and teaching others the depth of God's love has become her life's work. She has been married, divorced, and widowed. She is not defined by the journey of life, but by the powerhouse God designed her to be for His purposes.

When she is not writing or speaking, you can find her riding her Harley Davidson Sportster 48, flaunting new healthy gluten free recipes on her Facebook group The Recovering Southerner, painting, reading, watching movies with her family, and spending time outdoors. She has launched a family reunion a.k.a. "Church" called The Garbage Can. The goal of The Garbage Can is to raze hell and build the kingdom of God by answering the questions: who, what, when, where, why, and how for scripture. She is also a teacher and coordinator for The First Heavy Metal Church of Christ (Dayton, OH) and the FHMCC Worldwide family.

Other titles by Stephanie:

Believing in Boundaries
Using Biblical Teaching to Understand and Establish Healthy Modern Boundaries

Purchase here:
https://www.amazon.com/dp/1958441007

The Death Tsunami
An Unexpected Journey into Widowhood and How I Met Death

Purchase here:
https://www.amazon.com/dp/B0CM7ZXWVF

Follow her social media: @thestephaniejordan

Instagram:
https://www.instagram.com/thestephaniejordan/

Facebook:
https://www.facebook.com/TheStephanieJordan

Linked In: https://www.linkedin.com/in/stephanie-jordan-b3374623b/

YouTube:
https://www.youtube.com/@thestephaniejordan.
(don't forget to add the period!)

TikTok:
https://www.tiktok.com/@the.stephanie.jordan?lang=en

CAN YOU HELP ME?

I love hearing what you have to say and I need your input to make my future books better. Please leave me a helpful review (20 words or more) on Amazon, Goodreads, and/or wherever you purchased the book sharing your experience.

Each review helps encourage other readers to check out great books like this one. Thank you for your time. I look forward to meeting you between pages again.